RESTORATIVE JUSTICE

INTERNATIONAL AND COMPARATIVE CRIMINAL JUSTICE

Series Editors:

Mark Findlay, *Institute of Criminology, University of Sydney*
Ralph Henham, *Nottingham Law School, Nottingham Trent University*

This series explores the new and rapidly developing field of international and comparative criminal justice and engages with its most important emerging themes and debates. It focuses on three interrelated aspects of scholarship which go to the root of understanding the nature and significance of international criminal justice in the broader context of globalization and global governance. These include: the theoretical and methodological problems posed by the development of international and comparative criminal justice; comparative contextual analysis; the reciprocal relationship between comparative and international criminal justice and contributions which endeavor to build understandings of global justice on foundations of comparative contextual analysis.

Other titles in the series:

The Crime of Destruction and the Law of Genocide
Caroline Fournet
ISBN 978 0 7546 7001 8

The Criminal Law of Genocide
International, Comparative and Contextual Aspects
Edited by Ralph Henham and Paul Behrens
ISBN 978 0 7546 4898 7

The Genocide Convention
An International Law Analysis
John Quigley
ISBN 978 0 7546 4730 0

A World View of Criminal Justice
Richard Vogler
ISBN 978 0 7546 2467 7

Restorative Justice
Ideals and Realities

MARGARITA ZERNOVA
University of Hull, UK

ASHGATE

Published by
Ashgate Publishing Limited
Wey Court East
Union Road
Farnham
Surrey, GU9 7PT
England

Ashgate Publishing Company
Suite 420
101 Cherry Street
Burlington, VT 05401-4405
USA

Ashgate website: http://www.ashgate.com

British Library Cataloguing in Publication Data
Zernova, Margarita
Restorative justice : ideals and realities. -
(International and comparative criminal justice)
1. Restorative justice
I. Title
364.6'8

Library of Congress Cataloging-in-Publication Data
Zernova, Margarita.
Restorative justice : ideals and realities / by Margarita Zernova.
p. cm. -- (International and comparative criminal justice)
Includes bibliographical references and index.
ISBN 978-0-7546-7032-2
1. Restorative justice. 2. Reparation (Criminal justice) 3. Punishment--Philosophy. 4. Corrections--Philosophy. 5. Criminals--Rehabilitation. 6. Victims of crimes--Legal status, laws, etc. I. Title.

K970.Z46 2007
345'.001--dc22

2007021819

ISBN 978-0-7546-7032-2

Reprinted 2010

Mixed Sources
Product group from well-managed forests and other controlled sources
www.fsc.org Cert no. SA-COC-1565
© 1996 Forest Stewardship Council

Printed and bound in Great Britain
by MPG Books Group, UK

Contents

Acknowledgements *vii*

Introduction **1**
Introducing the theme 1
Aspirations of proponents and concerns of critics 2
What lies ahead 3

Chapter One Restorative Justice in Action **7**
Ancient practice and its revival 7
Victim-offender reconciliation/mediation programmes 8
Family group conferencing: New Zealand experience 10
Family group conferencing outside New Zealand 12
Sentencing circles 16
Navajo peacemaking 19
Vermont community reparative boards 20
Zwelethemba experiment 21
Community-based initiatives in Northern Ireland 23
Recent restorative justice developments in England 25
Some restorative trends and their implications 29
Present empirical research into restorative justice 31

Chapter Two Restorative Ideals **35**
Introduction 35
A new moral 'lens' 36
An alternative to punishment 38
An alternative to treatment 39
Victim-centred justice 42
Justice that repairs harm and restores peace and harmony 44
Voluntary justice? 46
Empowering, community-based deprofessionalized, justice 48
Restorative justice and the criminal justice system 53
Concluding remarks 57

Chapter Three Ideals and Practical Realities: The Gap **59**
Introduction 59
The empirical study 59
One restorative justice project 60

Is restorative justice punishment? 62
Restorative justice and offender rehabilitation 65
A victim-focused justice? 70
A voluntary process? 74
Empowering justice? 77
Community-based justice? 82
De-professionalized justice? 87
A new ethical orientation? 98
Conclusion 102

Chapter Four Problematic Ideals and a Problematic Relationship **105**
Introduction 105
The ideal of reparation 105
The ideal of peace and harmony 107
Restorative justice in the shadow of the criminal justice system 110
Conclusion 114

Chapter Five Restorative Ideals Re-examined **115**
Introduction 115
Restorative justice in the eyes of proponents and conference participants 115
Restorative realities 117
The gap 128
Search for a new ethical framework 135
Minimizing the gap? 138

References *143*
Index *159*

Acknowledgments

I would like to express my deepest gratitude to Gerry Johnstone who introduced me to the idea of restorative justice, ignited my interest in it, made it possible for me to write this book and has been my constant source of guidance and inspiration. Warm thanks to Martin Wright for his friendship, kindness, continuous support, encouragement and reading drafts of this text and providing useful comments. I am grateful to Keith Bottomley for his excellent advice on the empirical research and help with earlier drafts. I am indebted to all people whom I have interviewed for their invaluable help and to the practitioners in the family group conferencing project for their assistance and hospitality. Thanks to Brian Williams for the enthusiasm he expressed for my work and encouragement. I am grateful to my colleagues from the University of Hull for their encouragement and support. Thanks to Matt Moyer for the help with transcribing interviews. Finally, I would like to thank to my family for their love, incessant support and sweet care.

Introduction

Introducing the theme

This book is about restorative justice – a concept which has no single meaning (McCold 1998; Johnstone and Van Ness 2007), or a single practical application, yet which has attracted many sympathizers across the political spectrum and is rapidly gaining popularity. Some penal reformers see restorative justice as a promising way to redress problems within the existing criminal justice system[1]. Religious leaders, who pioneered the concept, are attracted to restorative justice as a humane and morally superior way of responding to crime (Zehr 1990; Consedine 1999; Hadley 2001, 2006). Conservative advocates find restorative justice appealing because it emphasizes family values and the interests of victims and promises cost savings and reduction of re-offending. Liberal thinkers view restorative justice as an individually empowering and less repressive response to crime. Some campaigners for social justice see restorative justice as having potential to create a more just society (Morris 1995, 2000; Sullivan and Tifft 2001, 2006).

Explaining the concept of restorative justice is not a straightforward task, as proponents are still debating how restorative justice should be conceived and defined[2]. Quite often restorative justice is defined by reference to what it is not[3]. It is not the 'traditional' way of thinking about crime and justice. Advocates claim that restorative justice understands crime not only as a violation of an abstract entity – the state – but also, and mainly, as a violation of people and human relationships. Proponents argue that in the aftermath of an offence restorative justice is concerned not with punishing offenders, but with repairing harm caused by the crime. It is emphasized that restorative justice requires that the key decisions about how the crime should be responded to must not be taken by state officials and legal professionals alone. Ordinary people who are directly affected by the wrongdoing should take an active part in deciding what should happen in the aftermath of an offence. It is also stressed that, unlike the formal coercive legal process, the restorative justice process is characterized by informality and voluntariness. In short, it is claimed by a number of restorative justice campaigners that restorative justice is a radical alternative to

---

1 See, for example, Van Ness 1989, 1993; Wright 1996, 1999; Walgrave 1995, 1999, 2000a, 2000b, 2007; Bazemore and Walgrave 1999b; McCold 2000; Braithwaite 2003b; Van Ness and Strong 2006.

2 For some of these debates see McCold 1998, 2000; Bazemore and Walgrave 1999; Johnstone 2004; Johnstone and Van Ness 2007b; Zernova and Wright 2007.

3 However, this way of presenting restorative justice has been criticized as too simplistic, crude and empirically unfounded (Daly 2000, 2002; Van Ness and Strong 2006, 50-53; cf. Zehr 2002, 8-13).

the traditional way of understanding crime and justice and dealing with criminal behaviour[4]. It is a new pattern of thinking, or a particular 'lens' through which crime and justice could be looked at, or a new 'paradigm' of justice (Zehr, 1989, 1990, 1995, 2002, 2003).

In practice restorative justice may appear under different names and guises (such as victim-offender mediation, family group conferencing, sentencing circles) and may be found both within and outside the criminal justice system. It may be used at different stages in the criminal justice process (Dignan 2007; Lawrence and Strang 2007) and may involve various degrees of 'restorativeness' (McCold 2000; Van Ness and Strong 2006). Yet, despite their diversity, what these practices tend to have in common is that they involve a participatory 'process whereby all people with a stake in a particular offence [victims, offenders and their 'communities of care'] come together to resolve collectively how to deal with the aftermath of the offence and its implications for the future' (Marshall (1998) quoted in McCold 1998, 20). Such process is guided by a set of values: victim healing, offender accountability, individual empowerment, reconciliation[5], reparation of whatever harm has been caused by the crime, community-orientation, informality, de-professionalization, consensual decision-making and inclusiveness[6].

Aspirations of proponents and concerns of critics

Restorative justice proponents have ambitious aspirations. They envisage the creation of a radical alternative to existing ways of thinking about – and responding to – crime. They aspire towards developing a way of doing criminal justice which would place crime victims and their needs at its centre and which would be characterized by individual empowerment of crime stakeholders, de-professionalization, community-orientation and, some argue, voluntariness[7]. If these aspirations were put into practice, they would most certainly lead to revolutionary changes for the way crime is traditionally dealt with, and, according to proponents, restorative reforms could produce various benefits for victims, offenders, their communities and society in general.

In recent years restorative ideas have influenced criminal justice policies, practices and legislative reforms around the world and expanded to non-criminal contexts (schools in particular), provoking an enormous amount of interest among criminologists and academics from related disciplines, researchers, criminal justice practitioners, educationalists and policy-makers and resulting in abundant literature. The rapid expansion of restorative practices and the growth in popularity of the

---

4 See Bazemore 1996; Wright 1999; McCold 2000; Braithwaite 2003a; Van Ness and Strong 2006.

5 However, some question whether reconciliation is central to restorative justice (Zehr 2002, 8).

6 See Pranis (2007) for a discussion of restorative values.

7 For discussions of aspirations of the restorative justice movement see Zehr 1990; Wright 1996, 1999; McCold 2000; Morris 2000; Sullivan and Tifft 2001, 2006; Braithwaite 2003a; Van Ness and Strong 2006.

restorative ideas has been accompanied by an increasing interest in the critique of restorative justice[8].

Critics have expressed considerable scepticism about the aspirations of restorative justice advocates and raised numerous concerns about possible dangers of pursuing the restorative ideals in practice (Johnstone 2002, 25-33; 2003, part E; 2007; von Hirsch, Roberts et al 2003). One source of danger identified by critics is that restorative justice philosophy is based on questionable and mistaken assumptions and suffers from fundamental flaws, tensions and limitations. So, many critics have questioned the accuracy and desirability of a sharp contrast drawn by many proponents between restorative and retributive justice[9]. Advocates have been accused of exaggerating certain claims about restorative justice (Daly and Immarigeon 1998; Daly 2002). The lack of clarity and coherence of restorative goals has been highlighted (von Hirsch, Ashworth and Shearing et al 2003). The departure of restorative justice from fundamental principles of justice has been identified (Ashworth 2002). The conservative nature of restorative ideals has been noted (Pavlich 2005; Johnstone 2007, 607-10).

Another common concern is that even if restorative ideals are not intrinsically flawed, restorative reforms may go astray and result in something not only different from what was originally envisaged but even worse problems than those which the reforms were designed to remedy[10]. There are historical precedents of criminal justice interventions which got sidetracked, resulting in undesirable consequences and serving functions rather different from those that had been intended (Martinson 1974; Rothman 1980; Cullen and Gilbert 1982). And there are no guarantees that restorative justice will escape the fate of earlier well-intended criminal justice reforms. In fact, there are good reasons to predict the likelihood of restorative ideals being diluted and distorted when implemented within – or closely related to – the hierarchical and coercive criminal justice system. Restorative values do not fit very well with the values of the traditional justice system. Indeed, using the words of Sullivan and Tifft (2006), restorative justice is 'subversive' in nature, or 'an act of insurgency', in the sense that it competes with the state's way of responding to harms and defining what harms should be given attention in the first place. Consequently, restorative justice 'must be put down, contained, co-opted, or modified in some other way to meet the state's ideological and administrative requirements' (Sullivan and Tifft 2006, 2).

What lies ahead

This book aims to contribute to the growing critique of restorative justice by analyzing certain current trends within the current practice and examining aspirations

8 Some examples of the critical works are Pavlich 1996a, 1996b, 2001, 2002a, 2002b, 2004, 2005, 2007; Daly 2000, 2002; Ashworth 2002; Johnstone 2002; 2003, part E; 2007; Duff 2002, 2003; Crawford and Newburn 2003; von Hirsch, Roberts et al 2003.

9 For this criticism see Zedner 1994; Barton 2000; Daly 2000, 2002; Duff 2002, 2003; Dignan 2002; Johnstone 2002; Roche 2007.

10 For discussions of this view see Zehr 1990, 232-6; Levrant et al 1999; Mika and Zehr 2003; Toews and Zehr 2004, vii-viii.

of advocates. Drawing upon the author's qualitative research – which involved observations within a family group conferencing project in the UK and numerous in-depth qualitative interviews with those who participated in the conferences (including interviews with victims, offenders, supporters of each and organizers and facilitators) – the book demonstrates the existence of a significant gap between the ideals of proponents of restorative justice and the objectives being pursued in practice. However, rather than seeing this gap as more or less inevitable in the implementation of any set of ideas, this book suggests that, to some extent, the way restorative justice has developed in practice can be attributed to the problematic nature of restorative ideals. Some of them are based on questionable and mistaken assumptions. Others are simply unrealistic. Hence, building upon the empirical work, the book goes on to examine critically the aspirations of the restorative justice movement, exposing key limitations and contradictions in the basic project of restorative justice. However, this will not be a purely negative critique. It will be suggested that it may be possible both to reformulate the aspirations of the restorative justice movement and to develop practices which express a coherent set of restorative ideals.

Some important points need to be made about the empirical study forming the basis of this book. First, whilst the empirical work is absolutely central to the book, the book itself is not simply a report of an empirical project. Rather, it contains a mixture of theoretical reflection and empirical analysis. Empirical findings are used to examine theoretical arguments of restorative justice proponents and generate new discussions. Secondly, the empirical study was confined to one restorative justice project and the number of interviewees was rather small. So it is important to look at the arguments, criticisms and claims made on the basis of the findings in the light of this fact. Thirdly, this empirical research is rather different from many other current evaluations of restorative justice programmes (see Chapter One for a discussion of problems in most present empirical research into restorative justice). The major difference lies in that this study was not designed primarily to answer questions posed by governments or any other bodies pursuing particular interests. Nor did it intend to measure 'success' of practical applications of restorative justice with reference to the standard criteria, such as re-offending rates and cost-effectiveness. Rather, the study aimed at letting people who have had a first-hand experience of restorative justice speak for themselves and explain what was important for them. The objective was to invite participants in restorative justice conferences to express their views and opinions, raise concerns and criticisms and bring their unique insights and perspectives to the restorative justice debate. How did participants in restorative justice interventions interpret what they saw and heard during restorative justice encounters? How does the understanding of the restorative justice process by its participants fit with the ideas of restorative justice advocates? How close does restorative justice, as practised in this family group conferencing project, come to the ideals of campaigners for restorative justice? Can insights of people who participated in restorative justice interventions shed some light on how realistic aspirations of restorative justice advocates are? Can experiences of participants help to identify problems which are likely to arise when restorative justice ideals are pursued in practice? These are some of the questions to which this book seeks answers.

Chapter One will describe practical applications of restorative justice. The main models of restorative justice – victim-offender reconciliation and mediation programmes, family group conferencing and sentencing circles – will be discussed. Other examples of restorative justice in action, in particular, Navajo peacemaking, Vermont community reparative boards, Zwelethemba experiment in South Africa and community-based restorative initiatives in Northern Ireland, will be provided. Then the chapter will outline recent restorative developments in England and some implications of current restorative policies. It will also discuss some problems inherent in most present empirical research in the area.

Chapter Two will discuss the key aspirations of restorative advocates and some disagreements and debates within the movement. The following aspirations and debates accompanying them will be examined: to create a new moral 'lens' through which crime and justice could be looked at; to develop an alternative to punishment and treatment models; to craft a way of doing criminal justice which would be characterized by victim-orientation, voluntariness, individual empowerment, deprofessionalization and community-orientation; to create a model of justice that would aim at reparation of harm and restoration of peace and harmony in the aftermath of an offence. Additionally, the debates within the restorative justice movement concerning the relationship between restorative justice and the criminal justice system will be outlined.

In Chapters Three and Four the key aspirations of restorative justice advocates will be looked at in the light of empirical findings. It will be demonstrated that the realities of restorative practice do not match the ideals of the advocates. It will be suggested that some aspirations have not been thought through by the advocates very well. They may be unrealistic or undesirable. Chapter Four will also discuss the relationship between restorative justice and the criminal justice system and argue in the light of empirical findings that dependence of restorative justice on the system is problematic.

Chapter Five will summarize the findings and discuss the implications of this empirical study for the key ideals of advocates and some debates that have taken place within the restorative justice movement. A significant gap between restorative ideals and practical realities will be identified and possible explanations for the existence of that gap will be offered. Finally, suggestions will be made as to how restorative justice practices could be brought closer to the ideals of advocates and how some ideals could be reformulated so as to avoid some present problems, tensions and dangers.

Chapter One

Restorative Justice in Action

This chapter will trace the emergence, evolution and expansion of restorative practices around the globe in the last 30 years or so. Three major models of restorative justice and some other restorative practices will be described. Then the chapter will proceed to discuss some present restorative policies and distinctive features of most current empirical research into restorative justice.

Ancient practice and its revival

According to its proponents, restorative justice is not a new invention. Rather, it is a return to traditional patterns of dealing with conflict and crime that had been present in different cultures throughout human history (Braithwaite 2002a, chapter 1). It is argued that in the era pre-dating modern states, crime was conceptualized in personal terms and was responded to in a fashion more in line with restorative justice, with the emphasis placed on restitution and reconciliation[1]. The state-administered retributive response to crime that dominates today's justice systems and governs our understanding of crime and justice is a phenomenon just a few centuries old[2]. The punitive system of crime control evolved and achieved its full development in the second half of the eighteenth century, and, as other parts of the world were colonized by Europeans, the Western model of justice was imposed on colonized peoples. Once Western legal systems were established, the informal, community-based forms of conflict resolution survived to some degree – openly or secretly – in many countries, but in public discourse they were generally considered as practices inferior to law. However, since the 1960s, there has been a sea change. Attempts have been made to begin reversing the historical process and revive ancient conflict resolution traditions. A variety of social and political movements have contributed to this reversal, such as the informal justice movement[3], the restitution movement (Barnett 1977, 1980), the victims' movement (Dignan 2005; Williams 2005; Green 2007), penal abolition[4], peacemaking criminology (Pepinsky and Quinney 1991), the women's movement (Harris 1989, 1991; Daly and Stubbs 2007), the growth of interest in native justice traditions of indigenous people[5]. These diverse influences

1 Some commentators challenge this view, as will be discussed below.

2 For this view see Zehr 1990, chapter 7; Bianchi 1994; Wright 1996; Cayley 1998, chapter 7; Weitekamp 2003; Van Ness and Strong 2006, 7-9.

3 See Christie 1977, 1982; Abel 1982; Auerbach 1983; Matthews 1988.

4 See Mathiesen 1974; Bianchi & van Swaaningen 1986; Bianchi 1994; Cayley 1998.

5 For discussions of indigenous roots of restorative justice see Griffiths and Hamilton 1996; Pratt 1996; Stuart 1996; Yazzie and Zion 1996; Nielsen 1996; Taraschi 1998; Yazzie

directly or indirectly contributed to the emergence of the restorative justice idea and practice.

The main broad categories of 'modern' restorative justice practices include victim-offender reconciliation and mediation programmes, family group conferencing and sentencing circles. These models of restorative justice will be discussed below. Also, some other examples of restorative practices will be provided, in particular, Navajo peacemaking, community reparative boards in Vermont, the Zwelethemba experiment in South Africa and community-based restorative justice projects in Northern Ireland.

Victim-offender reconciliation/mediation programmes

In 1974, in the Canadian town of Elmira, two young men vandalized twenty-two properties. At the request of their probation officer the judge ordered that they meet their victims and bring back a report of the damage they have suffered. The offenders visited their victims and reached restitution agreements with them (Peachey 1989). This spontaneous experiment was the first documented instance of what today is called victim-offender reconciliation and led to the establishment of a victim-offender reconciliation programme under the auspices of the Mennonite Central Committee in Kitchener, Ontario. Soon the idea and the practice spread through the Mennonite community into other parts of Canada and the USA (Zehr 1990, chapter 9).

Victim-offender reconciliation[6] is based on the idea that following a criminal offence, the victim and the offender have a shared interest in righting the wrong. The emphasis is placed on reconciliation, assisting victims in the aftermath of an offence, helping offenders to change their lives and, more generally, humanizing the criminal justice system (Zehr 1990). Victim-offender reconciliation programmes typically involve a face-to-face encounter between the victim and the offender[7]. With the help of a neutral third party – a trained mediator – they are provided with an opportunity to talk about what has happened and express their feelings. Victims can tell offenders how crime has affected them and ask questions. Then the parties may decide together what needs to be done about what happened and reach a mutually satisfying agreement. An agreement may involve the offender making financial restitution, working for the victim (or the community), undertaking to behave in a particular way or attending some rehabilitation programme, such as anger management. The mediator facilitates the mediation process, but does not impose outcomes upon the

1998; Zion 1998; Zion and Yazzie 2006.

6 The early programmes were known as 'victim-offender reconciliation programmes', however, some objected to the term 'reconciliation', because it was value-laden. Victims' rights advocates believed that the term implied that victims need to reconcile with their offenders. They preferred the term 'mediation'. Today most programmes are referred to as 'victim-offender mediation'.

7 Sometimes victim-offender reconciliation/mediation programmes take form of 'shuttle diplomacy' between the victim and the offender. They do not meet face-to-face, rather a mediator meets with them separately and acts as an intermediary in negotiating a restitution settlement.

parties. The idea is to promote a dialogue and empower victims and offenders to solve the conflict the way they like (within certain limits)[8].

Such face-to-face encounters between victims and offenders provide victims with a unique opportunity to receive answers to questions, some of which can only be answered by offenders. Victims may express how the offence affected them and how they feel about it and express it to people who committed the offence against them (Umbreit 1994). Face-to-face encounters with offenders may also help challenge stereotypes which victims may have about offenders and possibly reduce victims' fears. Victims may receive compensation for their losses, and, importantly, have a say over their desired compensation or reparation. All these opportunities may provide victims with a sense of empowerment and assist in the healing process (Zehr 1990).

Offenders are given an opportunity to see whom they have wronged and how the person was affected by their actions. They may have their stereotypes of victims and rationalizations of their actions challenged. They are invited to take responsibility for their actions and put things right. They may also express remorse and ask forgiveness (Zehr 1990).

Victim-offender reconciliation/mediation takes place within the context of the criminal justice system as an exercise of police, prosecutor or judicial discretion. The programmes can be located in the police or prosecuting departments or in non-profit community-based or church-based organizations.

As mentioned above, one of the major historical roots of victim-offender reconciliation/mediation were programmes initiated and developed by the Mennonite community. There were some other important roots. One of them was the early neighbourhood dispute resolution programmes, which emerged in the 1960s and 1970s in the USA (Wright 1996, chapter 4). Another important source of influence was the victims' rights movement (Umbreit, Coates and Vos 2001). Some proponents of the victims' rights movement worked closely with victim-offender reconciliation/mediation advocates in order to ensure that the process was conducted in a victim-sensitive fashion. However, it needs to be pointed out that many proponents of victims' rights were sceptical about – and some even opposed – the idea of bringing victims and offenders together. It was feared that such encounters may compound victims' injuries. It was also believed that victim-offender reconciliation/mediation programmes may lead to a reduced punishment for the offender. Some within the victims' rights movement still hold that view (Umbreit, Coates and Vos 2001).

In 1980s victim-offender reconciliation/mediation programmes were transplanted to Europe (Wright and Galaway 1989; Marshall and Merry 1990; also see relevant chapters in Messmer and Otto 1992). Today the victim-offender mediation movement is international in scope. Numerous programmes operate in North America and Europe[9] (Umbreit 1996; Wynne 1996; Claes 1998; The European Forum for Victim-Offender Mediation and Restorative Justice 2000). There are also some programmes

8 For detailed discussions of victim-offender mediation see Chupp 1989; Umbreit 1989, 1994; Zehr 1990; Marshall and Merry 1990; Umbreit, Coates and Vos 2001.

9 Umbreit (1999, 213) estimates that there are more than 1000 programs throughout North America and Europe. Two-thirds of these programs are private community-based or

in Australia, New Zealand, and South Africa (Umbreit 1999; Umbreit, Coates, Vos 2001).

Numerous studies of victim-offender mediation programmes have been carried out. The research findings have been largely positive. In particular, a high level of satisfaction and perception of fairness with the mediation process for both victims and offenders has been consistently reported (Coates and Gehm 1989; Marshall and Merry 1990; Umbreit and Coates 1993; Umbreit 1994, 1996). For instance, following a two-and-a-half-year study of VOM programmes in California, Minnesota, New Mexico and Texas, Umbreit and Coates reported that 79 per cent of victims and 87 per cent of offenders were satisfied; 83 per cent of victims and 89 per cent of offenders thought that the process was fair. It was found that victim-offender mediation had a significant impact on the likelihood of offenders successfully completing their restitution obligations (81 per cent), compared with similar offenders who completed court-imposed restitution obligations and did not participate in mediation (58 per cent) (Umbreit and Coates 1993; Umbreit 1994). It has been also reported that victim-offender mediation led to the reduction of fear and anxiety among victims (Umbreit 1994).

Family group conferencing: New Zealand experience

Up to the 1990s, restorative justice functioned by way of isolated experiments. Dramatic changes occurred after the Children, Young Persons and their Families Act was passed in New Zealand in 1989. This piece of legislation created a new forum called 'family group conferences' to address juvenile offending and made family group conferences an official response to juvenile crime.

According to its proponents, family group conferencing has ancient roots[10]. It was adapted from the 'whanau conference' practised by the Maori people. The Maoris did not have anything similar to the Western criminal justice system. Rather, their way of dealing with conflicts and wrongdoings was embedded in everyday life. The Maoris saw conflicts and wrongdoings as affecting extended families and clans of victims and offenders. So, in the aftermath of crime extended families of the victim and the offender came together and negotiated a conflict resolution (Maxwell and Morris 1996; Pratt 1996; Consedine 1999).

British colonization brought with it the Western criminal justice system, and the traditional Maori way of responding to wrongdoings almost disappeared. In the 1980s a number of developments (such as growing crime rates and imprisonment among Maoris, disenchantment with the formal legal process and a resurgence of interest in the rights and cultures of indigenous peoples) lead to publication in 1988 of a report by Moana Jackson, commissioned by the New Zealand Department of Justice. This report suggested that racial bias was endemic in the criminal justice system (Pratt 1996). The report also advised that Maoris should be allowed to deal with conflicts

---

church-based, and about a fourth operate under the auspices of probation and corrections (Umbreit, Coates and Vos 2001).

10 Some critics, however, dispute this (Zellerer and Cunneen 2001; Cunneen 2003).

and crimes that affected them in a way which was culturally appropriate, which meant returning to the pre-colonial methods of dispute-resolution.

The resulting legislation was the Children, Young Persons and their Families Act 1989. It brought forth a number of important developments, among which was the introduction of family group conferencing as a new forum to address juvenile offending. After the implementation of this legislation, only really serious offences by juveniles go to court. Other cases are diverted from the criminal justice system and referred to youth justice coordinators. Youth justice coordinators convene family group conferences, and normally the matter will be handled as decided by the conference without going to the court. There are two routes to family group conferences: (1) 'direct referral' to a youth justice coordinator, or (2) where there has been an arrest and charges have been laid, a case can be referred from the Youth Court.

A family group conference is attended by the offender, his or her relatives, friends, the victim (or a victim representative), a youth advocate, a police officer and possibly a social worker. The youth justice coordinator (who works for the Department of Social Welfare) organizes and usually facilitates the conference. At the beginning of the process, the police describe the offence, and the offender is invited to admit or deny involvement. If involvement is admitted, the conference proceeds with victims describing the impact of the offence on them. Victims have an opportunity to tell how the crime affected them, describe their experiences, express their emotions and ask questions directed at offenders. If the victim is represented by someone else, that person reports on behalf of the victim. People who come to conferences to support the victim can tell how they were affected by the offence and ask questions. The offender's familiy and friends are also allowed to speak. Participants will discuss how the injuries caused by crime could be repaired. Then the offender's family deliberates in private to develop a plan concerning what needs to be done to put things right and prevent further offending. The plan should take into account the views of victims, the need to hold the offender accountable and include measures necessary to prevent re-offending. The most common outcomes involve an apology to the victim(s) and work for the community. Then the meeting reconvenes and the plan is presented to victims and professionals for discussion. If the plan has been agreed by all those attending a family group conference and, for court referred cases, is accepted by the Youth Court judge, it is binding on those involved (Morris and Maxwell 2000, 207). If a conference is court-ordered, the Youth Court usually accepts recommendations made by conferences, but in serious cases it can impose additional sanctions (Maxwell and Morris 1994; McElrea 1996). The Youth Court may also decide cases if the family group conference recommends it or where the family group conference could not reach an agreement.

After the introduction of the 1989 Act evaluations of family group conferences were carried out (Maxwell and Morris 1993, 1994, 1996, 2000). A rather high level of satisfaction was reported among participants, except victims. Maxwell and Morris (1993, 115) found that 84 per cent of offenders and 85 per cent of their parents attending family group conferences were satisfied with the outcomes of conferences. Only half of victims were satisfied, and about a quarter of victims felt worse after the conference. However, it has been suggested that low levels of victim satisfaction could be partly due to lack of experience in working with victims and the fact that the processes were not established with victims in mind, rather than anything inherently wrong with the system itself (Maxwell and Morris 1993). It was argued that to a large degree victims' views were influenced by dissatisfaction with the process external to family group conferencing (for example, failure by professionals to inform victims about what happened after the conference and to make necessary arrangements for reparation). It was also suggested that there was no comparable information on victims' satisfaction levels with court outcomes, so the relatively low satisfaction figure could signify a relative success (Maxwell and Morris 1996).

It was found that restorative justice conferences could reduce re-offending, especially if offenders apologized to their victims and felt truly sorry for what they have done and provided the reintegrative aspects of restorative justice were achieved (Maxwell and Morris 2000, Morris and Young 2000, Morris and Maxwell 2003). For instance, it was found that in a sample of young offenders who took part in family group conferences in 1990-91, about three quarters were not reconvicted within a year, and more than two fifths had not been reconvicted at all or had been reconvicted only once within six years (Morris and Young 2000).

Before leaving New Zealand and looking at restorative justice in other jurisdictions, it is important to point out that unlike in cases of juveniles, the provision of restorative justice in cases of adult offenders has been very piecemeal. There are several pre-trial diversion and pre-sentencing programmes, however, it appears that judiciary do not always view outcomes of restorative justice encounters favourably. For example, *R v Clotworthy* [1998] 15 CRNZ 651 was a case which involved wounding with intent to cause grievous bodily harm, robbery being a motive. After this case was brought to a conference, the victim and the offender agreed that the offender would pay the victim $25,000 to cover the costs of cosmetic surgery. The sentencing judge, however, ordered the offender to pay the victim $15,000, and imposed 200 hours of community service and a two-year prison sentence suspended for two years. The prosecution appealed on grounds that the sentence was an insufficient response to a serious crime. The Court of Appeal reduced the reparation to $5,000 and imposed a term of three years' imprisonment. Critics suggested that this sentence obviously did not meet the victim's wishes (Bowen and Thompson 1999; Mason 2000; Morris and Young 2000).

Family group conferencing outside New Zealand

In 1991 an experiment started in Wagga Wagga – a town in New South Wales, Australia – which involved the police in the exercise of their common law powers of cautioning organizing and conducting family group conferences (Moore and O'Connell 1994; O'Connell 1998). Developments in New Zealand provided one source of influence for the Wagga Wagga conferences. However, one obvious difference between the New Zealand model of conferencing and the Wagga Wagga model was that the Wagga Wagga model was entirely police-based, without any other agencies involved in its functioning. The police were the only gate-keepers and undertook the organization and facilitation of conferences. Another source of influence was John Braithwaite's theory of reintegrative shaming (Braithwaite 1989). Family group conferences were conceived as instances of reintegrative shaming in practice (Moore 1993; Moore and O'Connell 1994; Braithwaite and Mugford 1994). In accordance with Braithwaite's theory, the distinction between 'reintegrative' shaming and 'stigmatising' shaming was made by practitioners, and the aim was to ensure that the conferencing process complied with principles of 'reintegrative shaming': shaming is conducted within a continuum of love and respect; the disapproval is aimed at the wrongdoing, rather than the wrongdoer; and shaming is finite and followed by gestures of forgiveness and reacceptance.

Wagga Wagga conferences were evaluated, and findings were positive (Moore and O'Connell 1994). Offenders and their families found conferences an effective and appropriate way of dealing with first-time offending. The research concluded that many offenders had gained an empathic understanding for the victims, and families of offenders noticed positive changes in their children (Moore and O'Connell 1994, 69). It was concluded that conferences resulted in improved communication between child-offenders and their parents. It was also found that conferences improved relationships between parents of offenders and police officers. Parents changed their perceptions of police officers and saw them not just as authority figures but as people offering guidance and help (Moore and O'Connell 1994, 70).

The Wagga Wagga conferencing received considerable attention and was seen by the police as a promising way of dealing with juvenile offenders. At the same time the model attracted criticisms. Concerns were expressed that the process gave police too much power (Sandor 1994) and that legal rights of offenders could be violated (Warner 1994). Besides, conferencing could lead to net-widening, that is, the expansion of the number of people caught in the net of penal control. It was suggested that when the Maori conferencing practices were transplanted to Australia, this intensified the police controls over Aboriginal people. Also, bringing the Maori practices to Australia was based on a false assumption that all indigenous people were amenable to conference-style resolutions and operated within shaming structures of social control (Blagg 1997).

In 1994, the Wagga experiment was abolished, because it was seen as a soft option for juvenile offenders (Blagg 1997, 2001; O'Connell 1998) and was superseded by the creation of a state-wide programme under the auspices of the Department of Juvenile Justice.

In the early 1990s, conferencing spread across Australia, with legislation authorizing conferences being passed by separate states (Miers 2001, 61). The overarching goal in the Australian legislative frameworks is to keep young offenders out of the formal justice system as much as possible. In addition to legislation-based schemes, conferencing is used in other contexts, such as schools and workplace conflicts, family and child welfare and care and protection matters (Cameron and Thorsborne 2001; Morrison 2001, 2007).

A considerable amount of research involving conferencing schemes in Australia has been carried out. Most findings have been positive, showing a high level of satisfaction with the fairness of the process and its outcomes (for an overview of Australian research see Daly 2001). One of the most interesting studies was the Reintegrative Shaming Experiments (RISE) Project carried out in Canberra, ACT

(Strang et al 1999, Strang 2002). This was a 5-year study, where RISE-eligible cases were randomly assigned to court or conference. This ensured that the control and comparison groups were equivalent on known and unknown variables, so any post-intervention differences between the conference and court groups could be attributed to the intervention, rather than to characteristics of individuals making up each group. One objective of RISE was to measure the impact of restorative interventions on offenders' and victims' perceptions of procedural justice and on offenders' post-conference offending. Offences included within the study were drunk driving, juvenile property offences and juvenile violent crime. It was found that offenders participating in conferences reported a higher level of satisfaction and greater procedural justice (which was defined as being treated fairly and with respect), than offenders who were processed by the court. The findings show that conferences increased the respect of offenders towards police and law more than the court did. There was a significant level of victim satisfaction, although there was a degree of dissatisfaction. The findings suggest that victims of more serious crimes are more likely to attend conferences, but at the same time are more likely to be dissatisfied. It was also found that conferences could have different impact on different forms of offending. For example, there seemed to be a greater impact on violent offenders (Strang et al 1999).

Restorative justice conferencing proliferated rapidly around the world, and in mid-1990s they were transplanted to the UK where the Thames Valley Police experiment received an extraordinary amount of publicity. It used the Wagga model of conferencing instead of traditional cautioning (Young and Goold 1999; Pollard 2001; Young 2001; Young and Hoyle 2003). The project became operational across the Thames Valley Police force in April 1998. The clients of the programme are all first-time offenders and some second-time offenders, both adult and juvenile, who fit the criteria for a caution or reprimand. The criteria involve the following: there must be sufficient evidence of guilt to give a realistic prospect of conviction, the offender must admit the offence, and the offender (or, in the case of a juvenile, a responsible adult) must give informed consent to the caution.

Police invite all affected by the offence to the cautioning sessions. A caution is delivered by police officers in accordance with a script which helps to facilitate a structured discussion of the harm caused by the offence and how it can be repaired. In accordance with the theory of reintegrative shaming (Braithwaite 1989), the facilitators are trained to ensure that the focus of shaming is on the offending behaviour, rather than the offender him- or herself.

The police officer delivering a caution would begin by saying some words of welcome and describe the purpose of the meeting. Then the offender is invited to provide their side of the story. The facilitator would ask questions in order to focus the offender on the harm caused, for example, 'Who do you think has been affected by your actions?' 'How have they been affected?'. Then the victim would be invited to present their side of the story. The facilitator would ask questions to encourage the victim to explain how they were affected by the offence and what harm has been caused. Where the victim does not attend the conference, the facilitator would present the victim's point of view, stressing the harm caused by the wrongdoing. Then people attending the meeting as supporters (usually parents of offenders) are invited to speak and explain how the offence affected them. After all the participants have spoken in turn, the facilitator would ask the offender if he or she wants to say anything to anyone present. At this point the offender may apologize. Then the facilitator would shift the focus of attention on to the issue of what needs to be done to repair the harm caused by the crime. Where victim(s) participate in the conference, an agreement may be made as to how the offender could compensate the victim(s) or repair harm caused to them in some other way. Then the facilitator would address the offender, emphasizing that the offender has begun the process of putting things right, that the offender is in a web of caring relationships, that the offender is not a bad person and their actions represented an out-of-character mistake. The session is concluded with the facilitator explaining the legal aspects of the caution and asking the participants to fill in a questionnaire seeking their views on the session (Young and Goold 1999; Hoyle et al 2002; Young and Hoyle 2003).

Research has shown that during the early stages of the implementation of restorative cautions the process was often deficient. Police officers delivering cautions sidelined other participants and occasionally asked questions inconsistent with the purpose of restorative justice. Later, overall the implementation improved, although this was not always the case (Hoyle et al 2002, 14-17; Young and Hoyle 2003, 286-9). Nevertheless, victims, offenders and their supporters were generally satisfied with the fairness of the process and the outcomes achieved (Hoyle et al 2002, 25). Offenders were very impressed when others present at conferences listened to them. Almost two-thirds of the victims said they felt differently about 'their' offenders as a result of the meeting. Two-thirds of all participants and three-quarters of offenders thought that cautioning helped the offenders understand the consequences of their offending behaviour (Hoyle et al 2002, 30-1). In most cases an apology was offered by offenders. However, it was found that in some cases facilitators pressurized offenders into apologizing (Hoyle et al 2002, 35-36). About two-fifth of offenders and a third of all participants said that the process made the offender feel like a bad person, which was precisely what the process was meant to avoid (Hoyle et al 2002, 34). It was also found that over two-thirds of offenders and 44 per cent of offender supporters felt coerced into participation in a conference. Researchers linked the quality of facilitation to the impact on participants' experiences and outcomes of the process (Hoyle et al 2002, 34-5). It was also concluded that restorative cautioning appeared to be more effective in reducing the risk of re-offending (Hoyle et al 2002, 48-56).

There are various other police-led restorative justice schemes around the world, which employ models similar to the Thames Valley experiment. One of them is the RISE experiment in Canberra, ACT, mentioned above. Another similar scheme is a programme in Bethlehem, Pennsylvania. The Bethlehem scheme deals only with juveniles arrested by the Bethlehem Police Department, who are first time offenders. Research into the scheme has been carried out, where both violent and property offenders were randomly assigned to conferencing or traditional court referral. Cases being conferenced were compared with those referred to court. It was found that offenders were equally satisfied with court or conferencing, with 95 per cent expressing some satisfaction. However, conferencing had higher ratings among crime victims, with 97 per cent satisfaction, compared to 81 per cent satisfaction with the court process. Victims and offenders both felt that they experienced fairness and that offenders were adequately held accountable by either courts or family group conferences (McCold and Stahr 1996; McCold and Wachtel 1998).

Sentencing circles

In the early 1990s another model of restorative justice emerged in Canada – sentencing circles[11]. This forum was pioneered in Canadian native communities and was informed by native practices. The first use of a sentencing circle took place in 1992. The offender (who was apparently a habitual one) pleaded guilty to carrying a baseball bat with the intention to assault a police officer. The prosecution insisted that 'the community' wanted him to be sent to jail. Judge Barry Stuart presided over the case. He adjourned the case, and when it was resumed, he reconfigured the court as a circle and invited the family and friends of the offender to find out what the offender's community really wanted. Family and friends of the offender made it clear that they did not want him to go to jail. It was also made clear that they were willing to help in his rehabilitation. The judge made a court order consistent with the wishes of the family. The offender successfully changed his life. This case gave a beginning to the model of restorative justice which today is known as sentencing circles.

The basic model used in sentencing circles is derived from aboriginal peacemaking practices in North America, mediation and consensual decision-making. Circles involve facilitated community meetings attended by victims, offenders, their families and friends, interested members of the community and usually representatives of the criminal justice system. Participants may be organized in one large circle or split into an inner and outer circle. The inner circle includes the victim, the offender, their supporters and criminal justice professionals who are normally involved in court. The outer circle is composed of professionals who may be called upon for specific information and interested members of the community. The 'keeper', or the facilitator of the process, keeps the process orderly, periodically summarizes what has been said for the benefit of those present in the circle, ensures respect for the teaching of the circle, mediates differences and guides the circle towards a consensus.

A circle is often opened with a prayer, which heightens the spiritual awareness of participants and calls them to reach beyond their immediate emotions in seeking responses to problems. Most prayers stress the interconnectedness of all things and all people and induce in the participants a feeling of being a part of the community. The participants start feeling that suffering of people directly affected by the crime is shared by others as well, that the disharmony caused by the offence affects the entire community, and that everybody in the circle shares responsibility for finding solutions to the problems.

Then the keepers of the circle make welcoming statements, introduce themselves and invite other participants in the circle to introduce themselves and explain why

11 For discussions of this model of restorative justice see Griffiths and Hamilton 1996; Stuart 1996; Cayley 1998, 182-198; Roberts and Roach 2003 and Ross 2003.

they are in the circle. Keepers discuss the teachings of the circle and extract guidelines from them, such as speak from the heart, allow others to speak by speaking briefly, respect others by not interrupting them, remain until the end of the circle and so on.

The circle enables its participants to be heard, express their views and feelings about the offence and propose solutions. Those who participate in the process speak one at a time and may discuss a wide range of issues regarding the crime. The issues discussed may help to understand why the offence occurred and what needs be done to meet the needs of the victim, hold the offender accountable and prevent similar incidents in the future. The discussions need not focus exclusively on the offence committed. They may go beyond immediate issues and uncover deeper problems. The judge, who is present during the process, passes a sentence and makes recommendations on the basis of what has been said in the circle.

It is argued that the circle process empowers its participants to take ownership of the process and to develop solutions to problems in accordance with their values and customs. It is also argued that the circle process reconnects offenders to their communities, rebuilds broken relationships and addresses victims' needs. The process educates the community about its problems, fosters a sense of belonging to the community, develops participatory skills of those who attend the process, helps to build communities which can work together, promotes the ability to mobilize local resources and generate community-based solutions to problems. It also helps to reveal underlying causes of crime, which in turn generates community initiatives aimed at redressing the needs of victims and offenders as well as addressing adverse social conditions (Stuart 1996).

The importance of circles also lies in the fact that they help to prevent the culture shock which many First Nation people experience when they have to appear in court. When native people follow their traditional ethic during court appearances (such as avoiding making eye contact, showing anger and confronting or criticizing others), their behaviour is regularly interpreted as indifference or uncooperativeness. Circle processes circumvent these problems, because they create settings where people can behave in a culturally appropriate fashion.

Today circle sentencing is widespread among aboriginal communities in Yukon, Canada. Circle sentencing is available to offenders who pleaded guilty and are motivated to comply with a plan created by a circle. One example of a circle sentencing programme is the Kwanlin Dun Community Justice Project, funded by the federal and territorial governments (Cayley 1998, 187).

Another Canadian example of a project utilizing the circle process is the Community Holistic Circle Healing Program in Hollow Water, Manitoba (Ross 2003). This is a healing programme which was designed to deal with high rates of sexual and family abuse among the aboriginal community. It is based on values of the First Nation peoples and has been implemented in four Native communities in Manitoba.

In 1980s, the Native communities in Hollow Water began to realize that alcoholism and incest had reached epidemic proportions within them. A group of social workers mobilized the community to deal with the problem, and a 'community holistic circle healing' was created as an alternative to conventional criminal justice processing for sex offenders. A protocol was negotiated with the Manitoba Department of

Justice that allowed a diversion and non-custodial sentencing of sex offenders. The underlying idea was that the traditional process of prosecuting and jailing offenders is counter-productive. It is believed that instead the problems can be dealt with more effectively within the community context. Offenders are given an option of going through the regular criminal justice system or taking responsibility for their actions and participating in the circle healing. Those who choose the latter are diverted from the court, and sentencing is delayed while a 'healing contract' is worked out.

Before the event called the Special Gathering (involving the victim, the offender and the community) takes place, a lot of preparation work is done with the offender and the victim. The first circle involves a meeting of the circle organizers with the offender. The offender is invited to tell as much as possible about what he has done and to begin to take responsibility for his actions. The next circle is with the family of the offender, when the offender tells his family about his activities. Another circle is with the victims. At this point the victim tells the offender about the impact of his actions. The fourth circle is the sentencing circle, where the whole case is open to the community, and where judicial authorities also participate. A healing contract would be signed during the process and the offender would publicly apologize to the victim(s) and their communities for the harm caused. The community has an opportunity to speak directly with the victim and the offender and make recommendations to the judge concerning sentencing. Assuming the offender takes responsibility for his actions and is willing to change, the sentence would not involve imprisonment. Rather, it would keep the offender in the community.

There is some evidence that circles may be effective in preventing re-offending: out of forty-three sex offenders who participated in the healing circle programme only two re-offended over a ten year period (Cayley 1998). However, it has been suggested that what may be even more important is the healing effect the circles have on communities. This is so because the circle offers a process which restores peace and order in the community. The programme heals not only victims and offenders, but the community as well. It was also suggested that perhaps circles could be used outside the native communities and viewed not as an 'aboriginal justice alternative', but as a practice that fits for everybody – just as the Maori traditions have been applied to the whole society in New Zealand through family group conferencing (Cayley 1998).

However, it has been argued that circle sentencing might involve dangers: it may make weak parties even weaker. It may lead to a situation where vulnerable members of the community may find themselves at the mercy of those in positions of power and influence (Griffiths and Hamilton 1996; Cayley 1998, 199-208).

Women's groups in particular have challenged the idea of delegating decision-making to the community and the adoption of community-based alternatives to imprisonment, because they believe this may help perpetuate the inferior status of women in native communities. Concerns were expressed about high rates of sexual and physical abuse in Native communities, and it was argued that local justice initiatives may not provide adequate protection for women (Cayley 1998, chapter 11).

It has been pointed out that communities are segmented by such considerations as wealth, gender, family connections, and authority. Unless these inequalities are addressed, the assumption underlying sentencing circles that the participants in a circle have an equal voice is highly questionable. It has been also suggested that the presumed homogeneity of the community submerges the interests of victim: the victim is persuaded to comply with the community interest, rather than insist on her or his own satisfaction. The emphasis within the sentencing circles that the problem is not located within the offender, but rather it is a problem of the community, seems to suggest that the victim (who is also part of the community) shares responsibility for the offence. In effect, within circles victims are encouraged to speak in a context where their voice is denied (Griffiths and Hamilton 1996, 187-8; Cayley 1998, 201-208).

Navajo peacemaking

There are various other practices consistent with restorative justice principles which currently operate in different parts of the world. Some examples will be provided below. One such practice is Navajo peacemaking. Similarly to the sentencing circles, it is based on Native American traditions.

For centuries the Navajo people had a traditional justice system which consisted of their common law and consensus-focused judicial procedures. However, since the end of the 19th century that justice system started crumbling, and the process finalized in 1959 when a Western court system was adopted. The Western justice system did not fit well with the Navajo culture, and in the 1980s the Navajo Supreme Court started integrating traditional Navajo law into the justice system.

In 1982, the Navajo Peacemaker Courts were created, which represented a court-annexed system of popular justice. Within Peacemaker courts, respected community leaders organize and preside over the traditional Navajo process to resolve problems and conflicts, which the Western culture conceptualizes as criminal. Peacemaker court decisions are made by the participants in accordance with Navajo values and thinking.

According to its proponents, Navajo peacemaking is a horizontal, egalitarian system of justice, where everybody is equally important in the peacemaking process. There is no pyramid of power or powerful people making decisions for others (Yazzie and Zion 1996). The Navajo solve their conflicts in the context of families and clans. When there is a dispute, a person who claims to be injured or wronged makes a demand on the accused to put things right. If individuals are unable or unwilling to make a direct demand, they may seek the help of relatives. Alternatively, a complainant may approach a *naat'aanii* and request his or her assistance in resolving a problem. *Naat'aanii* is a leader who is chosen because that person earns the respect of others and who is 'usually someone who thinks well, speaks well, plans well, and shows by his or her behaviour that the person's conduct is grounded in spirituality' (Yazzie 1998, 125).

The *naat'aanii* would invite interested parties for a group discussion of a problem, in particular, the clan of the victim and the perpetrator. The peacemaking process begins with a prayer in order to summon supernatural help and to focus the participants in the process on the conciliation. After a prayer, a complainant presents their grievances and makes a demand as to what she or he wants to happen. Relatives also have an opportunity to participate and express their views about the dispute. The accused has an opportunity to speak as well.

The *naat'aanii* is not a 'neutral' party in the peacemaking process. He or she has a persuasive authority and acts as a guide or teacher. One of the tasks a *naat'aanii* would perform is 'The Lecture'. The *naat'aanii* would

> ... pull wisdom from ancient Navajo journey and creation narratives to show how the same problems arose in the past and how [the] traditional figures dealt with them. Those stories reach inside people to revive the things they learned or should have learned as children. During the lecture, a peacemaker will apply the teachings to the problem and show how and why the excuses [put forward by the perpetrator] are false.
>
> (Yazzie 1998, 126)

The *naat'aanii* would draw upon the traditional teachings and propose what the parties involved in a dispute need to do to resolve the problem. After the lecture, disputants would move to discussing the problem and solutions to it. Following the discussion, the parties would make a decision about what to do. It may be decided that the offender makes restitution or reparation. If the offender has no money, members of the offender's family or clan would pay on his or her behalf. When necessary, relatives assume supervisory obligations towards the offender and use social pressure to ensure that the offender behaves in an appropriate fashion.

Peacemaking agreements can be reduced to, and enforced by, court judgement. However, in practice Navajo people prefer informal agreements. In Yazzie and Zion's words, Navajo peacemaking 'is not a system of law that relies upon authority, force and coercion, but one that utilizes the strengths of people in communities' (1996, 171).

Vermont community reparative boards

Another practice inspired by restorative justice principles which will be discussed here is community reparative boards in Vermont (Karp and Walther 2001). The programme was set up in 1996. The mission of the initiative was to enhance social control at the local level by involving citizens in the justice process. Community boards are an option for offenders convicted of minor offences who would otherwise receive probation or short-term prison sentences. Cases are referred to community boards by judges. Community volunteers serve on boards, and victims are encouraged to attend. Boards are open to the public, so it is not uncommon for observers to be present in addition to board members. Typically three to seven board members attend a meeting. Unlike other restorative justice encounters, community boards are not facilitated by professionally trained mediators or facilitators.

Board meetings start with personal introductions. After that the programme's mission and goals are reviewed. The meeting will then discuss the offence and its impact on victims and the community. It will also discuss strategies for reparation and reintegration and negotiate an agreement with the offender. The agreement may include various activities, such as writing a letter of apology, doing community service or participating in some competency development courses.

Usually offenders return to the board for a mid-term review (half the probationary period) and a final meeting before the offender is discharged upon completing the agreement. Offenders who are unwilling to sign an agreement or fail to comply with the terms of an agreement are returned to court.

Boards have limited power. They cannot retry cases or overturn judicial determinations of guilt. All they can do is recommend a sanction. Boards cannot create contracts that continue beyond ninety days. Neither can they stipulate any formal terms of supervision or imprisonment. There are also limits on the length of community service and the amount of other types of activities which the boards may assign. Also, only the court can order restitution or financial compensation. Yet, boards have considerable latitude in negotiating agreements tailored to a particular offender.

Research into the community boards has been undertaken, and it was found that 52 per cent of offenders successfully completed terms of the agreements. Some other findings were rather negative. Only 15 per cent of victims attended board meetings. Various explanations have been offered for low victim attendance: victims do not understand potential benefits of the programme; offences which are referred to boards are minor, and victims prefer to forget about the experience, rather than belabour it; and victims are primarily interested in receiving restitution, which is court-ordered in Vermont, so their needs might have been sufficiently met before board meetings (Karp and Walther 2001, 211).

Concerns have been raised that boards contain an imbalance of powers between older, middle-class, well-educated board members and more youthful, working-class, less-educated offenders. It is questionable whether the process really empowers offenders and whether their participation and contribution to decision-making is meaningful (Karp and Walther 2001, 214). The boards were also criticized on grounds that, unlike other restorative justice programmes, they do not employ professionally trained facilitators, and 'community volunteers involved in the boards often appear amateurish, undiplomatic, and less knowledgeable about restorative principles than trained mediators' (Karp and Walther 2001, 215).

Zwelethemba experiment

Another interesting restorative justice initiative is the Zwelethemba experiment in South Africa (Shearing 2001; Roche 2002; Froestand and Shearing 2007). The experiment known as the Community Peacemaking Programme started in 1997. With funding from the South African government and overseas governments, the programme began working with local community. The idea was to develop a community-based conflict resolution process centred around the use of peace committees.

There are two aspects to problem-solving within the Zwelethemba model. The first aspect involves peacemaking and peacebuilding. Peacemaking refers to problem-solving in relation to on-going conflicts that will establish peace with respect to particular disputes. Peacebuilding refers to problem-solving with respect to more broad issues. The second aspect is concerned with sustaining the processes of peacemaking and peacebuilding over time (Shearing 2001; Roche 2002).

After a complaint is made to a peace committee (a local group of peacemakmers), the committee convenes a meeting where the complainant, the accused, people whom the complainant and the accused have invited and those who were not specifically invited come together. Members of peace committees – or peacemakers – act as facilitators who have no authority to resolve disputes or insist that agreements are kept (Shearing 2001, 27). Yet, peacemakers can actively participate in the conflict-resolution process and make suggestions. The role of peacemakers is to facilitate the process and ensure that the agreements that have been reached conform to the Code of Good Practice and the ethical and legal framework it embodies[12] (Shearing 2001, 33). Peacemakers come from the same township as participants in a conflict and have six-months renewable license. Failure to follow the Code of Good Practice is a ground for not renewing a peacemaker's licence.

The overall objective of peacemaking forums is to bring together local knowledge and resources and provide solutions to the dispute by mobilizing the local capacity to deal with problems:

> In both the Peacemaking and Peacebuilding Forums the emphasis is not on problems but on the knowledge and capacity available within circles for solving them. The model's technology seeks to 'make people up', 'to hail them out', not as people who have problems – and certainly not as people who give their problems away ... to others experts, state or non-state – but as people who are capable of developing solutions. ...The model views disputes as occasions around which to demonstrate to people that they have the capacity and knowledge required to self-govern.
>
> (Shearing 2001, 22)

Importantly, the emphasis is not on reaching particular outcomes, but on empowering participants to handle their problems themselves:

> It is this bringing together of knowledge and capacity to seek a solution, rather than any particular desired form of outcome (for example, 'restoration as a healing component' for victims, restoration as 'accepting responsibility' for offenders and restoration as 'denouncing wrongful behaviour' for communities...), that is at the heart of the model.
>
> (Shearing 2001, 20)

A distinctive feature of the experiment is that it does not operate by way of diversion from the criminal justice system. Rather, a complainant brings a matter to a peace committee. This helps to avoid situations where cases come to the programme with definitions already attached by the criminal justice system (for example, what constitutes 'crime', who is a 'victim' and who is an 'offender' in the situation), and a framework within which the case will be responded to is already pre-established by the system and will direct the process and outcomes. The consequence of cases coming directly to the programmes is that

---

12 One of the principles enshrined in the Code is a prohibition against the use of force or violence to solve a problem. If it is decided that a coercive response is necessary to resolve a dispute, the matter has to be referred to the police or some other state authority (Shearing 2001, 21).

> Events are firmly embedded in a wider and deeper terrain. Thus, for instance, a stabbing is not 'pulled out' of the context of daily life as an 'assault' that has an offender and a victim. Rather it is located within a wider context of often ongoing and long-established patterns of action that include groupings such as families, neighbours and so on. Within this broader context, who is the 'offender' and who the 'victim' very often oscillates depending on just when a snapshot of events is taken – a 'victim' today may well have been an 'offender' yesterday.
>
> (Shearing 2001, 24)

A person accused of a wrongdoing is not required to make any admission before a peace committee gathering. Nor are they required to make any admission during a gathering. As a consequence, responsibility may swap between – or be shared by – people involved (Roche 2002, 528).

Peace committees receive cases directly from complainants (as opposed to the criminal justice system). So, the committees deal with actions which may be illegal, as well as those which are legal, although may be objectionable (for instance, infidelity, excessive noise late at night, the passing of insults). On one view, intervening in such cases is problematic because it results in net-widening (that is, bringing into the system of social control people who may have otherwise stayed out of it). On another view, such interventions are justifiable because they may prevent more serious harm from occurring. Early interventions may resolve conflicts, which, unless addressed by peace committees, may escalate into 'state-attention problems' (Shearing 2001, 24; Roche 2002, 527).

Yet another remarkable feature of the model is the income-generating mechanisms built into it. Peace committees are paid for every peace gathering conducted in accordance with the Code of Practice. A proportion of the money is invested into local development projects in an attempt to address the problems identified in the course of the peace-making process. For instance, the peace committee in Zwelethemba built a desperately needed children's playground and purchased sleeping mates for a new child care centre in the township. Also, 30 per cent of the money earned from peacemaking is used for loans to fund micro-businesses in the township (Roche 2002, 525). Peace committees can be viewed as small businesses which meet local demands for conflict resolution and earn money which they spend partly on themselves and partly on others (Froestand and Shearing 2007, 548).

Community-based initiatives in Northern Ireland

Community-based restorative justice initiatives in Northern Ireland were established mainly to respond to systems of informal justice developed in the last three decades[13]. In those informal justice systems both Republican and Loyalist paramilitaries assumed responsibility for the 'policing' of their communities through violent and brutal punishments and banishments (McEvoy and Mika 2001). The restorative justice projects were designed to provide alternatives to paramilitary punishment attacks.

13 There is a number of state-led restorative justice schemes in Northern Ireland as well, but they have not been so high-profile (McEvoy and Mika 2002, 534).

Following heavy criticisms by international human rights organizations and single-issue pressure groups in 1990s, Republicans and Loyalists have permitted intervention on behalf of those under threat of punishments. In 1996, a programme was devised at the request of activists from Republican areas which provided training on issues concerning informal justice (McEvoy and Mika 2001; McEvoy and Mika 2002). Following extensive consultations with Republicans, statutory agencies, community representatives and political parties, a discussion document ('The Blue Book') was produced in 1997, which outlined a model based upon 'community restorative justice' (Auld et al 1997). Following the publication of the document, NIACRO provided funding for four pilot projects in Republican areas.

The model proposed in the Blue Book was designed to meet several specifications, such as non-violence, meeting the needs and responsibilities of victims, offenders and communities; community involvement in the delivery of the programme; acting within the law; proportionality between sanction and infraction; due process and consistency; inclusive and transparent approach to the management and staffing of the project (Auld et al 1997).

Between the publication of the Blue Book and the projects becoming operational several of the proposed features have not been incorporated. For instance, it was originally envisaged that projects would have investigation powers and the power to 'boycott' persistent offenders, but these proposals have not been implemented. Instead, the work of the projects includes 'normal' restorative justice activities, such as preparation of victims and offenders, mediation, family group conferences and the monitoring of agreements (McEvoy and Mika 2001, 369; McEvoy and Mika 2002, 538).

The projects operating in Republican areas are known as Community Restorative Justice Ireland. Cases are usually referred to a local office by aggrieved parties or another local organisation or aired with local members of the management committee or the volunteer mediators of the service anywhere they might be found (McEvoy and Mika 2002, 538). Community members are encouraged to approach restorative justice projects where they would previously have approached the IRA seeking punishment or threats. Cases involving both criminal and anti-social behaviour are accepted by the projects, ranging from minor disputes (such as noise) to serious matters, including paramilitary threats (McEvoy and Mika 2002, 538-9). Assuming that a matter is within the remit of the service[14], the project staff assigns the case to teams of trained volunteers who either carry out indirect mediation or prepare parties for – and conduct – face-to-face mediations or conferences. The local service attempts to monitor compliance with agreements made during restorative encounters. Research has demonstrated that large group conferences are not uncommon, and many disputes are long-standing and complex in nature (McEvoy and Mika 2002, 538).

The project operating on the Loyalist side is known as 'the Greater Shankill Alternatives'. Its focus is to provide an alternative to punishment violence for young offenders in their community. Upon receiving a referral, the project stuff contact the Ulster Volunteer Force to verify that the threat exists and then negotiate lifting the threat of punishment from those who successfully participate in the Alternatives

14 Some types of conflict, for example, domestic violence and child abuse, are referred to other community or statutory resources (McEvoy and Mika 2002, 538).

programme. A young person is assigned a caseworker and a contract is drafted specifying victim restitution, community reparation and measures aimed at offending behaviour. A young person has a regular contact with a community panel which monitors the completion of the contract. After the contract is completed, the young person is discharged (McEvoly and Mika 2002, 540).

How did the state respond to these community-based restorative programmes? The projects received a cautious welcome. A 'Protocol on Restorative Justice' issued in June 1999 emphasized a complete state control over all aspects of any restorative justice process. The various prerogatives of the police were repeatedly raised. It postulated that

> ...any community-based initiatives in this area can only be pursued in full cooperation with the police and other criminal justice agencies. This means that any group or structures organised by the community should include provision for full cooperation and communication with the police.
>
> (Northern Ireland Office 1999, quoted in McEvoy and Mika 2002, 542)

So, complete and unconditional support for the police was demanded of communities with regards to restorative justice programmes. Only schemes making structural provisions for the full participation of the police were allowed.

This situation gives rise to the criticism that restorative justice is 'the co-option of revolutionary struggle and the legitimation of the state' (McEvoy and Mika 2001, 378). McEvoy and Mika quote from Saoirse, the magazine of Republican Sinn Fein:

> Community Restorative Justice is British double speak for collaboration with Crown Forces... NIACRO is dedicated to recruiting ex-prisoners into a new police force which will serve as an auxiliary wing of the RUC... It is clear that the establishment of a new British police force in the guise of community justice is the initiative of a British colonial agency operating from Stormount.
>
> ('Blue Book form New British Police', Saourse, September 1998, quoted in McEvoy and Mika 2001, 378)

It has been suggested, however, that even if this argument has some validity, it is not a good justification for continued brutal paramilitary punishments (McEvoy and Mika 2001, 378).

Recent restorative justice developments in England

Changes introduced by legislative provisions

There were some restorative justice projects operating in England since the 1980s[15], however the widespread development of restorative justice practices did not begin until recently. Important changes relating to youth offenders in England were brought

15 For some examples see Davis, Boucherat and Watson 1988; Marshall and Merry 1990; Dignan 1992; Miers et al 2001.

about by the Crime and Disorder Act 1998 (hereafter CDA) and the Youth Justice and Criminal Evidence Act 1999 (hereafter YJCEA). These two pieces of legislation establish some elements of restorative justice as a mainstream response to youth offending.

Section 67 of the CDA introduced reparation orders which require offenders to make some reparation either to the victim(s) or to the community at large. A reparation order may include such activities as writing a letter of apology to the victim(s), undertaking some form of practical activity that benefits the victim or the community, mediation or a restorative justice conference. Section 68(1)(b) requires that before making a reparation order, views of the victim(s) should be sought. Section 69 CDA introduced action plan orders. This order may require offenders to make reparation to the victim(s) or to the community at large. Reparation to the victim(s) or the community at large may also be included as a requirement of a supervision order (section 71(1) CDA). Additionally, offenders who have been given a final warning (section 66 CDA) may be required to take part in a rehabilitation programme, which may involve some form of a reparative activity either for the benefit of the victim or the community. It is also possible for some form of mediation or the Thames-Valley-style restorative cautioning to take place at this point.

Under the YJCEA 1999, all first time offenders who plead guilty (with the exception of those who are given an absolute discharge or who are sentenced to custody) must be referred to youth offender panels. The panels are set up by youth offending teams and comprise three members. One of them must be from the youth offending team (hereafter YOT), and the others are drawn from a panel of trained community volunteers. The youth offender panel involves a conference-type approach and holds a discussion between the young offender, their parents or guardians, the victim(s)[16], two trained members of the community, a YOT worker and anyone else that the panel considers to be capable of having a 'good influence' on the offender. The youth offender panel agrees on a contract with the offender. The contract involves activities aimed at preventing re-offending for the duration of the referral order and which, importantly, should always include reparation to the victim(s) or the community.

It has been argued that the philosophy behind the two pieces of legislation is broadly consistent with restorative justice principles (Dignan 1999; Dignan and Marsh 2001; Crawford and Newburn 2002). This is so because the measures introduced by the CDA and the YJCEA emphasize making offenders accountable by requiring them to undertake some form of reparation for the victim or the community. Also, the legislation provides a greater scope for victims' involvement in reparative sentencing. It is required that victims' views must be sought before reparative interventions. It may be possible for victims to participate in restorative conferences or restorative cautions. Victims may attend youth offender panels' deliberations. Notably, youth offender panels adopt a conference-type approach, which is based on the idea of inclusion, participation and consensual decision-making. The intention is

16 Where there is no direct victim, the panel may invite someone else who could bring the victim's perspective to the panel discussions.

that offenders, victims and community members should be empowered to reach an agreement. Emphasis is placed on reparation and reintegration.

In relation to adult offenders, Criminal Justice Act 2003 provides a legal basis for the use of restorative justice through the introduction of conditional cautions (Sections 22-27). Section 22(3) specifies that the condition(s) which may be attached to a conditional caution must have as their object either the rehabilitation of the offender or the making of reparation for the offence or both. Reparation may involve participation in a form of restorative justice.

Major empirical research

Research into the innovations introduced by the CDA and the YJCEA has been carried out. The Home Office evaluation of the pilot YOTs has identified problems relating to the requirement by the CDA to consult victims and, where they so wish, to arrange for them to receive direct reparation from the offender (Holdaway et al 2001). It has been found that victims of offenders who had been given a final warning were not usually involved in final warning process. Victims were contacted in only 15 per cent of cases. Just four per cent of victims had some form of direct involvement in reparative or mediating activity. Three per cent had indirect involvement (Holdaway et al 2001, 80). It has been also found that in relation to reparation orders, victims were contacted in 66 per cent of cases. Of those victims who were contacted, exactly half consented to some form of reparation being made by their offender. Just under two-thirds of those who consented agreed to some form of direct reparation to victims, just over one-third agreed to indirect reparation to the community. There were interesting variations in response rates across the pilots. The proportion of victims who consented to some form of reparation ranged from 20 per cent of those contacted in one of the pilots to 75 per cent in another. The proportion of victims who were willing to consent to direct, as opposed to indirect, reparation ranged from a low of 53 per cent to a high of 90 per cent (Holdaway et al 2001, 86).

The Home Office evaluation has found that virtually all YOTs were able to facilitate at least some form of direct reparation for victims. However, some YOTs used 'tokenistic' or 'formulaic' reparative interventions (for example, dictating letters of apology).

Another important finding is that not all victims felt that their needs had been met by the reparation they had received and most felt that the offenders' interests were seen as paramount. Nevertheless, the majority of victims were pleased to have been invited to take part in the process and felt that meeting their victim or providing direct reparation might help to discourage the offender from further offending (Holdaway et al 2001, 81).

The evaluation has concluded that all the pilot YOTs were strongly committed to using mediation where appropriate, but all have expressed strong concern at the speed with which they were expected to conduct the assessment and consultation process. Many have expressed strong doubts about the extent to which magistrates and their clerks are fully in tune with the restorative justice ethos that underpins this aspect of the CDA reforms (Holdaway et al 2001, 39).

Research into referral orders has also been undertaken, and early findings identify a number of problems (Crawford and Newburn 2002; Crawford and Newburn 2003). One of them is that youth offender panels are hardly representative of the community. Community volunteers willing to take part in panels are predominantly female, middle class and middle aged. There is a lack of correspondence between community representatives and communities which they seek to represent. It has been suggested that 'there is a danger that community panel members come to constitute something of a 'new magistracy', whose normative appeal may be undermined by their empirical lack of representativeness' (Crawford and Newburn 2002, 483).

Another problem is low victim attendance at the time when the research was carried out. It was found that victims attended panel deliberations in only 13 per cent of cases where a panel was held and where there was an identifiable victim. Research shows that working with victims poses a significant challenge for youth offending teams, for whom integrating victims and their perspectives into the core of their services is not an easy task and 'may appear to sit awkwardly alongside concerns for the young people with whom they work' (Crawford and Newburn 2003, 238).

A tension was found between managerial concerns (such as speed, cost reductions, performance measurement and so on) and communitarian appeals of local justice (that is, local people contributing to handling cases in their own local area). Managerial demands often led away from local justice and encouraged professionalization and centralization (Crawford 2006, 132-3). Lay members of the public had less involvement, and government departments and related agencies governed local practices. It was also suggested that the emphasis on speed and the reduction of delay may undermine victim input into the process. It is doubtful whether victims would want to attend the first panel meeting which is required to be held within 15 working days after court appearance and potentially soon after the offence (Crawford and Newburn 2002, 492; Crawford, 2006, 131-2).

Concerns have also been expressed over the fact that referral orders are coercive, which 'offends cherished restorative ideals of voluntariness' (Crawford and Newburn 2003, 239). However, research evidence from pilot sites shows that despite the coercive nature of the orders it was possible to engage offenders and their parents in the process in a more positive and constructive way than that found in criminal courts (Crawford and Newburn 2003, 239). It was also pointed out that by making referral orders an almost mandatory sentence of the court for first time juvenile offenders, referral orders ensure a steady supply of cases to youth offender panels, and thus help to avoid one of the main problems for most restorative justice initiatives – insufficient referrals. Crawford and Newburn argue that '[c]oercion provided the capacity to move certain restorative values to the very heart of the youth justice system, and the loss of voluntariness was the price paid' (2003, 239).

The most recent large study in England is the on-going evaluation of three restorative justice schemes funded by the Home Office as part of the Crime Reduction Programme (Shapland et al 2006a, 2006b). The study involves evaluation of restorative justice events, including conferencing, direct mediation and indirect mediation with both adult and young offenders. The study has found that unlike previous restorative justice initiatives which have found difficulty in engaging victims and obtaining victim attendance, the schemes achieved victim participation for over 90 per cent of conferences in one of the schemes and all direct mediations in the other two schemes. However, little community involvement was found. Victim and offender supporters tended to be family members, and representation from wider local community was very rare (Shapland et al 2006a, 71).

Another important finding is that both victims and offenders tended to display altruism, with offenders wanting to help victims and victims wishing to help offenders to stop offending. The rehabilitative priorities tended to dominate the restorative events. It was also found that most participants did not go to restorative encounters wanting financial compensation or direct reparation. They were more interested in preventing re-offending (Shapland et al 2006a, 72).

Some restorative trends and their implications

The growth of restorative justice in popularity in the past 30 years or so has been remarkable, and today practices and policies influenced by restorative justice ideas can be found on every continent and have a statutory basis in many countries (Johnstone and Van Ness 2007, Part 6). Restorative justice has secured a place not only in national legislations, but also at the level of international protocols and instruments. In 1999 the Committee of Ministers of the Council of Europe adopted a recommendation on the use of mediation in penal matters (Council of Europe 1999). In 2002 the United Nations Economic and Social Council endorsed a Declaration of Basic Principles on the Use of Restorative Justice Programmes in Criminal Justice Matters (United Nations 2002). As restorative justice is expanding in its influence, some noticeable trends are emerging.

Restorative justice as a criminal justice programme One such trend is that restorative justice often becomes equated to particular programmes operating either within – or in close alliance with – the criminal justice system. Such programmes typically depend on the system for legal framework, funding and referrals. The empirical study forming the basis of this book was carried out in one such programme. As will be noted in Chapter Two, some critics have argued that equating restorative justice to criminal justice programmes operating either within – or as an extension of – the criminal justice system is problematic. Chapter Four of this book will provide empirical evidence which may offer support to the arguments of these critics. The critics have also argued that restorative justice should not be restricted to criminal justice programmes and could have much wider application. These views will be discussed in Chapter Two and re-visited in Chapter Five.

Restorative justice and youth crime Another noticeable trend in the current development of restorative justice is that restorative initiatives have been particularly widespread in relation to juvenile offenders. A possible explanation is that proponents have been quite successful in persuading governments that restorative justice may be a more effective way of preventing re-offending among young offenders than the 'traditional' approaches. As a result, some elements of restorative justice have been given legislative force and adopted as a mainstream response to juvenile crime. An

English example of such legislation is the Crime and Disorder Act 1998 mentioned above. This Act defines the principal aim of the youth justice system as prevention of offending by children and young persons. One consequence of incorporating restorative techniques through legislation, the overarching aim of which is prevention of re-offending, is that it has shaped the style and focus of much empirical research into restorative justice which typically evaluates restorative justice by reference to its ability to reduce offending (see section 'Present empirical research into restorative justice' below). Another consequence is that it has influenced restorative justice practice and altered the original vision of restorative justice by over-emphasising offender rehabilitation (as will be demonstrated in the subsequent chapters of this book by reference to one restorative justice project).

Another explanation of the popularity of restorative justice in the context of juvenile crime is that the response to youth crime has been differentiated from the response to adult crime for a long time, but the traditional welfare rationale for the distinction is becoming more and more difficult to defend. So, if the distinction between responses to juvenile and adult crime is to be retained, a different rationale is needed. Policy-makers and practitioners see restorative justice as an attractive new rationale, because it allows holding juvenile offenders accountable without abandoning welfare concerns completely (Johnstone 2002, 166). It permits politicians to "talk tough' whilst behind the scenes enabling sometimes more enlightened practices to be developed and promulgated' (Crawford and Newburn 2003, 11). In the context of rising levels of juvenile crime and a popular belief that juvenile justice is ineffective, restorative justice seems to offer a governmental policy which is likely to win votes due to its emphasis on 'responsibilizing' juvenile offenders and their families and the communitarian appeal[17].

A consequence of developing juvenile restorative justice without a corresponding development in the context of adult offending is the distortion of the original vision of restorative justice (Johnstone 2002, 166-7). As will be pointed out in Chapter Two of this book, proponents of restorative justice aspire to develop a way of doing criminal justice which would place victims at its centre. If victims are to be central, the age of 'their' offenders seems an illogical basis for allowing or refusing victim participation. Enabling victims of juvenile offenders to derive benefits from restorative justice, while failing to provide similar opportunities to victims of adult offenders seems to unfairly discriminate between victims. In subsequent chapters of this book this danger will be illustrated with reference to empirical findings from the empirical study forming the basis of this book.

A universal practice? Yet another important trend in the current development of restorative justice relates to the claim made by some proponents which has been referred to at the beginning of this chapter. This is the claim that restorative justice has been a dominant way of 'doing' criminal justice in pre-modern societies and therefore presents a more 'natural' form of justice. Advocates of this view believe that it would be highly desirable to return to the pre-modern restorative justice

17 For instance, the reparation orders introduced by the Crime and Disorder Act 1998 require the young offender to make reparation either to a specified person or 'to the community at large'.

traditions and apply them throughout the whole of today's society. Consistently with this view, restorative justice is being marketed by some proponents as a universally appropriate practice.

However, some critics find this trend deeply problematic. They argue that the proponents who claim that restorative justice was an almost universal tradition present a misleading and biased account of pre-modern conflict-resolution practices (Daly 2002; Bottoms 2003; Cunneen 2007). Contrary to the assumption by proponents, conflict-resolution procedures in pre-modern societies were much more diverse. Even where restorative processes were used, they were frequently accompanied by threats of social sanctions and a strong degree of social pressure to reach settlements (Bottoms 2003).

Also, the assumption that restorative practices can be easily transferred from one cultural setting to another has been questioned, because the existence of restorative practices is connected to – and dependent on – certain cultural conditions (Crawford 2002; Bottoms 2003; Daly 2006). It has been argued that when attempts to transplant conflict resolution mechanisms from one society to another are made, elements of traditional practice are uprooted and consumed without acknowledging their deeper cultural meaning, purpose and significance (Blagg 1997, 2001). The failure to understand how the traditional practices were woven into the fabric of certain cultures results in a misinterpretation and distortion of those practices when they are moved into a different social context (Wonshe 2004).

Present empirical research into restorative justice

As restorative justice grew in popularity and its practice expanded, a vast amount of literature has been produced, explaining and promoting the idea of restorative justice, describing its practical applications, debating theoretical issues and presenting findings from evaluations of restorative justice programmes[18]. Yet, at present most empirical research tends to pursue a very narrow agenda[19].

Often the 'success' of restorative justice interventions is measured by reference to cost-effectiveness of programmes and 'outcome' criteria (such as a percentage of encounters resulting in some kind of a settlement, victim satisfaction, restitution compliance rates and reduction in re-offending)[20]. One reason for this style and focus

---

18 Much research into restorative justice is contained in edited volumes, such as Wright and Galaway 1989; Messmer and Otto 1992; Galaway and Hudson 1996; Walgrave 1998; Bazemore and Walgrave 1999a; Morris and Maxwell 2001; von Hirsch, Roberts, Bottoms, Roach and Schiff 2003; Elliott and Gordon 2005 – to mention just a few; in book-length studies, such as Marshall and Merry 1990; Umbreit 1994; Strang 2002; Crawford and Newburn 2003; in research reports, such as Miers 2001; Miers et al 2001; and in various articles.

19 Some research, however, goes beyond that limited agenda, for example, Young 2001; Strang 2001; Shapland et al 2006a, 2006b.

20 It needs to be noted that recently there has been an increasing interest in the agenda for empirical research into restorative justice which is informed by principles more in line with restorative justice ideals, rather than technocratic criteria (Toews and Zehr 2003; Zehr 2006; Bazemore and Elis 2007).

of empirical research is the following: to justify their existence and funding, restorative programmes must persuade governments and funding agencies that progress towards certain goals is being made (Marshall and Merry 1990, 16-17; Brookes 1998). For example, restorative encounters must be shown as superior to the 'traditional' criminal justice because they reduce re-offending, decrease the cost for taxpayers, increase participant satisfaction and reduce court caseload and prison population. Another reason for evaluating the 'success' of restorative justice on cost-effectiveness and 'outcome' grounds is that most of the data for such research is easy to collect. Programme management will keep records of cost per case, caseloads, percentage of agreements reached, and percentage of restitution compliance. It does not take much effort to add up these numbers and to produce figures which may impress the audience for which the evaluations are primarily designed (Brookes 1998).

However, measuring 'success' of restorative programmes by reference to 'outcome' criteria is problematic for a number of reasons. A typical evaluation would involve a comparison between a group of offenders who have been diverted to a restorative programme and a group who have been processed through the 'traditional' justice system. The problem with such research is that its value and reliability depend on the use of randomized samples, but finding and composing appropriate control group (subjected to a 'traditional' intervention) and experimental or treatment group (undergoing a restorative intervention) is extremely difficult. As a rule, offenders are not assigned to restorative programmes on a random basis. Offenders of a particular type tend to be referred to restorative justice programmes. They are usually first-time offenders committing trivial crimes and who are less likely to re-offend. Also, many evaluations compare cases where restorative interventions took place with those in which restorative justice was offered but refused by offenders or victims. It may well be that victims and offenders who agree to participate in restorative programmes are different from those who refuse. For instance, offenders refusing to participate may be more likely to re-offend. Victims agreeing to meet their offenders may be people with a high sense of social responsibility towards offenders and a strong desire to help them. So, the differences in outcomes may be attributable not to differences between restorative interventions and their alternatives but to intrinsic characteristics of victims and offenders.

Even where genuine attempts are made to equalize the experimental and control groups by selecting eligible offenders (by reference to the type of offence, prior offending history, the age and sex of offenders) and then assigning them randomly to the two groups, it is still difficult to achieve true equivalence between the groups. Many such experiments involve small sample sizes, impeding generalizations of findings. Also, some offenders who are randomly assigned to a restorative intervention may not attend it, creating a risk that those who remain in the experimental group may no longer be representative of the group as a whole (Wilcox, Hoyle and Young 2005; Hayes 2007; Sherman and Strang 2007, 14).

Many restorative programmes are carried out by highly motivated and highly skilled staff, whereas the 'traditional' criminal justice responses are often delivered in very routine and malfunction-prone settings. Staff commitment and motivation, rather than restorative interventions per se, may produce the differences in outcomes between experimental and control groups.

It has been suggested that the relevance of the criteria for evaluation of restorative programmes, such as participant satisfaction and impact on recidivism, to the purposes to be achieved by restorative programmes is far from obvious and rarely explained (Von Hirsch, Ashworth, Shearing 2003, 23).

One difficulty with evaluating restorative programmes by reference to 'outcomes' is that data produced by such research does not necessarily signify very much (Brookes 1998). For example, widely used evidence for the 'success' of restorative justice is the ability of participants to negotiate some kind of settlement, such as monetary compensation, or an agreement that the offender would work for the victim or community. However, the fact of reaching an agreement may not tell much about its significance for participants. An encounter may be classified as a 'success' if it results in a settlement between the victim and the offender, but an offender's only motivation for settling may be a desire to get the process over with. Alternatively, an encounter may be classed as a 'failure' due to the lack of any reparation settlement. Nevertheless, the participants may have acquired a better understanding of each other's position (Marshall and Merry 1990, 30), the victim's fears and sense of disempowerment resulting from crime may have diminished, and the offender may have felt remorse and empathy towards the victim.

Measuring 'success' of restorative programmes by reference to other 'outcomes' of restorative interventions is equally problematic. In effect, it involves testing restorative justice against unrealistic and, some would argue, inappropriate goals. The best example would be using recidivism data to evaluate restorative interventions. It may be unreasonable to expect that an hour-and-a-half restorative encounter would turn around what are quite often life-time problems. Also, evaluation of restorative justice against re-offending rates may be inappropriate because even if restorative justice did not reduce re-offending, there could be other important gains, such as victim healing, individual empowerment, development of participatory skills, strengthening communities, moral growth of participants in restorative justice encounters, participants in restorative justice encounters practising self-government and learning to handle their problems themselves, without resorting to the help of professionals and experts (as suggested by some writers, such as Christie 1977, 1982; Johnstone 2002, 144-150; Bush and Folger 2005).

The result of the research agenda into restorative justice which focuses on the reduction of re-offending rates, cost-effectiveness of restorative justice programmes, participant satisfaction and other criteria which are of interest to governments and funding providers is that many facets of the phenomenon of restorative justice remain largely unexplored, and many important issues which are capable of being researched have been scarcely investigated.

As has been already noted in the Introduction, the empirical study forming the basis of this book was different from most research in the area in its style and focus. This study will be analyzed in Chapters Three, Four and Five.

This chapter has discussed practical applications of restorative justice. It outlined recent restorative justice developments in England and identified some noticeable trends in the evolution of today's restorative practices and empirical research in the field. Now the discussion will switch from restorative justice practice to theory.

Chapter Two

Restorative Ideals

Introduction

The focus of this chapter will be the ideals of restorative justice theorists. Restorative justice has been described as a 'deeply contested concept' (Johnstone and Van Ness 2007b, 9). There is no single agreed meaning of restorative justice: proponents' views differ on exactly what kind of transformation their movement seeks to achieve. For example, some primarily want to create a way of doing criminal justice which involves crime stakeholders in the decision-making about what needs to be done in the aftermath of an offence (Marshall 1996; McCold 2000). Others see developing a form of justice which seeks to repair the harm caused by crime as a priority (Bazemore and Walgrave 1999b; Walgrave 2000a). Yet others view transformations of individual selves and of the whole social context in which crimes are committed as the main objective (Morris 2000; Sullivan and Tifft 2001). However, despite these differences, it may be possible to identify key aspirations and ideals of the restorative justice movement, many of which will be discussed below. This chapter will look at the following restorative aspirations:

- to create a new ethical orientation;
- to develop an alternative to punishment and treatment;
- to craft a model of criminal justice which will place victims at its centre;
- to design a way of doing criminal justice which will aim to repair harm and restore peace and harmony in the aftermath of a criminal offence;
- to construct a justice paradigm that will be characterized by voluntariness;
- to develop a model of criminal justice which will be de-professionalized, community-based and empowering for crime stakeholders.

The chapter will conclude by discussing the relationship between restorative justice and the criminal justice system in the writings of key proponents.

It needs to be noted that no suggestion is made that the restorative ideals which will be analyzed below are accepted by all proponents to the same extent. Individual advocates may attach different degrees of importance to certain ideals. They may embrace some ideals wholeheartedly, while contesting others or subscribing to them only partly. Such diversity of thinking creates tensions and debates within the movement. Some of these tensions and disagreements will be highlighted in this chapter.

A new moral 'lens'

There is a broad agreement among its advocates that restorative justice offers a new metaphorical 'lens' through which crime and justice could be looked at (Zehr 1990). Proponents frequently refer to restorative justice as being a 'very different way of thinking', or a 'new paradigm', or a 'radical alternative' that implies revolutionary transformations of the existing way of responding to crime and other types of wrongdoing.

The aspiration to produce changes of such a magnitude can be traced back to writings which preceded and inspired today's restorative discourse. One such early influence was proposals of the American legal and political theorist Randy Barnett. Barnett rejected the existing paradigm of criminal justice on the grounds that none of its declared goals – deterrence, retribution and rehabilitation – could justify punishment. Instead he proposed a new paradigm based on the idea of restitution (1977, 1980). Barnett's proposals to discard the punishment paradigm of justice and replace it with a new one have helped shape the idea of restorative justice, even though many of today's restorative justice campaigners probably will not agree with the exact vision of the new restitutive paradigm proposed by him. Yet they are likely to agree with the general spirit of Barnett's ideas: punishment may be understood as a paradigm of justice, and restorative justice may be viewed as an alternative paradigm (rather than an attempt to salvage the existing punishment paradigm) (Johnstone 2003, 22).

Another major source of inspiration for restorative justice advocates may be found in the works of the Norwegian criminologist Nils Christie (1977, 1982). His critique of the traditional criminal justice process, where the main actors on the criminal justice stage are legal and other professionals and ordinary people who are directly affected by the crime are excluded from participation in their own conflict, has found a wide acceptance among restorative justice campaigners. Christie puts forward a model of participatory justice which is characterized by victim-orientation and lay participation and operates through neighbourhood courts (1977). In making proposals for change, Christie admits that he raises more questions than answers. He argues that '[i]t is questions we need. The gravity of our topic makes us much too pedantic and thereby useless as paradigm-changers' (Christie 1977, 9-10).

There is a clear parallel between Christie's reference to paradigm-changing and Randy Barnett's idea of a restitutive paradigm. The proposals of both implied a totally different way of constructing reality, a radical shift in perspective.

The same theme of shifting paradigms emerges in – and becomes central to – another work highly influential in the development of restorative justice – *Changing Lenses* by Howard Zehr (1990), who directed the first Victim Offender Reconciliation Programme in the USA. That book was one of the first to articulate the idea of restorative justice. Zehr argues that when something is identified as crime in our society, we tend to make a number of assumptions. We assume that crime is a violation of the state, the lawbreaking defines the offence, guilt must be fixed, the guilty must get their 'just deserts', just deserts require infliction of pain and justice should be measured by the process. These assumptions shape our response to crime and our understanding of justice.

According to Zehr, our criminal justice system fails to meet needs of victims and offenders, and the reasons for this failure can be traced back to the assumptions we make about crime and justice. However, this is not the only way of thinking about crime and justice. This is simply one possibility, one moral 'lens' through which crime and justice could be looked at, or one possible paradigm. Zehr proposes to change the 'lens' through which we look at crime and justice and adopt a totally different way of thinking about them. He begins the exploration of this alternative vision by contrasting it to retributive justice. When looked at through a retributive 'lens', crime is seen as 'a violation of the state, defined by lawbreaking and guilt', and justice – as requiring determination of blame and administration of pain in a legal contest between the offender and the state (Zehr 1990, 181). Crime is seen as creating a moral debt which offenders must repay, and justice – as a process of righting through punishment of the offender a methaphysical balance that has been upset by crime (Zehr 1990, 74). Within this moral framework, the offence and guilt are defined in purely legal terms, and justice becomes determined by following correct rules and procedures. In the criminal process, offender is pitted against the state, which in practice means that one proxy professional representing the offender (defence lawyer) is pitted against a professional representing the state (prosecution), with another professional (judge) acting as an arbiter (Zehr 1990, 81).

This ethical orientation to crime and justice is contrasted with restorative justice which understands crime as 'a violation of people of relationships' (Zehr 1990, 181). If crime is essentially an injury, within this moral framework, justice becomes a process of healing and putting things right. This framework views reparation as a goal (Zehr 1990, 186-190) and aims to right the balance which crime violates by raising the victim to his or her pre-crime level (Zehr 1990, 183). It requires that offenders are held accountable for the harm they have caused, and their accountability involves 'understanding and acknowledging the harm and taking steps to make things right' (Zehr 1990, 201).

Zehr further argues that the restorative ethical orientation recognizes that not only what happens in a particular case, but also how the decisions are taken is of fundamental importance: justice has to be experienced and not simply done by others and reported to those who have been directly affected by the offence. So the process of doing justice puts power and responsibility in the hands of the victim and the offender, leaving room for community involvement: it 'involves the victim, the offender and the community in a search for solutions which promote repair, reconciliation, and reassurance' (Zehr 1990, 181). This process should address the relationship between those directly involved and focus on problem-solving (Zehr 1990, 203-4). Zehr proceeds to construct a detailed table in which the restorative and retributive moral frameworks are presented in oppositional terms (1990, chapter 10).

Such polarization of retributive and restorative justice has been very influential within the restorative justice discourse. Many proponents portray restorative justice as a radical alternative to the 'traditional' way of thinking about – and responding to – crime and argue that the values which underlie restorative practices are very different from those which guide conventional criminal justice interventions[1]. Although in his

1 See, for example, Wright 1996, 1999; Bazemore 1996; Bazemore and Walgrave 1999b; Walgrave 1999; McCold 2000; Braithwaite 2003a; Van Ness and Strong 2006.

subsequent writings Zehr has modified the view of restorative justice as a polar opposite of retributive justice (2002, 13), many leading restorative justice advocates continue to talk of developing a 'third model' (Braithwaite 2003a, 86), or a 'fully fledged alternative' (Walgrave 1995), or the 'replacement discourse' (Dignan 2002, 2003), or a 'truly different paradigm' (Umbreit 2001) which 'should in the long run replace the punitive or rehabilitative responses to crime' (Walgrave 2000a, 417-18). The conceptualization of restorative justice by reference to its alleged alternative – the traditional response to crime – has become so deeply entrenched within the restorative discourse that, as one critic points out,

> ...the very coherence of this alternative governmentality rests on the presupposition of difference: restorative justice announces itself as ethically, ontologically and practically distinct from the rationales, images and practices of state criminal justice.
>
> (Pavlich 2005, 17)

Although the development of the idea of restorative justice to a large degree has relied on – and been shaped by – the sharp contrast between restorative and traditional, retributive, values, a number of critics have questioned the accuracy and desirability of such polarization. It has been argued that the extent to which restorative justice really rejects criminal justice values is questionable (Pavlich 2005; Johnstone 2007). It has been further pointed out that an approach combining the best of restorative and criminal justice values could take the restorative justice movement into a more fruitful direction than the approach involving a wholesale rejection of the criminal justice values (Johnstone and Van Ness 2007b, endnote 7). The arguments of the critics of the oppositional presentation of restorative and criminal justice will be discussed in more detail below.

An alternative to punishment

A key feature of the restorative way of thinking about crime and justice is its rejection of the response to crime which considers imposition of pain on offenders normative and balances harm which an offender has caused by harm done to him or her. It is argued that the punitive response is 'unacceptable and ineffective' (Wright 2003, 2006). In contrast, restorative justice is portrayed as a more constructive and humane approach aimed at reparation of harms and broken social bonds, rather than involving 'deliberate infliction of pain' on offenders (Wright 1996, 27).

The advocates who contrast restorative justice to punishment do not deny that offenders may experience restorative sanctions as painful and unpleasant. Rather, they argue that it is the perspective of the person imposing pain, not the person receiving pain, that defines punishment: '...if [an offender] feels the obligation to repair as being hard and calls it 'a punishment', it actually is no punishment if the intention of the judge was not to make the juvenile suffer, but rather to request from him a reasonable contribution to reparation' (Walgrave 2003, 63). Because restorative sanctions do not involve a deliberate imposition of pain and are intended as reparative measures, they are not punishments (Wright 1996, 2003; Walgrave 2002, 2003, 2007). On this view, there are critical ethical differences between punishment and restorative justice because 'the intentional obligation to make up is ethically superior to the intentional infliction of pain' (Walgrave 2003, 64). So, it is wrong to equate painful obligations imposed with a view of reparation after a criminal act with punishment.

There has been a strong opposition to the view that restorative justice constitutes an alternative to punishment (Barton 2000; Daly 2000, 2002; Duff 2002, 2003; Dignan 2002; Johnstone 2002). This view has been criticized on the grounds that it seems to define 'deliberate infliction of pain' very narrowly. Even if causing pain is not the primary intention, as long as pain is an inevitable, or even highly probable, consequence, imposition of pain is intended, at least to a certain degree, when offenders are subjected to restorative sanctions (Johnstone 2002, 110). Besides, punishment is probably best defined not by reference to the intentions of the punisher, but the element of hard treatment, so that it would include 'anything that is unpleasant, a burden, or an imposition of some sort on an offender' (Daly 2000, 39).

It has been also suggested that the presentation of retributive justice by restorative justice proponents is misleading and over-simplified. It involves either an implication that hurting offenders is the sole purpose or an equation of punishment with a crude form of deterrence (Johnstone 2002, 107). However, many advocates of punishment offer rather different justifications for the practice. Some of them are not inconsistent with the restorative ideal, in particular, a moral education theory of punishment (Hampton 1984; Morris 1984; Reitan 1996; Duff 1999a, 1999b). Consequently, the belief that restorative justice and punishment are incompatible is mistaken. The goals of restoration and retribution are not mutually exclusive; indeed, restorative justice requires punishment as a component of an educative and reintegrative process (Daly 2000, 2002; Duff 2002, 2003; Johnstone 2002). So it has been argued that restorative justice is not an alternative to punishment. Rather, it is an alternative *form* of punishment (Duff 1992; Daly 2000, 2002).

It has been further noted that to present restorative justice as an alternative to punishment would be not only misleading but also counterproductive. Offenders tend to experience restorative justice as painful and burdensome (Daly 2000; Johnstone 2002), so they would view the claim that they are not being punished when they are subjected to restorative justice interventions as disingenuous and hypocritical. If victims are told that restorative justice is not punishment, they may see restorative justice as denying the validity of their 'legitimate emotions of anger and resentment' which they feel towards offenders (Daly 2000, 41). From the point of view of the community, if certain actions are not punished, it may amount to condoning and trivializing them. Thus there could be advantages if restorative justice were presented not as something different from punishment, but rather as a more constructive use of punishment (Daly 2000).

An alternative to treatment

Some proponents have extended the contrasting analysis between restorative justice and the conventional response to crime to encapsulate the rehabilitative approach, with the result that restorative justice is contrasted with not only the retributive, but also the treatment model (Walgrave 1995; Bazemore 1996; McCold 2000). The rehabilitation model is criticized on the grounds that it takes a one-dimensional, offender-driven approach. It focuses on identifying and meeting needs of offenders, while ignoring needs of victims and denying them meaningful participation in the justice process. It views offenders as victims of an underlying psychiatric disorder who are not responsible for their criminal behaviour and fails to hold them accountable. Offenders are assigned a passive role in the treatment process, where professionals play a dominant role, using their expertise to diagnose the disorder and prescribe suitable treatment. Being administered by professionals who 'do not see themselves as being in business of moral evaluation' (Johnstone 2002, 94), the treatment model shields offenders from social condemnation of their offending behaviour. According to restorative justice advocates, this prevents offenders from realizing the wrongfulness of their criminal activities and consequently changing their attitudes and conduct.

It is argued that, unlike the treatment approach, restorative justice holds offenders accountable and requires them to take responsibility for their actions. It attaches fundamental importance to meeting needs of victims and enables them to actively participate in the justice process. The restorative model aspires to change the offending behaviour not through therapeutic methods, but through other very distinctive means.

One essential element of the restorative approach to reforming offenders is encouraging them to experience a genuine remorse for their criminal behaviour. This is achieved through making offenders hear from victims how crime has affected them so as to enable offenders to realize the human costs of their actions and repent their wrongdoing (Zehr 1990; Retzinger and Scheff 1996, 39). This needs to be combined with subjecting offenders to moral condemnation by community members, which performs an educative function (Braithwaite 1989; Braithwaite and Mugford 1994). It is argued that disapproval by ordinary citizens is much more effective than that by authority figures (which occurs in the criminal trial), because offenders are more likely to listen to people who are significant in their lives and whose opinions they care about (Braithwaite 1989).

Another vital element in reforming offenders restoratively involves reparation by them of the damage they have caused (Bazemore and Walgrave 1999b; Walgrave 2000a). Reparation of harm obviously benefits victims and possibly community members, but, it is argued, it may benefit offenders as well in the sense that it may increase their chances of being reintegrated into the community. Firstly, it can help offenders realize the full extent of the damage they have caused, and this understanding is an important step in the reintegration process. Secondly, victims and community members are more likely to reaccept offenders who have earned their redemption, because reparation of harm may appease the anger which community members may feel towards offenders (Johnstone 2002, 102). The process of reparation may also allow offenders to gain valuable skills, which may help improve their self-esteem and promote their rehabilitation through 'competency development' (Bazemore 1996).

Restorative advocates are critical of the highly professionalized, expert-driven treatment paradigm, which, they claim, undermines the informal social mechanisms of crime control (Bazemore 1996). They argue that rehabilitation is highly unlikely to occur outside of the community or relational context and emphasize the need for a collective approach to offender reintegration. Successful reintegration requires ordinary people becoming actively involved in reaccepting offenders who have repented their wrongdoing and put things as right as they could[2].

In the light of the apparent differences between the restorative and rehabilitative models, certain restorative justice proponents emphasize the importance of maintaining a clear distinction and are critical of proposals to merge them:

> Incorporating rehabilitation as a goal of restorative justice legitimates as restorative the vast majority of existing juvenile justice programs where rehabilitation is an operational priority. Failure to distinguish the treatment paradigm from the restorative justice paradigm only adds to the confusion as to the parameters of restorative justice as a genuine alternative.
>
> (McCold 2000, 389)

It is argued that it is desirable to maintain the purity of the restorative ideal by 'includ[ing] only elements of the restorative paradigm and exclud[ing] the goals and methods of the obedience and treatment paradigms' (McCold 2000, 272-3).

Other restorative justice proponents take a different view on the relationship between restorative justice and offender rehabilitation and want to combine them[3]. The two models are seen as compatible, if not mutually supportive. One such advocate argues that since many victims want the offender to do something to make it less likely that he or she will offend again, taking part in a rehabilitative programme may be a way of making reparation (Wright 2004, 247).

Another advocate (Braithwaite 1998) argues that restorative justice is often rehabilitative, although it does not have rehabilitation as its primary purpose. It is rehabilitative precisely because it does not directly set out to change people and thus avoids the risk of psychological reactance on the part of the offender. Yet, when it directly pursues restorative objectives, rehabilitation is a likely spin-off. On this view, the key to the rehabilitative potential of restorative justice is the 'plurality of deliberation' found in restorative forums. Most crime problems have numerous sources, so when a problem is discussed by a group with knowledge derived from being affected by the offence in different ways, this may lead to a nuanced understanding of the causes of crime. This wisdom may make it possible to discover the best ways of preventing its reoccurrence. When the solution is provided by the support group around the offender and is coupled with a professional advice on what has worked and what has failed in the past with this kind of problem, the chances of offender reintegration are increased (Braitwhaite 1998; 2002a, 99-102). According to this proponent,

---

2 For a discussion of conditions needed for reintegration see Braithwaite 1989; Braithwaite and Mugford 1994; Bazemore 1996, 1999; Bazemore and Dooley 2001; Bazemore and O'Brien 2002; Bazemore and Bell 2004.

3 For this view see Bazemore 1996; Wright 1996, 1999; Braithwaite 1998, 2002a; Bazemore and Walgrave 1999; Bazemore and Dooley 2001; Bazemore and O'Brien 2002; Bazemore and Bell 2004; Van Ness and Strong 2006.

> Restorative justice does not involve a rejection of the rehabilitative ideal. ... It does mean reframing it. ... My hypothesis is that the marriage of rehabilitation programs to restorative justice will increase their effectiveness.
>
> (Braithwaite 2002a, 101)

Some critics of restorative justice have also expressed scepticism towards an approach drawing a sharp distinction between restorative justice and offender rehabilitation. It has been noted that the oppositional presentation of the two approaches by some proponents is not reflected in real life restorative experiments: elements of rehabilitative justice are clearly present in restorative practices (Daly 2000, 2002). Also, presenting the two models as incompatible has been criticized on the grounds that it is based on a caricature image of rehabilitation (Johnstone 2002, 111). That image is of a highly 'medicalized' model where offenders are passive recipients of psychiatric and other treatments administered by experts. In reality, many proponents of penal treatment reject that model and prefer socio-therapeutic interventions where offenders play active roles and are encouraged to develop personal responsibility for their actions (Johnstone 1996a, 1996b). There is a considerable overlap between the goals and assumptions underlying such programmes and restorative justice (Johnstone 2002, 111). Restorative justice aspires to reintegrate offenders into the community of law-abiding citizens, and similar objectives have been pursued for a long time by advocates of 'reform' or rehabilitation (Johnstone 2002, 96). It has been proposed that the restorative goal of offender reintegration would be more likely to be achieved if the methods of restorative and therapeutic interventions were combined (Johnstone 2002, 111).

Consistently with this suggestion, certain restorative proponents advocate the creation of 'a fully restorative model of rehabilitation', which is an approach 'based on the premise that rehabilitation is important, but not in isolation from a community or relational context' (Bazemore and Bell 2004, 120). The proposed model emphasizes the role of citizens as 'natural helpers' and the need to build networks of informal social support (Bazemore and Bell 2004, 120; Bazemore and O'Brien 2002, 33), and at the same time recognises the importance of professional treatment 'as needed' (Bazemore and Bell 2004, 121). It is argued that the rehabilitative agenda influenced by restorative values and goals would be 'more empowering, effective and marketable' (Bazemore 1996, 42).

Victim-centred justice

It is a fundamental tenet of the restorative philosophy that 'crime ... is at its core a violation of a person by another person' (Zehr 1990, 182), rather than a violation of an abstract entity – the state. Such redefinition of crime leads to victims becoming the key stakeholders in the justice process whose needs are the primary concern of justice. Restorative justice is presented as a way of responding to crime which would place victims at its centre and 'include as many opportunities for participation, voice, and choices for victims as possible' (Achilles and Zehr 2001, 90).

The aspiration to create a victim-oriented alternative to the conventional way of doing justice was prominent in the early theoretical works which have inspired today's restorative justice movement. So, justice as restitution proposed by Barnett, in his own words

> ...views crime as an offense by one individual against the rights of another. The victim has suffered a loss. Justice consists of the culpable offender making good the loss he has caused. It calls for a complete refocusing of our image of crime. ...Where we once saw an offense against society, we now see an offense against an individual victim. In a way, it is a common sense view of crime. The armed robber did not rob society; he robbed the victim. His debt, therefore, is not to society; it is to the victim.
>
> (Barnett 1977, 286, original emphasis)

In a similar spirit, Christie (1977) develops a model of neighbourhood courts which will be victim-oriented. In these courts, after guilt of the offender has been established, the situation of the victim would be discussed: what can be done for the victim, firstly, by the offender, secondly, by the neighbourhood, and, thirdly, by the state?

The development of this line of thinking culminates in Zehr's articulation of the restorative paradigm:

> When a crime occurs (regardless of whether an "offender" is identified) the first questions ought to be, "Who has been harmed?" "How have they been harmed?" "What are their needs?" Such an approach would, of course, be far from that of retributive justice which first asks, "Who did it?" "What should be done to them?"
>
> (1990, 191)

While this remains the ideal, concerns have been expressed that restorative practice fails to live up to it (Achilles and Zehr 2001; Braithwaite 2002a; Johnstone 2002, 81-3; Green 2007). The source of these concerns is that restorative programmes tend to operate within the present criminal justice system which 'is fundamentally a business designed for processing offenders' (Achilles and Zehr 2001, 96). So, Zehr in his recent evaluation of restoratrive justice principles writes:

> One of my chief concerns is whether we are being as victim-orientated as we claim. Are we really delivering justice for victims or are we using victims for our own purposes? ... In theory, restorative justice offers a more central place to victims than probably any previous effort to correct the system. On the other hand, this claim could turn out to be primarily rhetorical. Many victims and victim service providers are deeply skeptical, and with good reason.
>
> (Zehr 2005, 298)

The worry is that victims in restorative programmes can be treated 'as no more than props for efforts to rehabilitate offenders' (Braithwaite 2002a, 139), and this concern is likely to remain as long as restorative justice operates either within or in close alliance with the traditional offender-oriented criminal justice system.

Justice that repairs harm and restores peace and harmony

Within the restorative justice theory it is axiomatic that crime causes harm, and doing justice involves repairing that harm[4]. Reparation of harm in the restorative justice discourse is not limited to material harm that can be repaired through offenders compensating victims for their losses or doing some work for victims. It also includes psychological and relational injuries. It is argued that crime takes away from victims a sense of personal power. It also ruptures social bonds and disrupts a peaceful communal equilibrium. Apology and forgiveness are viewed as highly desirable for successful restoration of the psychological and relational damage.

Thus, Zehr argues that both victim and offender need to be healed following the offence, and '[f]or genuine healing to take place, at least two pre-conditions need to be met: repentance and forgiveness. If healing is to occur, it is helpful, for victims to be able to forgive' (Zehr 1990, 45). Zehr explains that real forgiveness is liberating and empowering for victims because it signifies that the crime and the offender no longer control the victim. Forgiveness enables a person to move from a victim to a survivor (Zehr 1990, 47). Not only does the victim need an experience of forgiveness. The offender needs it too: it allows the offender to deal with guilt and move on (Zehr 1990, 49). It is argued that

> For offenders to be truly whole, they must confess wrongdoing, admitting their responsibility and acknowledging the harm done. Only then it is possible to repent, to turn one's life around and begin in a new direction. Confession followed by repentance is a key to healing for offenders…
>
> (Zehr 1990, 50)

Retzinger and Scheff distinguish material reparation from 'symbolic reparation'. In 'symbolic reparation' apology and forgiveness are the 'core sequence' which 'generates repair and restoration of the bond between victim and offender, after this bond had been severed by the offender's crime' (Retzinger and Scheff 1996, 316). Without the 'core sequence', settlement is difficult to achieve, and, even if it does happen, it leaves participants with a feeling of dissatisfaction.

Bottoms (2003), analyzing Tavuchis's text on sociology of apology (1991), concludes that where the victim and the offender are part of the same moral/social community, a genuine apology offers the best hope for repairing the social/moral breach and making the resumption of the previous set of relationships possible. Bottoms points out that such reparation is not easy to accomplish if the victim and the offender do not share the same moral/social community. Therefore, it is questionable whether restorative justice approaches can work in the contemporary anonymous urban societies where the victim and the offender may not be part of the same community.

Another critic, Pavlich (2005), expresses a different concern about the restorative ideal to repair harm caused by crime and heal broken social bonds. Pavlich notes the

---

4 See, for example, Zehr and Mika 1998; Declaration of Leuven 1997; Restorative Justice Consortium 2002; Bazemore and Walgrave 1999; Walgrave 2000a, 2000b; Bazemore and Schiff 2005; Van Ness and Strong 2006.

rhetorical appeal of restorative justice to the medical model. It seems to be assumed in the literature on restorative justice that healthy and ordered relations exist between people, that crime is a form of disease that destroys that healthy relationship and generates trauma, that restorative justice offers a medicine to heal the harms and restore the healthy pre-crime order. The medical model implies a technical resolution to a given problem, significantly restricting ways in which justice could be conceptualized, disabling discussions of moral dimensions of justice and masking ethical decisions as technical necessities (Pavlich 2005, chapter 2).

Additionally, viewing restorative justice as a way of repairing harms is inherently conservative and seriously compromises its potential to bring about meaningful social changes (Pavlich 2002a). A number of proponents and critics have argued that at present restorative justice is biased towards consensus and elimination of difference among community members (Mika 1992; Pavlich 1996a, 2005; Dyck 2000, 2006). It neglects social distances between people in their patterns of association and aspires to achieve peaceful relations between individuals whose interests may be fundamentally in conflict. Restorative justice favours harmony and stability of the established social order, rather than social change. It ignores the fact that many disputes and instances of criminal behaviour stem from much deeper and wider social problems (for example, inequalities of wealth and power, inequalities relating to race and gender, oppressions and marginalization of certain individuals and groups)[5]. Reaching reconciliation among the conflicting parties in such circumstances serves to restore and protect the status quo, no matter how unjust that status quo may be. It serves to quickly and effectively expunge from the society conflicts with social-structural roots.

In the light of such concerns, writing in the context of community mediation, Pavlich proposes to re-consider the significance of conflict and re-orient the aims of mediation practices accordingly:

> …conflict need not be seen as intrinsically destructive; it could also be an important way of locating and communicating contradictions, inequities and injustices that affect particular people in given power-knowledge-subjectivity formations. In other words, community mediation might, instead of trying to extinguish conflict in its proximate manifestation between individuals, seek to uncover wider dangers of given associative patterns. It could attend to these in forums designed to bring conflicts to the forefront of the political theatre in a manner quite unlike the artificial, expert-controlled environments of present mediation sessions.
>
> (Pavlich 1996a, 152)

There is a parallel between the arguments of these critics of the 'ideology of harmony' (Dyck 2000) predominant in today's restorative discourse and the ideas of the inspirer of the restorative justice movement Christie (1977, 1982). Christie similarly suggests that there is a tendency in our culture to think of conflicts as pathological, destructive phenomena. It is generally believed that conflicts require speedy resolution, so as to restore peace and harmony in human relationships. Christie does not subscribe

5 For this argument see Harris 1989; Mika 1992; Morris 1995, 2000; Pavlich 1996a, 2005; Sullivan and Tifft 1998, 2000a, 2000b, 2001; Dyck 2000, 2006.

to that belief and argues that conflict is not a 'bad thing' – conflicts are 'social fuel' (Christie 1977, 13). Too little conflict may paralyze the social system. Conflicts are a 'valuable commodity' which ought not be wasted (Christie 1982, 93). They need to be cultivated, used and become useful. When conflicts are 'stolen' from people affected by them, there are numerous losses. For Christie, the main loss is the loss of opportunities for norm-clarification:

> It is a loss of pedagogical possibilities. It is a loss of opportunities for a continuous discussion of what represents the law of the land. How wrong was the thief, how right was the victim? Lawyers are ... trained into agreement on what is relevant in a case. But that means a trained incapacity in letting the parties decide what they think is relevant. It means that it is difficult to stage what we might call a political debate in the court. When the victim is small and the offender big – in size or power – how blameworthy then is the crime? And what about the opposite case, the small thief and the big house-owner? If the offender is well educated, ought he then to suffer more, or maybe less, for his sins? Or if he is black, or if he is young, or if the other party is an insurance company, or if his wife has just left him, or if his factory will break down if he has to go to jail, or if his daughter will lose her fiancé, or if he was drunk, or if he was sad, or if he was mad?
>
> (Christie 1977, 8, original emphasis)

Christie concludes: 'There is no end to it. And maybe there ought to be none.' (1977, 8).

Christie's suggestion that perhaps the main value of the participatory dialogue resides in the opportunity it offers participants to 'stage a political debate' (1977, 8) distinguishes his position radically from that of most today's restorative justice proponents. Christie's conceptualization of conflict and his approach to conflict-handling seems to promise a possibility of a restorative justice process which is less biased towards peaceful resolutions. Instead of aiming at speedily neutralizing potentially disruptive disputes, it calls for cultivating and nurturing conflicts. Rather than solidifying and strengthening normative standards and thereby upholding and preserving the presumed consensual social order, it invites opening up political debates of contentious issues – debates which may potentially lead to social changes.

Voluntary justice?

Certain restorative justice advocates are critical of the coercive traditional criminal justice process and argue that restorative justice presents an alternative that utilizes a voluntary problem-solving approach: '[t]he ideal of RJ requires that for both sides, victim and offender, participation in the mediation procedure is voluntary. ...There should be no pressure, nor urging or persuasion on both sides, for the victim and offender to agree to mediation' (Pelikan and Trenczek 2006, 80). Likewise, the UN Basic Principles on the Use of Restorative Justice Programmes in criminal matters require that '[r]estorative processes should be used only with the free and voluntary consent of the parties. ... Agreements should be arrived at voluntarily by the parties...' (UN 2000, para 7), and criminal justice agents should merely 'encourage' the offender to take responsibility for his or her actions (UN 2000, para 10). It is believed that cooperative decision-making cannot be forced or accomplished on behalf of primary stakeholders in crime: 'restorative justice requires cooperation and cooperation cannot be compelled or imposed' (McCold 2000, 382).

However, some proponents are critical of limiting restorative justice to voluntary deliberations (Bazemore and Walgrave 1999b; Walgrave 1999, 2000a; Bazemore 2000). While they accept the superiority of voluntary agreements (Walgrave 2000a, 419; 2007, 560), they warn that as long as restorative justice is presented as a model of free settlements, 'it will be condemned to remain some kind of a "soft ornament" in the margin of "hard core" criminal justice' (Walgrave 1999, 131). So, voluntariness is viewed merely as 'a means of enhancing the quality of restoration' (Walgrave 2003, 62), not an essential ingredient in the restorative way of doing justice. While it is emphasized that restorative justice 'prefers' voluntary and co-operative responses to crime (Claassen 1996 in McCold 2000, 414), and voluntary participation by offenders should be maximized and coercion minimized (Mika and Zehr 2003, 143), it is accepted that where offenders refuse to participate in restorative programmes voluntarily, they should be subjected to coercive sanctions (Claassen 1996; Declaration of Leuven 1997; Restorative Justice Consortium 2002). Such sanctions should be employed primarily towards achieving reparative goals. This can be done through judicially ordered reparation or community service (Walgrave 1999).

Yet, some advocates continue to oppose models of restorative justice which define coercive practices as restorative, because, it is argued, such models reinforce, rather than challenge, the existing criminal justice system. They fail to challenge 'business as usual': 'the same laws, the same process, the same coercion, and the same goals – with one addition [that is, reparation]' (McCold 2000, 396).

At the same time, even the proponents who see voluntariness as an indispensable restorative value accept that where voluntary restorative justice is impossible or considered undesirable, judicially imposed coercive sanctions are acceptable, indeed necessary (McCold 2000, 394-5).

What then distinguishes the position of these restorative advocates from the position of those writers whose view they oppose on the issue of judicial coercion, given that both seem to accept that judicial coercion sometimes will be necessary? According to McCold, the difference lies in the fact that even though the model of voluntary restorative justice is prepared to fall back on judicial sanctions in certain circumstances, it does not define judicial coercion as a restorative practice. In his own words, '[t]he imposition of minimum force in some situations may be necessary, but that does not make the coercion restorative' (McCold 2000, 382).

The response of McCold's opponents who wish to define judicial coercion imposed with a view of reparation as a restorative practice is that 'coercion is basically accepted in most restorative thinking' (Walgrave 2000a, 422). It is acknowledged that court-ordered restitution and community service address the needs of stakeholders in crime 'rather weakly'. Yet it is argued that such sanctions 'seem better than the primary alternative: not attempting any repair by punishing the offender or ordering that he attend treatment that is disconnected altogether from victim and community' (Bazemore 2000, 471).

It has been also suggested that it is simply unrealistic to aspire towards absolute freedom of choice in the context of restorative justice. Voluntariness within restorative justice will always be qualified by enticements, inducements, perceived threats and availability of alternative courses of action (Crawford and Newburn 2003, 47). As Braithwaite admits,

> Very few criminal offenders who participate in restorative justice processes would be sitting in the room absent a certain amount of coercion. Without their detection and/or arrest, without the specter of the alternative of a criminal trial, they simply would not cooperate with a process that puts their behavior under public scrutiny. No coercion, no restorative justice (in most cases).
>
> (2002a, 34)

Perhaps all that choice within restorative justice involves is an opportunity for offenders to refuse to participate in a restorative intervention, or walk out of one following a referral, and consequently be processed in a 'traditional' way by the criminal justice system (Crawford and Newburn 2003, 47).

Empowering, community-based, de-professionalized justice

Another key aspiration of restorative justice advocates is to involve victims, offenders and their communities actively in the process of doing justice. This is another aspiration which has roots in writings of Christie (1977, 1982). Christie argues that

> ...in a modern criminal trial, two important things have happened. First, the parties are being represented. Secondly, the one party that is represented by the state, namely the victim, is so thoroughly represented that she or he for most of the proceedings is pushed completely out of the arena, reduced to the trigger-off of the whole thing. She or he is a sort of double-loser; first vis-à-vis the offender, but secondly and often in a more crippling manner by being denied rights to full participation in what might have been one of the more important ritual encounters in life. The victim has lost the case to the state.
>
> (Christie 1977, 3, original emphasis)

According to Christie, conflicts have been 'stolen' from people by lawyers and became the 'property' of legal professionals. Lawyers either prevent conflicts from arising in the first place or solve them for people who are directly involved in them. Other 'professional thieves' of conflicts are treatment professionals who define conflicts away by 'converting the image of the case from one of conflict into one of non-conflict' (Christie 1977, 4, emphasis omitted).

Christie is critical of the assumption popular in the modern society that the best way of dealing with problems is to delegate their resolution to professionals trained in handling disputes. He believes that people affected by the conflict should stop handing their conflicts over to professionals for quick and effective resolution. Instead, he advocates a participatory justice that would be characterized by 'an extreme degree of lay orientation'. It should be a 'court of equals representing themselves' (1977, 11). They should engage in lengthy – or maybe even endless – discussions, unrestricted by legal rules, 'external' interpretations of norms and 'outside' opinions of what information is relevant to the case. People directly involved in conflict should be at the centre of the conflict-handling process, and professionals should have a very limited role. According to Christie, '[e]xperts are as cancer to any lay body' (1977, 11), so the objective is to have 'as few ... experts as we dare', especially the ones specializing in conflict handling (1977, 12). If, however, we find experts unavoidable in some situations,

> Let us try to get them to perceive themselves as resource-persons, answering when asked, but not domineering, not in the centre. They might help to stage conflicts, not take them over.
>
> (Christie 1977, 12)

Actively engaging victims, offenders and their communities in the process of doing justice and returning to them conflicts 'stolen' from them by professionals has become one of the key aspirations of restorative justice advocates[6]. So, McCold argues:

> For restorative justice to be 'restorative' it must involve those most directly affected. Every effort must be made to maximize the involvement and exchange of information between the affected parties … Neither the state nor any individual or group appointed by the state can restore people by replacing the primary stakeholders, doing things to them or for them. … The essence of restorative justice is not the end, but the means by which resolution is achieved.
>
> (2004, 15)

The last sentence from the quote above deserves special attention. Although Christie's essay 'Conflicts as Property' (1977) has a status of a 'sacred text' within the restorative justice movement (Crawford 2002, 102), most restorative justice advocates subscribe to Christie's proposals to empower stakeholders in crime and place them at the centre of conflict-resolution process for reasons rather different from those put forward by Christie. Most restorative justice campaigners see the participatory and empowering restorative justice process as the best way of achieving restorative outcomes:

> Active participation of the parties concerned forms a core element of restorative justice. Thanks to its participatory nature, mediation is likely to produce a more comprehensive solution to the problems arising from the offence or which have led to the offense than the criminal justice system can do alone.
>
> (Pelikan and Trenczek 2006, 65)

It is argued that victims, offenders and their communities can usually come up with more meaningful dispositions than those developed by judges and other 'experts' who lack knowledge of, and connection to, the parties affected by crime, and therefore are

6 It needs to be noted that despite the rhetoric of de-professionalization within the movement, most proponents believe that restorative encounters require a trained mediator or facilitator guided by a set of principles. According to Sawin and Zehr, 'it can be asserted that the facilitator is a pivotal stakeholder who cultivates the safety and space to engage people in the hearing and telling of stories' (2007, 54).

incapable of meeting the real needs created by the offence. It is generally believed that the restorative justice process is more likely to lead to reparation of harm caused by the offence, reconciliation of conflicting parties, victim satisfaction and offender reintegration, than the 'traditional' criminal justice process. That is, most of today's restorative justice proponents view the participatory process as the best means towards achieving declared goals, rather than an end in itself.

In contrast, for Christie participation in itself is of fundamental importance. He argues that

> ...it is important not to presuppose that conflict ought to be solved. The quest for solution is a puritan, ethnocentric conception. ... Conflicts might be solved, but they might also be lived with ... maybe participation is more important than solutions.
>
> (Christie 1982, 92-3)

The implication of Christie's position is that even if no restorative outcomes are attained (no harm repaired, no reconciliation achieved) or if unrestorative outcomes are brought about (for example, the victim is dissatisfied, the offender is punished), the participatory process is still a supreme and a 'natural' way of doing justice simply because it restores to people control over their conflicts. It is intrinsically right that people should participate in handling their own conflicts, and even if they make decisions which are inappropriate or even repugnant by restorative standards, their conflict belongs to them, so it is for them to decide what they want to do with it.

Integral to the ideal of creating a form of justice that is characterized by de-professionalization and empowerment of crime stakeholders is the aspiration of restorative justice proponents to develop a community-based form of justice. Different understandings of the 'community' are present in the restorative discourse[7]. Some view it as a geographical entity, such as local neighbourhoods (Christie 1977). Others claim that community 'is not a place' (McCold and Wachtel 2003). Rather, it can be viewed as consisting of individuals connected through 'perception of connectedness to an individual or group' (McCold and Wachtel 2003, 300). On this view, restorative justice's communities are created by incidents of crime in efforts to respond to and prevent it. Yet others conceptualize community in symbolic terms.

Despite the diversity of meanings, it is clear that the 'community' is allocated distinct functions separable from those of the state agencies. So, Van Ness and Strong propose as a restorative principle that 'in promoting justice, government is responsible for preserving a just order and the community for establishing a just peace' (2006, 46).

Various rationales are proposed for the community involvement in restorative justice (Crawford 2002), among which are the claim that the community is a secondary victim of crime in need of restoration, the belief that it is a resource for achieving restorative goals and the hope that the process of conflict-handling will strengthen the community by developing its capacity to regulate itself (Johnstone 2002, 151-2). It is also suggested that community participation can add a sense of moral authority and legitimacy to the decision-making process and enhance democracy (O'Mahony and Doak 2006).

7 See McCold and Wachtel 2003; McCold 2004; Pavlich 2005, chapter 5.

Yet critics have identified various practical obstacles to community involvement in restorative justice (Crawford 2002, 121-123; Johnstone 2002, 152-3). They have pointed out that it is insufficient simply to offer people opportunities for participation in the criminal justice process. Community members may be too busy to participate, or they may be unwilling to get involved in criminal justice because it is generally associated with punishment, coercion and violation of people's freedoms.

Additionally, concerns have been expressed about the desirability of delegating decision-making powers to community members in the aftermath of crime. Empowering the community carries risks of domination, vigilantism, authoritarianism, totalitarianism, lack of accountability, transparency and disrespect for human rights[8].

One frequently quoted example of empowered communities effectively frustrating the achievement of restorative goals is a conference in Canberra where crime stakeholders agreed that the offender should wear a T-shirt declaring 'I am a thief' (Braithwaite 2002c, 2003b; Roche 2003). As Braithwaite explains, in cases of this kind, justice has not been done restoratively, even though crime stakeholders participated actively in the process and decided on its outcomes. In his own words,

> [i]f we have a conference in which all of the parties with a stake in the offense participate actively and it is decided to boil the offender in oil and criticize the victim for bringing the trouble on herself, for outcome reasons we would not want to say the conference was restorative.
>
> (Braithwaite 2000, 435)

Given the potential dangers of crime stakeholders reaching decisions inconsistent with the restorative philosophy, attempts have been made to impose limits on community empowerment within the restorative process. Braithwaite proposes to declare certain outcomes 'morally unacceptable' (2002c, 567) and 'uncontroversially bad practice' (2002c, 565), for example, an outcome such as in the 'I am a thief' T-shirt case should be banned (2002c, 567). Braithwaite develops a set of standards designed to guide and constrain the restorative process (2002c, 2003b). He acknowledges that the restorative aspiration to shift power to communities may be compromised by imposing on them a set of standards, but claims that this may not necessarily happen. He believes that whether or not the 'deliberative democracy' is enabled or disabled by the imposition of top-down standards depends on what the standards are and how they are used (2002c, 564). The standards Braithwaite proposes are derived from the republican perspective (Braithwaite and Pettit 1990; Pettit 1997) and values and rights embodied in numerous human rights instruments which he believes 'most restorative justice advocates would agree with' (Braithwaite 2002, 568).

Yet, it is far from obvious whether the standards proposed by Braithwaite are of a type that will enable the 'deliberative democracy'. What is problematic about his proposals is that the moral standards to which he wishes to subject crime stakeholders seem to be his own and perhaps those of other restorative justice advocates, but not necessarily of the crime stakeholders whose personal and local values might not be

8 See Dignan and Lowey 2000; O'Mahony and Doak 2006, 16; Shapland 2003; Pavlich 2001, 2004, 2005.

the same. Thus, in the 'I am a thief' T-shirt case, crime stakeholders agreed to the outcome, so it was obviously morally acceptable for them. Another example hinting at disparities between values of restorative justice advocates and those of lay crime stakeholders may be the Australian aboriginal practice that involves wrongdoers agreeing to submit to ceremonial spearing through their thigh as a way of symbolic reparation (Johnstone 2002, 20). Restorative justice advocates are likely to ban such a practice as unacceptable, yet for the aborigines volunteering to undergo such punishment it is an important way of demonstrating how remorseful a wrongdoer is.

There appears to be a tension at the very heart of the restorative philosophy between two competing value commitments: to the empowering process and to case dispositions promoting restorative goals (Johnstone 2004, 12). Braithwaite's response to this tension seems to be to insist that the rights and values to which he wants to subject crime stakeholders 'are also consistent with the empirical experience of what victims and offenders say they want out of restorative justice processes' (2002c, 569). Pranis (2007) makes a similar claim: the values identified by citizens she had worked with as components of a better way to resolve conflicts and harm are consistent with those proposed by restorative justice proponents. Such claims may well be true, however, they require proper empirical evaluation, because there is a contradiction between the restorative desire to promote the empowerment of stakeholders, while at the same time ensuring that limits are placed on their power so that it is used towards certain ends. There is an inherent conflict between, on the one hand, an aspiration to develop restorative justice as 'a bottom-up social movement', committed to 'combating oppressive state structures' (Braithwaite 2002c, 563), and, on the other hand, subjecting the citizen empowerment to 'top-down' standards.

Various other concerns have been expressed by both proponents and critics about the communitarian appeal of restorative justice. One common worry is net-widening (Braithwaite 2002a, 148-9; Johnstone 2002, 32; Morris 2002, 602), that is, the expansion of the number of people caught in the net of penal control.

Another worry is that community-based forms of conflict-handling may be the benign cloak under which the state sheds its responsibilities by dumping the management of problems on communities who may have neither resources nor capacities for regulating conflicts (Crawford 2002, 113). It has been further argued that restorative justice may be economic not only in monetary sense, but also in the sense of use of power. Within the restorative context, pressures and sanctions appear to come from community members, rather than state authorities, enabling the state to achieve effective control over troublesome subjects without revealing a heavy hand and risking resistance (Johnstone 2002, 32-3).

Pavlich (1996a, 1996b), building on Foucault's work on government (Foucault 1977, 1978, 1980, 1981), argues that community mediation needs to be understood as a form of power relating to – although distinct from – state power (1996a, 1996b). Community mediation is developed outside the state, but for the purpose of strengthening the state. Pavlich argues that mediation employs its own techniques of power (in particular, techniques of discipline and techniques of self[9]) directed at participants in mediation. In doing so, it allows the state to govern its subjects at a

9 That is, techniques aimed at creation of particular self-identities.

distance, exercising power in an invisible fashion in order to minimize resistance to the state power and maximize regulatory efficiency (Pavlich 1996a, 1996b).

Restorative justice and the criminal justice system

Many restorative advocates see transformation of the criminal justice system away from retributive and towards restorative goals as their main objective. However, different methods of achieving it are suggested. Some proponents locate restorative justice outside the system with only loose links to it (McCold 2000). These advocates propose that restorative programmes should operate by way of diversion of cases from the criminal justice system. They believe that this model is best capable of preserving the purity of the restorative ideals. Incorporation of restorative justice into the state justice system is considered undesirable because it would dilute the purity of the restorative ideals by bringing judicial coercion into the restorative paradigm. To be true to its values, restorative justice should remain informal and voluntary.

One proponent subscribing to this view, McCold (2000, 387-8), believes that there are likely to be three stages in the development of restorative justice. During the first stage it would operate by way of diverting cases from the traditional criminal justice system to programmes operated by NGOs. The second stage would be characterized by the transfer of responsibility for organizing and facilitating restorative justice encounters to the criminal justice system. At the third stage restorative justice will begin to permeate the criminal justice system, with the consequence that the system will be transformed in accordance with restorative principles.

Other advocates wish to position restorative justice firmly within the criminal justice system[10]. They argue that restorative justice should be made an integral part of it, and the system should be 'maximally', 'radically and systematically' reformed in accordance with restorative values. These proponents are critical of placing restorative justice outside the system and limiting it to informal voluntary practices, predicting that this would provide a recipe for marginalization and a missed opportunity to bring about broad and far-reaching reforms of the criminal justice system:

> ...if the definition of restorative justice is indeed tied to a particular kind of informal dispute-resolution processing the effect will be to drastically restrict the scope of restorative justice theory and practice. And restorative justice initiatives themselves are likely to remain confined for the most part to diversionary processes that will, at best, have a marginal status at the periphery of the regular criminal justice system.
>
> (Dignan 2003, 138)

However, despite their differences, advocates of both the diversion and integration models are united in that their formulas for the development of restorative justice presuppose a significant degree of dependence of restorative justice on the criminal justice system. There seems to be an agreement that the state justice system should

---

10 See Walgrave 1995, 1999, 2000a, 2000b; Bazemore and Walgrave 1999b; Dignan 2002, 2003.

provide a legal framework, funding and referrals for restorative justice programmes. Additionally, it should offer a back-up in situations where restorative justice is either impossible or undesirable. The system should also supply judicial oversight and legal safeguards.

Some writers, however, have expressed concerns about pursuing restorative justice through criminal justice agencies because restorative justice values do not fit well with the ideology underlying the system. One such writer sceptical about attempts to accommodate restorative justice within the existing ideological and structural framework argues: '[t]rying to patch restorative justice onto the existing fundamentally retributive system is a transplant the social body will reject' (Morris 1995, 288). Another critic of restorative reforms without a reduction in the power and the involvement of the state believes that granting victims and the community a more significant role in the criminal justice process would result in a situation where

> ...the offender [finds] himself or herself not only lined up in defence against the state, but also against the victim and perhaps ... some new entity or presence put there to represent 'the community'. ... Simply injecting into the status quo some kind of formal victim-offender confrontation, replete with lawyers on both sides, and providing for the victim to have a formal say in each step of the traditional process promises only to do more to further unbalance an already skewed system.
>
> (Harris 1989, 32)

An important criticism directed at those willing to affiliate restorative justice with the criminal justice system is that practising restorative justice under the auspices of the system commits restorative justice to the moral compass of the 'traditional' criminal justice. This is a consequence of an adoption by restorative justice of the important concepts forming the basis of the criminal justice system, such as 'crime' defined by criminal law. Pavlich (2002a, 2005) points out that despite its claims to present an alternative to criminal justice, restorative justice is 'parasitic upon legally defined crimes' (2005, 35). Consequently, the restorative aspiration to offer a new moral framework of criminal justice 'grounds itself in the very value orientation it seeks to redress' (Pavlich 2005, 35). Restorative justice's failure to contest legal definitions of crime results in avoidance of ethical discussions beyond the value framework of the criminal justice system.

Two advocates critical of restorative justice adopting the legal framework, Sullivan and Tifft, argue that criminal law is a product of a particular political economy and is designed to preserve existing power relations (1998, 2000a, 2000b, 2001). Criminal law divides the world into categories of acceptable and unacceptable harms and violence, culpable and non-culpable perpetrators, and worthy and unworthy victims, and such a division helps to maintain present social order. The legal system is structured in such a way that it is designed to deal mainly with interpersonal violence, and social-structural injustices usually do not even deserve the designation of crime:

> ...the harms created by social-structural violence are not taken into account by law because law, as an administrative derivative of power-based political-economic

> institutions, is structured to direct the eyes of all towards the acts of those who are marginalized or disenfranchised by power. The law directs our attention to their 'reactive' forms of violence, and away from the perpetrators and benefactors of structural violence, hierarchical relations, and an economy that is geared toward deficit creation for some in the interest or surplus enhancement for others.
>
> (Sullivan and Tifft 2001, 157)

Restorative justice accepting the authority of criminal law serves to perpetuate the existing social arrangements by focusing on interpersonal dimensions of crime and deflecting attention away from the deeper roots of crimes as found in class, race, gender-based and other social-structural conflicts (Mika 1992; Pavlich 1996a; Dyck 2000, 2006). So, Pavlich proposes that if an objective is to create a new paradigm of justice, this would probably imply searching for justice without crime (2005, chapter 6). Sullivan and Tifft (2001) advocate widening significantly the campaign for restorative justice in such a way that it is no longer limited to legally proscribed crimes. Rather, it should confront what they call 'social-structural violence'[11] at all levels of social existence.

There is a similarity between some ideas of these critics questioning the adoption of the concept 'crime' by most restorative advocates and the position of the inspirer of restorative justice Christie. Christie also questions the concept 'crime'. He argues that

> Crime is not a 'thing'. Crime is a concept applicable in certain social situations where it is possible and in the interests of one or several parties to apply it. We can create crime by creating systems that ask for the word. We can extinguish crime by creating the opposite types of systems.
>
> (Christie 1982, 74)

Christie re-defines crime as a 'conflict' requiring an active participation more than it requires solutions (as has been pointed out earlier) and claims that the main advantage of such an approach would be 'opportunities for norm-clarification' (1982, 93).

This approach suggests very radical implications for the concept and institution of law (Johnstone 2002, 146; Bottoms 2003, 86). In particular, it appears to transform the nature of dispute resolution process from judicial to political. It also appears to abandon principles of consistency in decision-making and equal treatment before the law. Christie's approach seems to be based on the premise that law can never cover every unique situation and that matters cannot be decided ahead of time by a mandate. It acknowledges that it is never possible to make final judgements with regard to the interpretation of norms and values among members of society and that interpretations of matters of right and wrong should be made in an endless process of discussion. It is through such a continuous discussion process that people develop their moral sense, their sense of justice.

11 'Social-structural violence' is defined as 'the kind of violence we do when we exercise power over each other, [as well as] the violence that derives from the way we organize our primary social relationships so that we set up patterns of interaction that allow some to thrive at the expense of others' (Sullivan and Tifft 2001, 122).

Other traditional concepts rejected by critics who are skeptical of restorative justice's reliance on the criminal justice system are 'victim' and 'offender'. It is argued that the roles of 'victim' and 'offender' are 'a result of a snapshot approach to justice' (Morris 1995, 290). As Sullivan and Tifft further suggest,

> ...to conceive and speak of others in terms of identity fixing and identity separating categories such as offender and victim is itself a source of harm because these designations are personally deconstructive and non-integrative. By using them, we force upon the person harmed and the person responsible for the harm a fixed, false identity. ...For the person who has harmed, an identity is created and placed so as to separate, brand, marginalize, control, and constrain. For the person who has been harmed, the assignment of victim status is often disempowering, one more harm to be transcended.
>
> (Sullivan and Tifft 2001, 80)

Pavlich also points out that 'for some cases that filter into both criminal and restorative justice systems, the designation of victim may not be sought by affected parties, or indeed may not be appropriate to the situation' (2005, 58). He argues that the label 'victim' presumes a disempowered identity, which contradicts the restorative aspiration to empower victims. Pavlich asks,

> ...what purpose lies behind attempts to empower subjects through an identity that is, by definition, disempowered? Is it not more appropriate to try to escape that identity, perhaps by 'empowering' subjects through another identity? Might it not make more sense to support those who have suffered in pursuing identities that are not, by definition, disempowered?
>
> (2005, 59)

Assigning the identity of a victim may amount to double victimisation as it fails to enable the subjects to alter the social conditions which might have generated their suffering in the first place (Pavlich 2005, chapter 3).

The label 'offender', according to Pavlich (2005, chapter 4), is equally problematic, because it implies that the offender is the main bearer of harm and places the responsibility for harm almost exclusively on offenders. Yet, in some cases it is the designation of crime itself that generates harm. It is argued that 'approaching the offender as the main bearer of harm deflects questions of justice away from wider power relations that might be as harmful as the act committed' (Pavlich 2005, 81-2).

Harris (1989, 1998) similarly criticizes models of restorative justice based on the assumption that crime is a problem attributable solely or primarily to individual lawbreakers. These models ignore the role of the social forces that promote crime and conflict. Harris argues that restorative justice which fails to address social injustices and is focused exclusively on getting the offender to repair the damage caused by his or her crime is likely to reinforce the existing social inequalities. She concludes:

> [Restorative justice] often seems to come back to putting everything on an individual offender ... That is, the rhetoric states that crime often represents and manifests structural and community and interpersonal problems, reflecting poverty, sexism, racism, inequality, segregation, and other attributes of lives too often lived in an atmosphere of hopelessness and despair, yet when we respond to it, we forget all that stuff. ... if we are serious in

> believing that such factors have effects, and that they are harmful and threaten domestic tranquility and security, then [restorative justice] has got to confront those forces with equal emphasis as confronting individual harm-doers.
>
> (Harris (1998) quoted in McCold 1998, 43-44)

These critics propose to break away from the paradigm of criminal justice that respects the right of criminal law to define what constitutes 'crime', who is the 'victim' and who is the 'offender'. The moral 'lens' which they suggest significantly widens the scope of the campaign for restorative justice and firmly grounds restorative justice in the commitment to fundamental social changes[12]. Their search for justice goes far beyond reparation of 'harms' resulting from legally defined crimes.

Concluding remarks

This chapter has outlined key ideals of restorative justice advocates and some debates which have taken place among them. These restorative ideals will be revisited in the subsequent chapters of this book and looked at in the light of findings from the empirical study upon which this book is based. To what extent have the aspirations of restorative justice advocates been achieved in one restorative justice project? Is there empirical support for some concerns of critics that have been outlined in this chapter? These are some of the questions which will be dealt with in what follows.

12 See Harris 1989; Mika 1992; Morris 1995, 2000; Dyck 2000, 2006; Sullivan and Tifft 2001; Pavlich 1996a, 2005; also Sullivan and Tifft 1998, 2000a, 2000b.

Chapter Three

Ideals and Practical Realities: The Gap

Introduction

As has been demonstrated in Chapter Two, restorative justice advocates have a number of rather ambitious aspirations. It is believed that restorative justice could present a new moral 'lens' through which crime and justice could be looked at (Zehr 1990). It is argued that it offers a 'fully fledged alternative' to both punishment and offender rehabilitation (Walgrave 1995, 1999, 2000a; Bazemore 1996). It is promised that restorative justice will place victims at its centre and treat their needs as the primary concern (Claassen 1995; Achilles and Zehr 2001; Mika and Zehr 2003). Proponents aspire to develop a model of criminal justice which empowers stakeholders in crime, 'restores the deliberative control of justice by citizens' (Braithwaite 2003a, 87) and offers a deprofessionalized, community-based alternative to the state justice system. Some argue that restorative justice offers a way of doing criminal justice which is characterized by voluntariness (Marshall 1996; Council of Europe 1999; McCold 2000; UN 2000). How realistic are these ideals? What happens when they are pursued in practice?

In this and the remaining chapters the aspirations of restorative justice advocates and theoretical debates outlined in Chapter Two will be looked at in the light of the findings of the empirical study carried out by the author. The implications of this study for the restorative justice theory and practice will be explored.

The empirical study

This empirical study has been carried out in one family group conferencing project in England[1]. As has been noted in the Introduction to this book, the study aimed at bringing into the debate about restorative justice insights and perspectives of people who had experienced restorative justice first-hand. The intention was to enable participants in restorative interventions to share their views about restorative justice, raise concerns and criticisms. One objective was to look at aspirations of restorative justice advocates (which have been outlined in Chapter Two) in the light of empirical findings and see to what degree those aspirations have been achieved within one restorative justice project. Another objective was to see how the empirical data informs some debates referred to in Chapter Two which have taken place among

1 The precise location of the project will not be disclosed to preserve confidentiality of the interviewees.

restorative justice proponents and critics. Yet another objective was to use empirical findings to identify potential problems and tensions which emerge when restorative justice ideals are pursued in practice.

This study involved in-depth qualitative interviews with 47 participants in family group conferences and six professionals. Out of the 47 participants, 13 were offenders, 17 victims, 13 offender supporters and four victim supporters. The professionals included a manager of a Youth Offending Team and a case worker from a Youth Offending Team (both of whom attended some conferences and had a role to play in making referrals to the family group conferencing project), two family group conference facilitators and two Victim Support representatives (who represented victims in some conferences).

Another research method employed was documentary analysis of files kept in the family group conferencing project containing information relevant to case studies (referral forms from Youth Offending Teams, copies of pre-sentence reports, copies of reports for family group conferences, copies of plans developed during conferences and copies of letters of apology).

One conference was observed as part of this study.

A very useful source of information was several informal conversations with a family group conference facilitator from the project who provided detailed background of the case studies and also generously shared experiences relating to the conferencing practice.

In total, 16 case studies have been examined. They involved a variety of offences, including assaults, a robbery, burglaries, thefts of a vehicle, theft and handling stolen goods and criminal damage.

It is important to note that this study was limited to one restorative justice project and the number of interviewees was rather small. It is not argued that the findings are true for other restorative projects. However, they may provide some general lessons applicable to other restorative justice experiments. They may shed some light on the important debates among restorative justice proponents and provide some empirical support for certain theoretical arguments made in the course of those debates. Additionally, it might help to highlight some dangers inherent in the current development of restorative justice.

One restorative justice project

After its establishment, the project of this study conducted family group conferences in child care and protection cases. Later it started working with young offenders (aged 10 to 17), following a successful application for funding made together with a Youth Offending Team (hereafter YOT) to the Youth Justice Board. The Youth Justice Board was the main funder, and other funders included the Social Services, Community Safety project, police, YOTs and the probation service. The project operated in partnership with the police, YOTs and Victim Support. The legislative framework was provided by the Crime and Disorder Act 1998.

By the end of the second year of dealing with criminal cases, the project received over 80 referrals from YOTs and carried out over 40 conferences. In the majority of cases victims attended the conferences. Where they did not attend, either a Victim Support worker or a police officer represented them. It was estimated that in the first year of the project operating 44 per cent of victims attended conferences and in the second year – 64 per cent[2].

The process worked as follows. In some cases conferences were court-ordered as part of reparation orders, action plan orders or supervision orders. In other cases, if the court had not seen the report detailing wishes of the victim at the sentencing stage, the court could make a flexible order, enabling assessment for a conference. If, following the assessment, it appeared that victims wished to be involved, a family group conference could take place.

All referrals had to be channelled through a YOT after a YOT manager had assessed the appropriateness of a referral to the project and had conducted a pre-referral discussion with a project senior practitioner. Before a referral was made, the young offender and his or her parent or guardian had to give consent to participation in a conference. The YOT police officer would contact the victim(s), explain the process and ask if they consented to participate in the conference.

The next stage was a meeting of representatives of four agencies: the family group conferencing service, YOT, police and Victim Support. The aims of the meeting were to pull together all relevant information related to the offence, to develop a plan of what needed to be done in the preparation for the conference, to identify and allocate roles and tasks among the professionals, and to set timescales for the conference.

Prior to the conference, a YOT worker would write a report for the conference. The report would have two parts. Part One would be focused on the offence and Part Two on risks of re-offending and the offender welfare issues. The offender and his or her family would have to sign the report and give consent to share the information contained in Part One with victims and other conference participants and Part Two with other professionals who would be involved in the conference.

During the preparation for the conference, a conference facilitator would meet in private with the victim(s), the offender and his or her parent(s) or a guardian at least twice, explain the process, and prepare them for participation. Together with the offender and his or her parent(s) or a guardian they would identify family members and significant others who should and who should not be invited to the conference. The facilitator would also make other arrangements necessary for the conference.

The conference would have two main parts. The first part is focused on the offence. During this part the victim(s) can tell how the offence has affected them, ask questions and express their feelings. The offender is provided with an opportunity to apologize. Then the victim(s) leave and the focus shifts to the prevention of re-offending. Professionals and the family discuss ways how to keep the offender out

---

2 The victim attendance rate in this project was much higher than in some other restorative experiments. For instance, in Vermont community reparative boards only 15 per cent of victims attended board meetings (Karp and Walther 2001). Holdaway et al (2001) found in their research of pilot YOTs that in relation to final warnings, just four per cent of victims had some form of direct involvement in reparative or mediating activity. In relation to referral orders, it was found that victims attended panel deliberations in only thirteen per cent of cases (Crawford and Newburn 2003).

of trouble. Then the professionals leave, and the family has private time to develop a plan. The plan needs to include details how reparation will be made to the victim and how the family will help the offender stay out of trouble. Then the plan is shared with professionals. After the conference the facilitator would contact the victim(s) and outline the reparation proposal. The plan needs to be agreed to by a YOT worker, but its implementation lies with the family.

The remaining part of this chapter will examine the extent to which the ideals of the restorative justice movement have been achieved in this family group conferencing project.

Is restorative justice punishment?

As argued in Chapter Two, restorative justice is frequently portrayed as an alternative to the 'traditional' way of responding to crime – punishment of offenders. However, there has been a strong opposition to advocates of this view. A number of theoretical arguments have been put forward to challenge claims that restorative justice presents an alternative to punishment. Rather, it has been argued, it is an alternative *form* of punishment (Daly 2000).

What did lay participants in restorative justice think on the issue? Did they understand restorative justice as a form of punishment?

One offender and three offender supporters interviewed as part of this study considered restorative justice conferencing punishment. Two offenders were not sure whether it was punishment. Other offenders and their supporters did not interpret the conferences they attended as punishment. Rather, they tended to conceptualize restorative justice as a strategy aimed at helping and educating offenders and thereby facilitating their rehabilitation. For example, in response to the question whether or not they considered the conference punishment, one offender replied: 'No, I didn't see it as a punishment, really, because they just helped me out, not punishing. They just wanted to help me out.' The older brother of another offender who participated in a conference similarly argued: 'No, I didn't see it as a punishment. I see it more as an experience that had to teach [the offender]. It was more of like a learning experience.' In another interview, after answering the question whether the conference was punishment negatively, an offender explained: 'The first part [of the conference] is basically to make you aware that property belongs to somebody else. It's to make you aware of that. But during the second part – the bit about re-offending – is how to put strategies in place to actually try and prevent that.' His mother also argued in the interview that: 'The conference wasn't a punishment. … I think the conference is a good thing – making them aware how the victim feels.'

The position of the vast majority of victims and their supporters on the issue of punishment was similar to that of most offenders and their supporters. They refused to view restorative justice as punishment and considered it an intervention aimed primarily at making offenders realize the consequences of their actions and helping them to stay out of future trouble.

Only two victims (both of whom were children) felt that restorative justice was punishment. One of these victims viewed a conference that way 'because it is very embarrassing' (in her own words). The other victim explained that he did so 'because [the offender] was the top guy in his gang, and now he goes straight back down, because he was caught, he was made to apologize.' Yet, both of these interviewees pointed out that punishing offenders was neither the only nor the main objective of the conference. They thought that the main objective was to make offenders understand the wrongfulness of their behaviour, to prevent them from doing similar things in the future and to make the victim feel better.

The finding that participants in restorative justice conferences – especially offenders – did not generally understand conferences as a form of punishment is rather surprising. The majority of offenders were ordered by the court to attend the conference and apologize to victims, and a refusal to comply with the order could lead to offenders returning to court and being penalized for breach of the order. Also, it was obvious from conversations with offenders that they found conferences a painful and unpleasant experience.

How can the refusal by offenders to interpret painful court-ordered sanctions as punishment be explained? One possible explanation is that the way conferences were prepared and conducted could have masked the punitive aspects of restorative sanctions (Zernova 2007). Despite the fact that conferences were usually court-ordered, conference organizers refused to resort to openly coercive and repressive methods in making offenders participate and apologize to victims in conferences. The consent to participate in a conference and apologize was secured through the use of much more subtle means. During pre-conference private meetings, conference organizers behaved towards offenders in a friendly, caring, sympathetic and understanding fashion. So, offenders interviewed as part of this study frequently described facilitators as 'friendly' and 'supportive' and expressed high levels of satisfaction with the way the facilitators treated them. The presentation by facilitators of themselves as 'caring friends' and 'helpers' of offenders discouraged resistance and opposition on the part of offenders and served to encourage them to reveal their thoughts and feelings and submit to the care and guidance of facilitators organizing conferences. Facilitators promised to offenders various benefits (for example, attending a conference will help to put the offence behind and move on; it would help the offender to stay out of future trouble and to make the most of their lives). Through skilful questioning, probing, reframing and rephrasing offenders' statements, focusing offenders on certain issues, praising and encouraging them and using other invisible techniques, conference organizers carefully constructed particular self-identities and subtly pressurized offenders to embrace them (see discussions in section 'De-professionalized justice?' below for more details). These identities were of empathic, repentant and forgiveness-seeking individuals who have realized their past mistakes and desired to make amends and change their behaviour and attitudes in the future. If offenders did embrace such self-identities, they would believe that they attended a conference and apologized to victims not so much because they had to, but because they wanted to do it.

Just like at the pre-conference stage, during the actual conferences, facilitators avoided using openly coercive and repressive methods. During the first part of the conference, they presented themselves as neutral parties, delegated the disapproval of the offending behaviour to victims and refrained from criticizing offenders and expressing their personal views on what had happened. During the second part of the conference, facilitators acted as people caring for the offender's well-being and willing to provide the best help they can to enable offenders to make the most of their lives. As a consequence, an image of conference facilitators as friends and helpers caring for their well-being, rather than punishers, was created in the eyes of offenders.

Other professionals participating in conferences – Youth Offending Team workers and social workers – also presented themselves as friends and carers, desiring to help offenders.

A somewhat similar image of victims – the image of altruistic helpers – seems to have been produced in a number of cases (probably not without the assistance of conference facilitators who, just like in dealings with offenders, had employed a whole array of subtle techniques to craft particular self-identities of victims, as will be argued in the section 'De-professionalized justice?' below). During conferences offenders met people whom they had wronged, but who, contrary to expectations of many offenders, instead of being abusive and revengeful, were respectful, understanding, forgiving and sympathetic towards offenders. So, a number of offenders said in the interviews that victims were surprisingly nice and not vindictive to them during conferences. As one such offender explained, 'I didn't expect they would be so nice. I thought they would be shouting at me'. Several offenders also said that if the roles were reversed, they probably would not be so nice towards people who have committed a crime against them[3].

In conferences offenders met people who had sacrificed their time and came to meetings from which a number of them did not seem to derive any obvious benefits for themselves. They came to conferences because they wanted to help offenders. Some victims shook offenders' hands after the conference and wished them well. Some even started crying, touched by the offenders' apology. Some victims tried to comfort crying mothers of offenders. One victim offered the offender an apprenticeship in his company. Another victim gave the offender a lift after the conference and offered him free driving lessons during weekends. Such forgiveness, kindness, generosity and altruism made it difficult for offenders in many cases to see victims as punishers.

The hospitable, informal and friendly atmosphere within which conferences were conducted could be another factor preventing offenders from interpreting conferences as a form of punishment. That atmosphere was designed to underscore the non-hierarchical, informal and participatory nature of the process. Participants usually sat in a circle, they usually introduced themselves by their first names, drinks and snacks were provided, during coffee breaks people could mingle and

---

3 Offender supporters were also surprised that victims were so kind and not vindictive towards them and their children. To quote a parent of an offender:

> ...I must admit when I first heard about [a possibility of attending a conference], I thought: "Oh, no", because they are really going to have a go at my son, and calling him names, 'cause I would. I mean, I think, I would. But hearing how it has gone in the past, I was quite surprised, really, that people are so forgiving and just how understanding they were. A couple of them said they have children who had gone through similar troubles...

chat, facilitators tried to make participants feel comfortable and relaxed. Offenders saw a marked contrast between the treatment they received during conferences and the treatment they were subjected to in the police station following the arrest, in the court and in prison (for those who were imprisoned)[4]. The hospitality and care they experienced during conferences could serve to discourage them from understanding conferences as punishment (Zernova 2007).

The finding that the vast majority of participants in restorative justice interventions did not conceptualize conferences as a form of punishment seems to offer some support to the view of those advocates who believe that restorative justice is an alternative to punishment and does not appear to strengthen the argument of critics that restorative justice is an alternative *form* of punishment. However, four points need to be noted in relation to this conclusion. First, six interviewees did see conferences as a form of punishment, consistently with the claim of the critics. Second, the suggestion made above that the punitive essence of restorative interventions could have been masked should not be overlooked. Third, while the understanding of the nature of restorative interventions by the vast majority of participants differed from the interpretation by critics (who believe that restorative justice is a form of punishment), the participants' interpretation of the substance of restorative encounters did not coincide with the interpretation by those advocates who refuse to see restorative justice as a form of punishment either. These advocates view restorative justice as a measure aimed at reparation of harm. However, conference participants tended to view it as an intervention aimed at offender rehabilitation (Zernova 2007). Finally, the findings that most offenders did not see the conference as punishment does not support the position of advocates claiming that restorative justice is an alternative to punishment because, according to those advocates, the perspective of offenders is irrelevant. It is the perspective of those who impose sanctions, rather than those receiving them, that determines whether the sanctions are punishment (Walgrave 2003).

Restorative justice and offender rehabilitation

As has been pointed out in Chapter Two, a number of restorative justice advocates present restorative justice as an alternative to the rehabilitation or treatment model (Walgrave 1995, 1999, 2002; Bazemore 1996; McCold 2000). It is argued that the rehabilitation paradigm focuses on identifying and meeting offenders' needs, assigns offenders a passive role in the treatment process, views sanctioning offenders as

4 A leaflet which offenders were given before conferences contained quoted statements by offenders from earlier conferences which could serve to re-enforce the contrast between the treatment which offenders get within the criminal justice system and restorative justice conferences: 'In court I didn't say nothin', let the lawyer talk. It seemed like no one cared – everyone just doing their jobs. Now with Restorative Justice people care – I speak up and it makes a real difference. Now I'm part of the community here.' Or: 'I had good intentions coming out of jail, but as you walk out … your only identity is as an offender. But in Restorative Justice you are recognised as a community member. You see people who are willing to help…'.

irrelevant and inappropriate and ignores the needs of victims. The aim of the criminal justice intervention becomes to meet offenders' needs and promote their welfare. In contrast, restorative justice holds offenders accountable, requires them to make amends for their actions and views needs and interests of victims as central. Other restorative justice proponents, however, see restorative justice and rehabilitation as mutually supportive and wish to combine them. What was the relationship between restorative justice and offender rehabilitation in the project of this study?

It appears that the vast majority of victims, offenders and supporters of both felt that restorative justice interventions were a form of offender rehabilitation. Several findings which will be outlined below lead to this conclusion.

One such finding relates to explanations by conference participants why they agreed to participate in conferences. When asked why they decided to take part, the majority of victims, especially adult ones, said that they came to the conference, hoping that their attendance might help to keep offenders out of trouble in the future[5]. Using the words of one such victim, 'we hoped [our attendance] would do the boy some good … and hopefully he won't get into trouble again'. Or, as another victim explained, 'we thought it was important for the boy, that it would help him in any way'.

A number of these victims believed that prevention of future offending could be achieved by making offenders understand the wrongfulness of their behaviour and the consequences of their wrongdoing. As one victim has put it, '[m]y reasons for agreeing to attend the conference were to try to help the boy to see that he'd done wrong. … I hope it will stop him from doing what he did again.' It was also hoped that invoking empathy and feelings of guilt in offenders could help them stay out of trouble. So, an elderly victim of burglary confined to a wheelchair explained her reasons for attending a conference, 'I wanted to say to [the offenders] … how would they have felt if I was their grandmother or relative … and also to see their reaction to seeing me being like this'.

Victims of motor vehicle thefts came to conferences because they wanted to make offenders understand that driving the stolen vehicles endangered their own lives and the lives of others, because the offenders were not good drivers. These victims hoped that in the future offenders would think more carefully about possible consequences of their actions.

Two victims got into trouble themselves when they were young. Using the words of one of them, he came to the conference to 'put this lad … in the right direction'. The other victim explained that he wanted to serve as a positive example for the offender:

> …when I was a lad, I also got into trouble. … [Yet] I ended up being a director of the company. So, you can get over these problems if you can put them behind you and take the lessons that you learn from these things … if [the offender] could put it behind him, then he could go forward and make good of himself.

5 Other common reasons why victims came to conferences were getting answers and expressing emotions.

Similarly to victims, one common reason why offenders' parents came to conferences was a hope that it might help their child understand the wrongfulness of her or his behaviour and its effects on victims and consequently prevent further involvement in crime. The mother of one offender explained: 'I hoped it would benefit [my son] ... it would benefit in helping him to understand what he had done and how it had affected people.' The mother of another offender justified her reasons for coming to the conference: 'I wanted him to face everything, as much as he was going to see. … So, I wanted him to see every corner of what crime does'.

Further evidence indicating that participants viewed conferences as a form of offender rehabilitation can be found in their response to the question about the rationale of conferences. The vast majority of victims thought that the purpose of the conference was to make the offender realise the consequences of their criminal behaviour and the wrongfulness of their actions. Many hoped that this realization, combined with a supportive attitude on the part of conference participants, would work toward stopping offending behaviour. The following quote from an interview with a victim summarizes this general assumption about the rationale for conferencing:

> I think that was the whole point of it: to stop the boy from doing another crime. ... I think what the purpose was – for him to be remorseful, to be sad for what he'd done, and to see that he shouldn't be doing what he did, and he wouldn't do it again in the future, you know, and with people being positive and encouraging him...

Similarly to most victims and their supporters, the vast majority of offenders and their supporters thought the purpose of the conference was to help offenders 'understand what they have done to people' (using words of a victim supporter). As one offender noted, 'normally if you are robbing someone, it's no one … until you see their face and you hear their feelings...'. It was hoped that the realization of the victim's hurt would, using words of an offender supporter, 'draw attention to what he's done and make him listen and to stop him doing it to anybody else.'

When asked whether the conference has achieved its purpose, the answer was generally positive and emphasised the rehabilitative impact of conferences on offenders, in particular, that offenders were made to understand human costs of their offences. For instance, one victim explained:

> I think [the offenders] have learnt their lesson. I think they've understood exactly the injustice they've done to us, how they came to our house and upset us, and what it meant to us, which, I think, they probably didn't realize without the conference.

Somewhat similarly, one offender supporter argued:

> I was hoping and I did actually get what I expected. The result I expected was for [my son's] attitude towards victims to change, and it did. It did, and it was very pleasant. Before we went there, he was like 'it doesn't matter who they are. I don't care.' It was

> all very much like that. But afterwards, after he had actually met the victims, his whole attitude changed, which was really nice[6].

Additional evidence shedding light on the role of offender rehabilitation in this family group conferencing project can be found in the pre-conference reports in the 16 cases which were examined as part of this study. The reports were divided into two parts. The first ('restorative') part was entitled 'The Offence and Righting the Wrong' and explained that the offender had recently committed an offence, detailed the court order and emphasized that the offender 'will need help and support to stay out of trouble in the future'.

The second ('rehabilitative') part of the report dealt with the offender rehabilitation and welfare. This part focused on identifying reasons for offending behaviour and needs of the offender. Typically, it would discuss at length problems within the offender's family and suggest ways of resolving them. It would deal with schooling matters, friendship groups, drugs-related issues, emotional well-being and self-image of the offender, as well as identifying other potential problems and deficits of the offender and possible solutions. In conclusion, it would instruct the family what the plan developed by them in the conference needed to include and list professional help which was available.

It was obvious from the reports that not only the 'rehabilitative', but also the 'restorative' part had the offender as its focus. Both parts were written in the offender welfare spirit, with a clear emphasis on the 'help and support' which the offender needed if he or she were to stop offending. The discussion of restorative matters typically was limited to specifying that the offender had to meet victims and apologize. While the offender's needs and possible ways of meeting them were discussed at a great length, typically the needs of victims were not even mentioned. On the basis of the pre-conference reports alone one could conclude that the project attempted to implement a correctional programme which had some elements of restorative justice added to it (Zernova forthcoming).

These reports formed the basis for the plans that had to be developed by families during conferences. Probably unsurprisingly, the resulting plans – at least the ones which were examined as part of this study – focused almost exclusively on issues relating to rehabilitation. If restorative matters were raised, they were restricted to writing a letter of apology.

Conferences, like the pre-conference reports, consisted of two parts. As was explained earlier in this chapter, the first, 'restorative', part focused on the offence that has been committed, and the second, 'rehabilitative', part – on prevention of re-offending and the offender welfare. Victims were not allowed to participate in

6 Parents of two other offenders claimed that the conference was much more effective than the court appearance because it helped the offenders clearly understand the seriousness of their actions. These parents said in the interview that their children responded to their arrest as if it was a joke. They were laughing and giggling when they were brought to the police station. They also laughed, shouted and talked to each other when they were placed in the adjacent cells. When they appeared in court, they behaved in a similar fashion. The conference, however, provided a totally different experience, which made the offenders realize the seriousness of their actions.

the second part of the conference during which, with the help of professionals, offenders and their families were expected to develop a plan how to keep offenders out of trouble[7]. Only offenders and their families could attend. Some victims said in interviews that they would have been interested in staying during the second part of the conference. The fact that victims were excluded from participating in the 'rehabilitative' part might suggest that victims were used during the first part of the conference to educate offenders about consequences of their actions. Once their presence was no longer necessary, they were sent back home.

There is some evidence suggesting that professionals in this project were not very enthusiastic about sanctioning offenders. As a result, several victims in this study complained that they felt uncomfortable during conferences because of what they saw as the conference facilitators' adoption of a non-blaming approach towards offenders. To quote one young victim of assault commenting on the conference preparation: 'It did make me feel as though [the offender] hadn't done anything wrong, though. It did. It did feel like [conference organizers] were sticking up for her.' Several victims wished that during the conference, professionals would actively express their disapproval of offenders' actions. Evaluating the approach taken by facilitators during the conference, one such victim said:

> I think [the way the conference was conducted was a] too soft approach. I think it could've been a harder and a more direct approach, without being offensive. … I felt [the conference facilitators] were … almost too accommodating, too sympathetic to the perpetrators, than the victim. It was almost conscious that here we have two young people who might be daunted by this situation, so we'll make them feel as comfortable as we can.

A somewhat similar view was expressed by Victim Support representatives who came to one of the conferences to represent a victim who was too ill to attend the conference. During the interview, they feared that if the victim came to the conference, she would have felt uncomfortable. The conference looked more like a birthday party for the offender, rather than a criminal justice intervention. There were huge amounts of food, and everybody was nice and kind to the offender, as this extract from the interview illustrates:

> Victim Support representative 1: ...what struck us was that the person coordinating [the conference] provided a great deal of food, and there appeared to be a party atmosphere at the conference.
>
> Victim Support representative 2: Yes. It was quite a young offender, so they tried to make it informal and relaxed.
>
> Victim Support representative 1: It was actually bizarre. I'm glad the victim wasn't there. I don't know how effective that was for the suspect and the family of the suspect, but I suspect they wouldn't have the same opinion that we had, because we're approaching it from a different perspective. … For Victim Support, it was clearly a serious matter, and yet here we were sitting around this feast.

---

7 Victims could not participate in the second part of the conference because the information that is private to the offender's family was shared there.

According to these Victim Support representatives, during the conference the offender read out a poem which he had written. He was praised by those in the room. It was also pointed out that the offender felt very comfortable in the conferencing room:

> Victim Support representative 2: The other thing that didn't help was that the premises that the conference was in – and I can't remember how, but – they were familiar to the young person, the perpetrator. So he felt comfortable there and was dashing in and out, saying: 'I'll go and get this!' and 'I know where that is!'. I don't think he should be beaten. Not 'beaten', that's not the right word. I don't think he should feel uncomfortable. He shouldn't feel frightened or intimidated. But to get the balance wrong – when he became so familiar, and it was so easy, and it was such a nice place to be – that the balance was out of kilter. ... I think, had the victim been there, it wouldn't have been funny. It would have been very seriously wrong.

The above findings seem to suggest that restorative justice, as practised within the project of this study, with its strong emphasis on offender rehabilitation, can hardly be seen as an example of full-blown restorative justice. At the same time it would be unfair to argue that the experiment fits perfectly well within the offender rehabilitation model. Some needs of victims did receive attention (in particular, the need to express feelings and a disapproval of the offending behaviour and the need to ask questions, as will be discussed later in this chapter). The issue of offender accountability was not totally ignored. Offenders were expected to acknowledge their wrongdoing and apologize to victims. In some cases, they were even asked to do some material reparation (see below). The project can be seen as a hybrid of the rehabilitation and restorative paradigms, as elements of both could be found within it.

A victim-focused justice?

As has been pointed out in Chapter Two, one of the most important claims made on behalf of restorative justice is that it is a victim-centred justice, the primary concern of which is healing those who have been hurt by crime. Proponents argue that the injury has been inflicted primarily on individual victims, so they are '[e]ntitled to be the primary beneficiary of reparation' (Restorative Justice Consortium 2002). Do findings from this study support the claim that restorative justice as practised in this family group conferencing project places crime victims at its centre and treats their interests as a priority?

Half of victims interviewed during this study felt that the motivation of conference organizers behind inviting them to the conference was less to benefit them and more to benefit offenders. The following quote from an interview with a victim represents a common answer to the question whether it was important to have a conference: 'yes, but more from the kids' point of view than ours. I think they got more out of the conference than we did'. Victims did not object to that and were happy to help. Yet, an argument can be made that victims were in effect *used* to rehabilitate offenders[8].

One factor that may cast doubt on the centrality of interests of victims is that this project was limited to juvenile offenders. The result of this limitation was that only those victims whose offenders happened to be juveniles could get an opportunity to participate in restorative justice encounters (and presumably to derive from them the promised benefits). The fact that the age of offenders determined the entitlement of victims to benefit from restorative justice programmes does not fit well with the aspiration to make the interests of victims paramount. If needs and interests of victims were indeed of fundamental importance, the age of offenders would seem a rather illogical basis for allowing some victims to take part in restorative justice encounters and denying others a chance to benefit from restorative justice (Zernova 2007). One of the conference facilitators interviewed as part of this study criticized the project on the grounds that restorative justice discriminated among victims. Her explanation of the situation related to the fact that the project was funded mainly by the criminal justice system, whose primary concern is prevention of re-offending, rather than victims' needs.

Another finding which puts into question the validity of claims that restorative justice is a victim-centred justice (within the project of this study) is that a considerable number of conferences went ahead, even though victims did not attend. Yet, no conference occurred without the offender attending[9]. It is noteworthy that in a significant number of cases it was assumed that a conference without victim participation could benefit offenders. Yet, it seems it was never believed that a conference without offender participation would be beneficial to victims.

Some findings indicate that certain actions and attitudes of conference facilitators made some victims feel uncomfortable. Some examples have been already provided earlier (for example, victims feeling that facilitators acted as if the offender had done nothing wrong and victims complaining that facilitators were too sympathetic and accommodating to offenders). Another example would be a conference in which the facilitator started by asking the offender if it was okay to begin. The victim (who was a child) was not asked a similar question. This way of starting the conference created an impression that the offender was the most important person in the room, and the victim did not even deserve an inquiry if she was ready to start the conference. As the mother of the victim explained in the interview,

> The conference facilitator asked [the offender] if they could start, and I said, 'hang on, we are not here for [the offender], we are here for [the victim]'. The conference facilitator said 'sorry' and asked [the victim], 'is it all right to start?' She said, 'yeah, fine'. … I think she should have asked, 'are you all comfortable to start? Shall we start now?', instead of asking [the offender] if she was comfortable to start.

---

8 Even if in reality victims were not used in order to benefit offenders, the victim perception that offenders were primary – or even the only – beneficiaries of the conferencing process is significant in itself, given the difficulties many restorative justice practitioners face when persuading victims to take part in restorative interventions.

9 This is consistent with Roche's findings resulting from a study of 25 restorative justice programmes (2003, 72).

Another source of discomfort reported by some victims (in particular child victims) was that their supporters were outnumbered by offender supporters. Child victims usually came to conferences with a parent and possibly a friend. Offenders, however, tended to come with several family members and quite often with members of their extended families. Bringing as many family members as possible was very much encouraged by conference organizers in the hope to mobilize the support of offenders' 'communities of care' to prevent re-offending (consistently with Braithwaite's idea (2002a, 100) that the 'plurality of deliberation' in family group conferences will increase the rehabilitative potential of restorative justice, as was explained in Chapter Two). Some child victims reported feeling especially uncomfortable and vulnerable because offenders brought more supporters[10].

One more factor that makes the centrality of victim needs and interests questionable within this restorative project is that too little importance was attached to material reparation. If restorative justice were indeed a victim-centred justice, it would probably be reasonable to expect that reparation of material harm caused to victims by offenders would be seen as an important issue. Yet, according to the interviewees, the issue of material reparation was not even raised in 12 out of 16 cases. In only two cases was compensation ordered by the court, and in only two other cases was a possibility of material reparation discussed in conferences. The project's official statement of principles claimed that '[t]he primary focus of conferences will be the offence that has been committed and reparation of harm'. It appears that if the reparation of harm was indeed 'the primary focus' (which was far from obvious), it was limited to *symbolic* reparation expressed through apology[11].

There is also some evidence that certain other needs of victims were overlooked. Some victims felt that they did not have a sufficient opportunity to discuss the conference thereafter[12]. Some of these interviewees wished that instead of offenders and their families staying after the first part of the conference and victims leaving, offenders and their families left, and victims stayed, so that they could share their views and opinions with each other and conference facilitators. Some victims felt that they were not given proper feedback[13]. So, during interviews they asked to call

10 This finding was mentioned to one of the conference facilitators in the project. Her response was that that was a mistake made in the past. Today steps are being taken to prevent situations where the offender supporters significantly outnumber the victim supporters. One way of doing it is to ask some of the offender supporters to stay outside the conferencing room during the first part of the conference and let them join the rest of the offender's family for the second part, after the victim and her or his supporters leave.

11 Shapland et al (2006b, 518) also found that financial reparation was very rare and symbolic reparation was prevalent in the three restorative schemes in England which they have evaluated.

12 After the conference victims were asked to fill in a conference evaluation form and send it by post to conference organizers. Also, conference organizers normally called victims after the conference to thank them for participation. Yet, that was clearly insufficient for at least some victims.

13 Shapland et al (2006b, 516) have similarly found that some victims wanted to keep in touch and find out how the offender was doing.

them if any information about how 'their' offenders were getting along became available and to share that information with them.

Yet, it is important to point out some evidence indicating that interests of victims, at least in one case, were put above interests of offenders. In that case, one of the four offenders had shown no remorse before the conference. Conference organizers decided that it would be better for the victim if the offender in question did not participate in the conference. This decision was made in spite of the fact that conference facilitators felt that attending the conference could potentially benefit the unremorseful offender.

Another finding that might suggest that restorative justice, as practised in this project, could claim the title of victim-centred is that several victims and their supporters believed that the purpose of the conference was primarily to benefit victims, or to benefit victims as well as offenders[14]. Several victims felt that confronting the offender was helpful because it enabled them to understand the reasons behind the offence and get an insight into whether the offender had any animosity towards them and was going to re-offend against them. It was believed that such insights could reduce victims' fears[15]. Several offenders and their supporters also thought that the purpose of the conference was to help victims by reducing their fears and making them feel safer. Using the words of an offender supporter, 'I think it is more or less to help the victims, really. They can see, you know, the people who came to their house, and it takes off worries from them, knowing that they wasn't actually personally picked on and chosen…'[16]

To summarize, some findings from this study make one doubt the centrality of victims' interests in this family group conferencing project. Other evidence suggests that at least in one case interests of a victim were given priority. While some interviewees thought that conferences were designed primarily to benefit offenders, others thought that the main purpose of conferences was to help victims or to help both parties.

---

14 As one victim supporter explained in the interview,

> I think the whole purpose was to see that the meeting was beneficial for both parties … seeing that it is beneficial to all concerned, seeing if it's good for the boys, seeing that it's good for people who have been offended against. … It is to see if the boys are repentant and to see if the people they offend are able to get back to the normality of life through contact with them and saying how they feel. I think this is what the conference was set out to do.

15 So, one victim described the rationale of the conference as he saw it:

> I think the reason it was done is to help the people who were affected during the incident. … if you are personally affected, as an individual … you always live in a fear. But if you actually confront the young man and understand that person, why they did it, you know, it's probably worthwhile.

16 Another offender supporter made a similar point:

> I think the focus was to alleviate the fear or some of the fears for the victims, to help them perhaps understand why [the offenders] did it, to help them see what is happening to the boys now [and] what is going to happen to them. [Also], hopefully, to help them see that [the offenders] had learned from it, and they are going to go on when they come out to not re-offend.

A voluntary process?

As discussed in Chapter Two, within the restorative justice discourse, the conventional way of doing criminal justice is frequently criticized for being coercive and violent, and some proponents present restorative justice as an alternative characterized by a voluntary process (Marshall 1996; Council of Europe 1999; McCold 2000; UN 2000). Others, however, find coercion necessary where voluntary restorative justice is impossible or considered undesirable[17]. What was the position within this family group conferencing project in relation to the issue of voluntariness?

The promotional leaflet given by conference organizers to participants claimed: 'Restorative Justice is *entirely voluntary* so if you do not want to take part you cannot be forced to' (emphasis added). As one of the conference facilitators has put it in the interview, '[i]f it is restorative, it has to be restorative. It can't be prescriptive. It can't be forced. ... if you were forcing people to be there, it wouldn't be real, and it couldn't be as impactive. ... It has to be voluntary in the purest sense of the word for it to be meaningful'.

However, a number of offenders said in interviews that their attending a conference was court-ordered, and a refusal to attend would lead them back to court for re-sentencing. Most of these offenders did not seem very enthusiastic about attending. It appeared that their attendance was motivated by fear of returning to court and being punished for breach of a court order, as this extract from an interview illustrates:

> Interviewer: Did you *have to* go to the conference?
>
> Offender: I had to go, because there was no other alternative. They said, 'there is no other alternative, so you have to go through it, otherwise you'll be in more trouble'.
>
> Interviewer: Why?
>
> Offender: People in the YOT said that. If I didn't go to the conference, I'd have to go to the court.

When asked whether they would have gone to a conference if it had been optional, opinions of offenders whose conferences were court-ordered divided. Some said they would have gone to say 'sorry', others said they would not.

For some offenders attendance was not court-ordered. This could happen if an offender expressed remorse, and a YOT, following the assessment of the case for conference suitability, referred it to the family group conferencing project. These offenders said in the interviews that they came to conferences because they wanted to apologize. So, one such offender explained that he came to the conference 'just to tell those people I didn't mean it. It'll make me feel better.' Another offender said he attended a conference 'because I thought it'd be nice, because [when I stole a bus and was chased by the police], I hit the ambulance as well, and the ambulance driver was there, so it gave me a chance to say sorry to him.'

---

17 See, for example, Declaration of Leuven 1997; Bazemore and Walgrave 1999b; Walgrave 1999; Claassen 1996; Restorative Justice Consortium 2002.

Some of the offenders whose participation was not court-ordered felt they were merely encouraged to participate. Others felt that when they were invited to participate, a degree of pressure was exercised over them[18], as the following extract from an interview demonstrates:

> Interviewer: Did you have a choice whether to go to the conference?
>
> Offender: Umm… Kind of yeah, but the YOT worker was quite pushy…
>
> Interviewer: In what way?
>
> Offender: Umm… Well, he kept saying it would be nice and everything… My mum didn't really wanna do it 'cause… I didn't really wanna do it because I thought I'd already done most of my sentence inside, and I had only one month left, and I thought that'd be it.

A number of offenders in the sample were simply unsure whether or not their attendance was optional. So, it seems that the neat distinction made by some academic commentators – voluntary vs. coerced – is not necessarily as clear-cut in the minds of participants.

As far as apologizing to victims is concerned, some offenders said they had to apologize. Others said they did so voluntarily. The latter category pointed out that they were encouraged by YOT workers and conference organizers to do so. Some offenders from the former group said that even if it had been optional, they would have apologized anyway.

Several offenders' parents thought that coming to a conference was obligatory not only for their children, but also for them. Some were not sure whether participation in the conferences was optional.

What did conference facilitators have to say about the issue of voluntariness in attending conferences and apologizing to victims? Conference facilitators argued that offenders should not be pressurised into – and during – the conferencing process, because coercion will provoke resistance on the offenders' part and will block their ability to empathize:

> I think if young people were … their arms twisted up behind their backs, and route-marched up to these things, there would be, I suspect, resistance to taking part in that process. That would block their ability to empathize. They would be sitting there feeling miffed that they were made to come. They wouldn't listen. If they can come to a conference with an agreed expectation, then they feel okay about coming. You can lead a horse to water, but you can't make it drink. I think it is important that it is voluntary in the purest sense.
>
> (From an interview with a conference facilitator)

When asked what happens if an offender who is ordered to attend a conference and apologize appears to be unwilling to do so, the facilitator responded:

> When you come to see an offender for the first time, you do not say, 'Well, I've come to see you today, because, you know, we are going to have this meeting and you're going

18 A finding similar to Miers et al (2001, 39).

> to say 'sorry' to the victim.' It isn't like that. It is not prescriptive in that sense. Mostly it comes from themselves.

To the question what conference facilitators do if it does not come from offenders themselves, the response of the facilitator was:

> When I go to see a young person, one of the first questions after a basic introduction is, 'Do you know why I am here, why I have come to see you?' Nine out of ten, they will say to me, 'yes'. So, I say, 'So, can you explain to me what your understanding of that is?' And they will usually say something about, 'Well, I'll meet the person whose house I've burgled, and I'll say 'sorry' to them'. Now, they may not say that. The one out of ten may not say that. So, then I might say, 'Can you tell me how you think the person might feel about what you did to them?' Some young people are more switched on than others. It is as any kind of interviewing skill, really. You are trying to gain an understanding of whether there is empathy there. For some it is immediate, and others it takes a little bit of pulling out.

The facilitator proceeded to provide an example of a boy who refused to go to the conference because he thought the victims, whose car he had stolen, would strangle him. The facilitator interpreted his fear as based on the ability to empathize with the victims, because the offender was able to put himself into victims' shoes and imagine what he would do to someone who had stolen his car. According to the facilitator, once the offender has demonstrated such ability to empathize,

> ...then you can switch into: 'So what you are saying is, if that had been your car, you would be really angry about that and you would want to strangle the person that did that to you. So, explain to me why you would feel angry about that?' And they maybe start talking about, 'Well, I saved up for the car...' So, you are pulling bits out to gauge whether there is empathy there, and there usually is, I have to say. Therefore you are giving them an opportunity to say to you, 'Well, you know, I want to say 'sorry''.

It appears from interviews with the conference facilitators and from observations during the fieldwork that restorative justice professionals employ a set of various subtle techniques (for example, multiple private meetings, skilful questioning, probing, reframing and restating what offenders are saying in a way that focuses them on certain issues, evoking empathy in offenders). These techniques are used to obtain the offender's agreement to participate in a conference and apologize to the victim(s). It seems this is done in such a skilful and subtle way that an appearance of a voluntary consent to participate and apologize may be created. Offenders may be made to believe that, despite the fact that attending a conference and apologizing was in their court order, they themselves freely chose to attend and apologize.

When it is claimed by its proponents that restorative justice involves a voluntary process, it is important not to overlook the subtle, virtually invisible, informal pressure exercised over offenders by restorative justice professionals. The claims that restorative justice is voluntary need to be looked at in light of the fact that coercion is not necessarily limited to court orders. It may come from different directions and be much more complex in its nature. It would be additionally a mistake to think of coercion within the restorative justice process in 'either/or' terms (that is, either the process is wholly coercive or wholly voluntary). Such thinking would be too crude and simplistic to capture the subtleties and complexities of what happens in practice.

Before concluding this section, the issue of voluntariness in relation to victims needs to be mentioned. There seems to be a consensus among restorative justice proponents that victims should not be coerced into participation in restorative encounters. However, as will be argued below (see section 'De-professionalized justice?'), there is some evidence that victims could be subjected by conference organizers to subtle moral and psychological pressures to take part in conferences.

Empowering justice?

It has been emphasized in Chapter Two that restorative justice advocates criticize the traditional criminal justice process on the ground that it disempowers stakeholders in crime. To quote McCold, '[l]awyers in courtrooms steal people's conflicts, taking from them the opportunity to resolve those conflicts themselves' (2004, 14). In contrast, restorative justice is presented as a process empowering stakeholders in crime to actively participate in developing their own solutions to their problems[19]. Did restorative justice in this family group conferencing project come close to this ideal?

Victim empowerment

When asked whether they felt involved during the conferencing process, the majority of victims and victim supporters answered positively. They could say what they wanted to say, as this quote from an interview with a victim illustrates: '...we had every opportunity to express what we felt, how it affected us personally, what our views were of the situation, and everyone made a comment.'[20] Can the finding that most victims felt involved during conferences be interpreted as evidence of their empowerment in the restorative justice process?

Important in this context is the fact that restorative justice conferences took place after sentencing, so even if they empowered victims, it happened after victims had been disempowered by the criminal justice system. Thus, one young victim of assault said in the interview that she wanted to come to court because she wished to hear the offender's side of the story there. In spite of this, she was told by the police

19 See, for example, Marshall 1996; Morris and Young 2000; McCold 1996, 2000, 2004; Braithwaite 2003a, 2003b; Bazemore and Schiff 2005; Van Ness and Strong 2006; Sawin and Zehr 2007.

20 However, some victims felt they could have been involved to a greater extent. Also, one victim supporter said that although she felt involved, she tried to not participate too much, because she thought the conflict was between her daughter and the girl who had assaulted her. This victim supporter believed the girls should be given maximum opportunity to resolve their conflict themselves.

that 'there was no need' for her to come. Another child victim of assault was invited to court and spent the whole day in the waiting room only to be told to go home, as the offender changed her plea to 'guilty' at the last moment. One young victim of robbery was forced to testify in court and was so traumatized by the process that he refused to attend a conference afterwards.

Prior to conferences victims were given a leaflet entitled 'Restorative Justice. Victims have a voice too' which consisted of a set of rhetorical questions:

> Do you want your say? To the offender? About how you feel? How the crime has affected you? Do you want to know? Why it happened to you? More about your offender? What you can do about it? What would they have done to me if…..? What has happened to my property? What have I done to deserve this? Was this a personal attack? Is it my fault in some way? Will they come back?

This leaflet concluded '[t]hese and other questions can be answered by Restorative Justice'. It effectively pre-defined the role of the victims, and it seems all that a victim's role involved was the following: ask questions and express emotions (as long as they did so within the ground rules imposed on them during conferences).

Victims had no real say over how crime should be responded to, or in defining offenders' obligations. The criminal justice system retained the monopoly over those matters. Without denying the value of an opportunity given to victims to ask questions and express emotions, it can be suggested that the functions which victims were allocated within the project of this study were narrowly restricted, and consequently the degree of their empowerment was limited. At the same time, by allowing victims to attend conferences, ask offenders a few questions, express emotions and receive an apology, an illusion may be created that victims play an active role in the criminal justice process and the restorative justice process 'belongs' to them.

Offender empowerment

This study has found that the vast majority of offenders felt they were involved in the conference and could say what they wanted to say. It may be argued that offenders were empowered in the course of family group conferences in the sense that they were given an opportunity to explain to victims and other conference participants the reasons behind their actions[21]. However, in three case studies offenders revealed in interviews that they did not even attempt to present their side of the story because they did not think they would be believed. This is hardly an indication of offender empowerment. In one case study, in order to avoid a trial, the offender pleaded guilty to something he claimed in the interview he did not do. The court ordered him to attend a family group conference and apologize to victims, which he did. If this offender indeed did not commit the crime, he offered a false apology.

---

21 So, the information pack given to offenders prior to conference listed benefits which attending a conferences could offer them. Among such benefits was the following: 'You can get yourself HEARD by the victim and the authorities to explain why you did it…' (original big print).

Another finding which makes the degree of the offender empowerment questionable is that several offenders said they wished they could invite friends to conferences as supporters, but they were not allowed to do so. Some offenders felt that their friends were in a better position than adults to understand them and could confirm the offender's version of the events, making it more credible. One such offender believed that a certain policeman acted unfairly, but had trouble convincing conference participants that this was the case. This offender complained in the interview: 'I would've liked to take a friend [to the conference], because then there would've been someone to talk to, someone who experiences the same as what I am going through ... but I wasn't allowed. Because when I was saying the policeman was nicking people, no one believed me. They were believing the policeman...'.

It emerged from conversations with conference facilitators that the reason they do not allow offenders to bring their friends to conferences is that they believe it is 'unsafe' to allow such people to attend restorative justice encounters. However, one conference facilitator pointed out that he would have no problem with allowing an offender to bring a friend to a conference, provided it was an adult friend who was likely to have a positive influence on the offender. It seems that offenders were 'empowered' to choose people whom they wanted to support them during a stressful experience only to the extent that their choices coincided with those of conference organizers.

Some further evidence suggests that the extent of offender empowerment in this project was limited. Several offenders felt they did not have much say over the rehabilitation plan which was developed during the second part of the conference mainly by professionals and offenders' families. In one case the rehabilitation plan was created while the offender was not even present[22]. During the second part of the conference which was observed in the course of this study, it was clear that the main participants in the discussion were the conference facilitator, the offender's mother and a YOT worker. The offender's father and brother made some input into the discussion, but the offender remained silent throughout the meeting and spoke only once very briefly.

Offender family empowerment

Some offender supporters felt they were involved in the conferencing process and could say what they wanted to say. Others believed that because of the victims taking a too dominant role they were not involved to the degree they desired during the first part of the conference. Some offender supporters thought that perhaps they should have been more active during the conference. Others reminded themselves that their role was to support and not to take over the conferencing process. Towards that goal, they simply sat back and let the victims and offenders speak. However, even those who felt insufficiently involved during the first part of the conference believed they were actively engaged in the second part, which aimed at creating a rehabilitation plan and required mobilizing family resources to prevent re-offending.

---

22 This offender left in the middle of the conference, but his family stayed to develop a plan.

The rehabilitation plan developed in the second part of the conference deserves special discussion. On the basis of the documentary evidence which was kept in the project and which was examined (in particular, pre-conferencing reports and conference plans) it can be suggested that the plan can hardly be seen as a pure creation of empowered families. The basis for the plan had been developed to a large extent by YOT workers in pre-conferencing reports. An example of a typical pre-conferencing report from one of the case studies will illustrate this. The report starts with describing the offence committed by the offender (let us name him Tommy), then it outlines the court order, provides a detailed description of the reasons why the drafters of the report think Tommy gets into trouble and proceeds to instruct the family what they need to do when developing the plan during the conference. The list of the ingredients under the rubric 'what the plan needs to include' is extensive and detailed and sets a clear agenda what the family should put in the plan. Here is an extract from the report:

> …the family and all the people involved will need to make a plan of action that addresses the reasons why [Tommy] gets into trouble. In order to think about how everybody can support [Tommy] in his efforts, we have to think about the following questions:
>
> Who can offer mom support in her day-to-day supervision of [Tommy]? Who can mom call on to back her up if she needs this? Is there someone [Tommy] can go to if there is an immediate crisis at home if mom needs a bit of time alone?
>
> … How can mom reward [Tommy] for positive behaviour?
>
> … Is there someone in the family that [Tommy] finds it easier to talk things through with? Does he need someone outside of the family circle to talk about how he feels?
>
> Who can support mom to put boundaries around [Tommy]? E.g. Who does he hang around with? What time does he need to be indoors? Which areas of [the town] does he hang out and may need to avoid? How will this be monitored?
>
> What should [Tommy] do when he is bullied? What safety net needs to be in place for when this happen [sic]? Who can he report this to? How will they deal with it? Which teacher can he go to if there is a trouble in school?
>
> What help does [Tommy] need in building his self-confidence?
>
> … What support can the following agencies give: Social Services, YOT … Youth Centre, Family Centre, School?
>
> What can [Tommy] do to constructively stay busy?...'

A plan devised by the family during a conference in that case study (which was examined as part of this research) consisted of answers to the questions posed in the pre-conferencing report. It postulated that '[Tommy] will be supervised at all times' and outlined detailed provisions of exactly how this would be accomplished. It also outlined how Tommy would be kept 'constructively busy' and described other methods of setting boundaries and managing Tommy's behaviour (for example, negative reinforcement: 'If Tommy's behaviour is bad then the plans for that week (like trips) will be cancelled').

It would not be correct to suggest that professionals writing a pre-conferencing report are the sole authors of the plan resulting from a conference. The family clearly make an input. However, that input is carefully restricted by the framework set out in the pre-conferencing report. Through the report, the professionals writing it pre-determine the nature and the focus of the plan which the family would develop in the conference, ensure that the plan satisfies certain criteria and aims to achieve certain outcomes and assign a specific role to the family (which is to help the offender stop offending). The professionals carefully guide the family in creating the plan, while delegating the task of fleshing out the detailed provisions of the plan to the family.

One implication of such separation of functions between the professionals and the family is that the resulting plan is likely to be better tailored to the circumstances of the family and, consequently, more effective in achieving its goals than a plan authored by professionals alone, because the family are the best judges of how they can mobilize their knowledge and resources in working towards the desirable outcomes. Yet, the separation of functions allows the professionals to retain an overall control of the nature and contents of the plan.[23]

The second implication is that allowing the family to develop the details of the plan (although within a framework set out by professionals) makes the family believe that they themselves developed the plan during the second part of the conference. That is, it serves to mask the fact that the input by the family was relatively minor, and the plan was based on a detailed report written by professionals long before the conference. This may create a sense of empowerment in family members and reinforce their enthusiasm in implementing 'their' plan.

It is also significant that offenders are given a chance to participate in the development of the plan because they may be more willing to comply with a plan in the creation of which they participated.

Importantly, if offenders violate the plan, the pressure to comply will come from their family, rather than the state authorities. Such enforcement of the plan can be very effective, and in its duration it may continue far beyond a court order. Thus, offenders' families may be 'empowered' to govern their children in such a way as to advance the agenda and goals of the criminal justice system[24].

---

23 The argument that professionals retain an overall control is supported by the fact that the plan must be approved by a YOT worker.

24 The rehabilitation plan created during the second part of the conference was not the only vehicle through which the criminal justice system 'empowered' parents to govern their children on its behalf. Another such vehicle was the so-called 'STOP' programme organized by YOTs, which a number of offenders' parents interviewed during this study were encouraged, or even ordered, to attend. It appeared from the syllabus and the study manual of this programme (which were examined) that the programme was designed to equip parents with an array of subtle techniques which could be utilized in managing their children and moulding their attitudes and behaviour (such as using positive and negative reinforcement and using 'I' statements instead of 'you' statements in communicating with their children). Parents who were interviewed believed that the programme had taught them useful skills. One parent liked the programme so much that she decided to attend the same classes for the second

To sum up, the findings from this study suggest that empowerment of crime stakeholders in this family group conferencing project was rather limited. There also may be a danger that an illusion of their empowerment could be created, while crime stakeholders could be used to promote objectives of the criminal justice system.

Community-based justice?

As noted in Chapter Two, proponents aspire to create a form of justice that belongs to the (differently defined) community and allocate the community a distinct role in the justice process, separate from the role of the state. Who represented the community in this restorative justice project? What was its role? Can restorative justice as practised in this project qualify as a community-based justice?

All potential conference participants in this project were given a leaflet which informed the reader that 'Restorative Justice seeks to balance the concerns of the victim and the community with the need to reintegrate the offender into society'. However, who constitutes the 'community' was nowhere explained. It appears from observations and conversations with project workers that community typically involved members of offenders' families, victims and whoever came to conferences to support victims (parents in cases of child victims and possibly friends).

Importantly, conference organizers had ultimate control over who represented a community in a particular case. With the help of offenders and victims they identified potential community representatives who were to be invited to conferences and had a power to exclude the undesirable ones. As has been noted above, offenders could not invite their friends, unless a friend was an adult who conference organizers believed could positively influence the offender.

The leaflets given to those representing the community in future conferences proclaimed in large print: 'You are a part of this crime. Now you can do something positive'. The leaflet also contained a number of quoted statements made by participants in earlier conferences encouraging members of the community to accept that crime is their problem for which they should take responsibility. Some examples: 'I never saw it as a community problem before. I always blamed the parents, but now I have seen the truth and responsibility lies with the community to support its people, especially families.' Or:

> Restorative Justice belongs to everyone. It is a chance to begin to do what we must as a community, to take responsibility for what happens in our community. We've got to do the best we can. It's not good leaving it up to others to do it. Judges' [sic] do care and want to help, but we've got to do it ourselves. These are not only Judges' problems, they are community problems.

It was further emphasized that '[a]ll of us must invest more time to take on more responsibility for the well-being of our families and communities'. The leaflet

---

time, even though she had to travel a very long distance from her village to the town where the classes were run.

concluded: 'Restorative Justice processes are not about fitting communities into the justice system, but rather are about fitting the justice system into the community'[25].

Some findings suggest that a number of community representatives were generally reluctant to assume a greater power in the justice process. Several victims were critical of the 'passive' attitude adopted by professionals during conferences, when the professionals refrained from expressing their personal views and delegated disapproval of the offending behaviour to victims. These victims wanted to hear the expert opinions and were mystified why the professionals (conference organizers and social workers in particular) present in the conferences did not contribute to the discussions their knowledge and expertise. For example:

> Victim: I can't remember anything said by the professionals organizing the meeting. They've only done the introduction, so I remember him putting the meeting in context… but can't remember anything said by any of other professionals.
>
> Interviewer: What did you expect them to say?
>
> Victim: Well, again, just to re-affirm what impact this had had on the victims. I felt … it was very shallow … not very effective … I think there were people there at that meeting who didn't have anything to say. … Again, what was interesting was that none of the professionals involved in a conference said 'what you have done is wrong'. No one said that. It was all 'we want you to hear it from the victim'. But no one of them expressed a concern at that meeting – a concern about what they have done.

From an interview with another victim wishing for more professional involvement:

> Interviewer: You said the social worker ... didn't speak during the first part of the conference, did they?
>
> Victim: No, as I say, it would have been nice to actually find out that side of it. You understand what I mean? All these people: child welfare, child social workers...
>
> Interviewer: Why would it be helpful?
>
> Victim: Perhaps you would have heard more coming from [the offenders], of why they did it, and, you know, they would have been better like that. Then we would have perhaps... We could have understood it more, why they did it. … As I say, you got all these professional people there ... [but] we didn't hear their side of their questioning and their opinions.

Clearly these victims wanted a much greater professional input to the conferencing process. These victims reported feeling uneasy, being the only people in the conference to express dissatisfaction with the offenders' actions. They wished people in a position of authority to join them in reprimanding offenders. It seems that these victims failed to understand the virtues of a community-based approach

---

25 Cynics may argue that the ulterior motive was to convince community members that crime prevention is *their* problem and make them rely less on the state for suppressing crime. State may be discarding its responsibilities by unloading them on communities who may have neither resources nor abilities to assume those responsibilities.

to offending and did not quite appreciate the benefits which a shift to a lay-oriented justice could deliver them and maybe others (as has been suggested by several writers, such as Christie (1977, 1982), Johnstone (2002, 144-150), Bush and Folger 2005)).

At the same time, this study has found evidence that a number of victims, especially adult ones, were willing to assume 'moralizing social control' (Braithwaite 1989, 9) over young offenders. So, one of these victims pointed out in the interview that she would not have come to a conference if the offender was an adult 'because an adult is old enough to know right from wrong, but children need some leading'.

Some victims confessed that they saw in 'their' offenders their own children or grandchildren, and this shaped their attitude towards offenders[26]. As one victim has put it, 'I've never had a bad attitude toward [the offender]. ... I've got grandchildren, and I don't know what they are doing. And I hope if they do something wrong, someone will be lenient with them, as I was with that boy.' Another victim argued in the interview: '[A young person] who is committing a crime – I see it as perhaps my own son or my own daughter ... I see it in a sort of relative way, you know ... stopping people from doing wrong because you are a little bit older.'

Further evidence indicates that some community representatives were willing to take a greater part in the process of offender reintegration after conferences. As has been already mentioned earlier in this chapter, one victim offered the offender an apprenticeship in his company. Another victim wished to give driving lessons to the offender who had stolen and wrecked his car. Some victims were willing to participate in the creation of the rehabilitation plan.

According to a conference facilitator who was interviewed, in virtually all cases, one of the reasons why victims came to conferences was a desire to help offenders. So, a facilitator explained: '...I think from experience of working with some victims of young offenders that they are motivated – and it is part of their healing – they can make something good ... and they are motivated to try to do something constructive that would help the young person.' Indeed, the presence or absence of that motivation may determine whether or not the victim agrees to come to a conference:

> I have to be honest with you. I think [the hope that it would benefit the offender] is an ingredient in all of them. It may not be the primary. But I honestly believe that is what gets them to the conference, I mean, ones I have been involved in – what I have seen – has always been an ingredient.
>
> (From an interview with a conference facilitator)

The facilitator has illustrated this point:

> ... A good example of that is recently with the young lad who damaged somebody's car. It was a company car that belonged to ... an adult male. ...My conclusion from speaking to him was actually he didn't see himself as a victim of crime. He wasn't particularly

26 Consistently with these findings, Marshall and Merry point out, '[a] striking feature of victims' accounts was the social concern that motivated most of [them]. In several cases this was enhanced by an imaginative sympathy with the offender's experience and by a feeling that 'it could have been my own son (or daughter)'' (1990, 148).

> agreeing that it was a nuisance. It hasn't had a lasting impact on him. ... Effectively, that is how our meeting concluded. But then I went on to say, 'So, the only thing left for me to ask of you is whether you would be prepared to come to a meeting purely in order that the young person might benefit from hearing some of those things'. And he said, 'Yeah, sure, I would.' So, he was going to get nothing from it, other than that important ingredient which, I think, is the difference between what makes victims come or not come, is that wanting to do something to help the young person. That might mean all that is left for the victim, the only reason. They might not want 'sorry'. They might not want to understand. ... But they might want to come to do something [to help the young person].
>
> (From an interview with a conference facilitator)

As noted earlier, victims could not participate in the 'rehabilitative' part of the conference where they potentially could be mobilized as a useful resource in offender reintegration process. It seems that the potential benefits that could be derived from a greater involvement of ordinary community members in the offender reintegration process were not fully appreciated within this project. It appears that rather than relying on citizens as 'natural helpers' and using professional help 'as needed' (Bazemore and Bell 2004), the approach to offender reintegration in this project relied primarily on professionals, using community members 'as needed' (in particular, to make offenders realize the wrongfulness of their actions during the first part of the conference with the help of victims and to mobilize offenders' families to implement rehabilitation plan which has been to a certain degree already developed by professionals in pre-conferencing reports).

Before concluding the section on restorative justice as a community-based justice, a concern expressed by some restorative justice advocates which has been mentioned in Chapter Two (section 'Empowering, community-based, de-professionalized justice') will be re-visited. This is the concern that the move towards a community-oriented approach may lead to dispositions of offenders which are unlikely to promote their reintegration, as in the well-publicized example of a conference where stakeholders decided that the offender should wear a T-shirt announcing 'I am a thief' (Braithwaite 2002b, 2003b; Roche 2003). Whether in order to avoid outcomes of this kind or for some different reason, it appears that the move towards a lay-oriented approach attempted during the conferencing process in this project was rather limited. The professionals stayed in control of the restorative process and its outcomes through determining who attends conferences and who does not, shaping conference outcomes with the help of pre-conference reports and certain other techniques which would be discussed in more detail later in this chapter.

However, this study has found some evidence hinting at attempts by lay stakeholders in crime to resist the authority of professionals. One piece of evidence is the case mentioned earlier where a facilitator started by asking the offender, but not the victim, if they could begin the conference. The victim supporter in this case found the courage to intervene to challenge the authority of the facilitator – an expert in matters relating to the conferencing practice – and attempted to shift the focus at the beginning of the conference from the offender to the victim. This intervention on her part is important because it may provide a degree of support for the claim made by some restorative justice advocates about the virtues of 'plurality of voices' as a safeguard against abuses of power in the restorative justice process (Roche 2003, 86).

For example, Braithwaite and Strang argue that '[w]elcoming plurality is the best way of guaranteeing that there will be someone who will speak up when domination occurs' (Braithwaite and Strang 2000, 205; Roche 2003, 86) makes a similar point). Arguably, had the victim supporter in this case study not attended the conference and had she not spoken up, there would have been a greater chance of the victim and her needs being marginalized in the course of the restorative encounter. The 'plurality of voices' might have reduced the probability of domination occurring.

Another piece of evidence pointing towards the same conclusion was a case study where one offender supporter felt uncomfortable about the fact that when he came to the conference, he discovered that there was no chair for him in the circle of main participants. So, he had to sit behind the main circle. He said in the interview that the sitting arrangements discouraged him from active participation, especially at the beginning of the conference:

> I would have liked to sit in the front. [I would have preferred] to be more central ... Once I got [to the conference], I sat at the back ... When I first sat at the back, I didn't say anything. But when people started letting me speak, I felt better about it, because I was still able to speak and put my point across.

The omission on the part of the conference organizer to provide a chair for the offender supporter in question in the circle of main conference participants was not accidental. The facilitator wanted to exclude this offender supporter from participation in the conference (this incident will be discussed in more detail below). Yet, at this stage it is important to point out that the facilitator's attempts to silence the person in question largely failed because victims started asking him questions and thus engaged him in discussions (as the above quote demonstrates). Perhaps this example can be viewed as offering support to the suggestion that the best assurance against domination in restorative meetings of some participants by others is widening the circle of participants, so that 'other voices will be raised against the voices of domination' (Braithwaite and Strang 2000, 205).

To summarize, a move towards a community-oriented justice in this family group conferencing project was incomplete. Strict restrictions were imposed by facilitators on who could attend conferences. Professionals stayed in control of the process, limiting the role of lay participants to expressing disapproval of offending behaviour (and possibly offering forgiveness) and developing a rehabilitation plan under the guidance of professionals. Some evidence indicates that some lay crime stakeholders were uncomfortable with their increased role in the criminal justice process and wished for a greater professional involvement. Other findings suggest that some victims were willing to subject offenders to moralizing social control and participate in their reintegration.

De-professionalized justice?

It has been noted in Chapter Two that restorative justice advocates are critical of the highly professionalized criminal justice process where legal and treatment experts have 'stolen' conflicts (using Christie's expression (1977)) from victims and offenders and turned stakeholders in crime into 'idle bystanders in their own cases in what, after all, is *their* conflict' (Barton 2000, 67, original emphasis). In contrast, restorative justice is presented by some of its proponents as a lay-oriented process empowering stakeholders in crime to actively participate in developing their own solutions to their problems[27]. To what extent has the aspiration to create a de-professionalized form of justice been achieved in this restorative justice project?

From the outset it needs to be noted that lay participants in restorative conferences did not perceive the process as de-professionalized. Many of them stressed in the interviews that they were impressed by the number of professionals present at conferences. The conference which was attended as part of this study did not look like an example of lay-oriented justice either. In addition to two conference facilitators, there were a police officer, two case workers, two other YOT workers (as well as a person from the Home Office and a YOT manager attending as observers).

Conference preparation

Restorative justice professionals engage in much preparatory work prior to the conference. This work is vital for the success of conferences, and, as will be argued below, to a significant degree shapes the restorative justice process and influences its outcomes. A facilitator interviewed as part of this study argued that if at this stage her job has been done well, she has little to do during the actual conference.

During an initial meeting with potential conference participants, restorative justice practitioners will explore and assess their attitudes in relation to the criminal incident. Then, under the guidance of conference organizers, certain individual identities would be constructed, which potential conference participants are invited, encouraged and subtly pressurized to embrace.

It is quite possible that prior to the conversation with conference organizers, at least some victims do not even see themselves as victims, as this quote from an interview with a conference facilitator illustrates:

> [Another conference organizer] and I went to see [a man] some time ago. He was driving his car, and his car got hit by a car that had been stolen. The very first thing he said to us was: 'I was quite amused by your reaction, because it refers to me as being a victim of crime'. He said, 'I didn't see myself as a victim at all'. I said, 'Oh, how do you see yourself?' He said, 'Well, I see myself as being in the wrong place at the wrong time. If I hadn't been at the junction he wouldn't have hit me'.

With the help of conference organizers, a person who did not originally see him- or herself as a victim and refused to participate in a conference may adopt an identity

27 Some, however, question the desirability of de-professionalization (Olson and Dzur 2003).

of a victim who has been hurt by crime and has specific needs which could be met through a restorative encounter with offenders. Once that identity is adopted, the person is likely to agree to attend a conference and play the assigned role.

Incidentally, victims were given leaflets prior to conferences with the following statement on them, printed in large red letters: 'YOU HAVE BEEN A VICTIM. Now is your chance to put it behind you'. This might be another technique used to persuade those who did not originally see themselves as victims that they indeed have been victimized.

A similar process applies to offenders. Some offenders could feel that in the circumstances their offence was the right thing to do and thus may not see themselves as offenders. However, following a private meeting with conference organizers, they may be convinced that they have harmed another person and start feeling empathy and a desire to apologize for their actions. Just like victims, offenders were given leaflets before conferences which instructed them (also in big print): 'WHAT YOU HAVE DONE IS WRONG. Now you can put it right and move on'. This may be a method of encouraging those who had previously denied the wrongfulness of their actions to embrace self-identities of wrongdoers and re-affirming the role which they were expected to play in conferences. The same leaflet informed offenders about the 'benefits' which the process could provide them with. For example, 'You can get to feel sorry about what happened … You can get to see the effects of your behaviour, how to repair the harm you caused … You can get to know how the victim feels, why you shouldn't commit crime, what you can do about it…'. The leaflet also quoted statements of remorseful offenders who had participated in earlier conferences. For example, 'Restorative Justice has made me realize what my victims suffered after the crime. It opened my eyes in a big way regarding my behaviour to get drugs. Thank you for changing my life before it was too late'. These statements could serve to encourage offenders to participate in conferences and invited them to adopt identities of repentant selves who have understood their past mistakes and wanted to make amends.

A conference facilitator during an interview provided numerous examples of victims, offenders and their supporters who initially refused to attend conferences, accept an identity desired by conference organizers and play roles assigned to them. However, following private meetings with conference organizers, these individuals changed their mind, attended a conference and left conference facilitators deeply satisfied with the way they performed the expected roles. This finding may indicate a possibility that such transformations of attitudes could be a consequence of conference organizers subjecting potential conference participants to moral and psychological pressures to change their views. In some situations such transformations could be ethically questionable. For example, some young people in this study felt that their offence was morally justifiable, yet they complied with the role of offenders assigned to them by conference organizers. One boy claimed that he had been falsely accused of his crime, but performed the part of an offender and apologized to victims to the satisfaction of conference facilitators. By encouraging these young people to adopt the identities – and play the roles of – offenders in conferences, facilitators could be participating in – and contributing to – miscarriages of justice.

This study has also found that it was not uncommon for conference organizers to ask victims to participate because their attendance would help young offenders.

Open or implicit appeals to their sense of social responsibility towards young people and the request to help offenders may induce a sense of guilt in victims who may be reluctant to participate, making them agree to take part. This may be traumatizing for at least some victims, as well as adding to their sense of vulnerability and loss of control which they may be already experiencing (Strang 2002, 152)[28].

What makes the process of obtaining victims' consent to take part in restorative encounters particularly problematic is that it tends to be conducted in a very subtle way, hiding the existence of the psychological pressures and inducements which victims may be subjected to. During an interview carried out as part of this study, a conference organizer was asked if, when faced with victims who refuse to participate in a conference, he would attempt to persuade them to attend. His response was: 'Very gently, because it would be a more successful conference'. What this facilitator described as a 'gentle persuasion' used to convince victims to take part could be conducted through examples from earlier successful conferences. As he explained in the interview, 'I just try and sell to them the benefits of the process. I'd give them examples of conferences that have been successful'[29].

Another conference organizer emphasized the importance of victims determining for themselves the benefits of participating in a conference and described some of the indirect methods that may be used to assist them in that process:

> ...You are not saying, 'Oh, this would be an opportunity for you to say how angry you feel'. Instead, you say, 'Clearly, there may be things that you would want to say to the young person.' Then that might provoke a response, 'Well, actually, I'd really like to tell them that they should have been locked up in prison and burned in water'. I would say, 'From that I gather you are really angry with them for what they did. So, would it be helpful to you if they understood that?'. So, you are prompting them to say what they think and feel.

Conference organizers claim that they merely assist victims to 'say what they think and feel'. However, it is far from obvious whether those thoughts and feelings are not induced at least partly by restorative practitioners through skilful questioning, probing, focusing victims on certain issues, re-framing and re-phrasing their statements and using other subtle psychological techniques. When employed correctly, such methods may entice victims to take part in restorative conferences, while creating an appearance that the decision to participate came from themselves.

Pre-conference private meetings with victims and offenders may be used for rehearsals of what participants say and how they behave during conferences. So,

---

28 It is also important to note that when victims in this project are approached for the first time, this is done in this programme by a police officer attached to a YOT. The fact that the contact is initiated by a state official may put an additional pressure upon victims, making them feel that they *ought* to participate in a new programme for the treatment of young offenders (Reeves and Mulley 2000, 139).

29 Incidentally, victims were supplied with leaflets which quoted statements by satisfied victims who had attended earlier conferences, detailing how helpful the process had been for them. The leaflet concluded with an extract from a letter written by a victim who claimed that '[i]t is a fabulous idea to make offenders confront their victims' and a proclamation (in capital red letters) 'RESTORATIVE JUSTICE WORKS!'.

some conference participants believed that the surprisingly kind and sympathetic behaviour and attitudes of victims towards offenders was a consequence of preparatory work done by conference facilitators:

> Offender supporter: I think ... the people who were actually in charge of this conference, I think they actually saw the victims. They saw the victims first, and, I think, they sort of told them, didn't they, not to bite the kids' heads off, I think. Do you know what I mean? I think they told them to be careful sort of thing, you know, what they say.

Conference facilitators said it was a common practice for them and offenders to prepare a written apology statement during a pre-conference meeting. At the conference the offender will read out the statement. Probably unsurprisingly, some victims have noticed that what offenders said in conferences was a result of preparation work, as the following quote suggests:

> Victim: I felt what [the offenders] were saying was what they've been told to say.
>
> Interviewer: Really? Told by whom?
>
> Victim: By their relatives, by their social worker… I think what they were saying was… another adult had sat down with them and said, 'when you are asked this question, you should say this'. I didn't feel it was a genuine… I don't think it was remorse… didn't feel there was any remorse. I think it was more of a 'if you are asked this question, you give the right answer.

Another victim similarly shared in the interview that 'I just felt it wasn't a remorseful apology. I felt it was a rehearsed apology'[30].

A conference facilitator interviewed as part of this study described her role in the pre-conference preparatory process as 'mediation, facilitation and information-giving'. However, some findings from this study which have been outlined above hint that conference organizers may play a much greater role.

---

30 Incidentally, this study found that to some victims and their supporters the sincerity of apology and expressions of forgiveness were very important. Other interviewees appeared to attach less significance to the sincerely of apology. So, one young victim of assault and robbery said he did not care whether the apology was sincere. All that mattered to him was the fact of apology:

> Victim: I respect him for saying 'sorry'. Whether or not he meant it is up to him – it's not my problem. … It's important to me that he said it, but I am not one of those people who think that forgiveness is everything, that apology has to be sincere. As I said, I had an apology, and it doesn't bother me whether it's true or isn't true. What matters is that I had him apologize. … What matters to me is that it brought him down.

It appeared from the interview that this victim was more interested in ensuring that the offender has fallen in the eyes of his gang as a result of being forced to say 'sorry', rather than making certain that the offender was remorseful. In a different case an offender made a false apology, yet he said he felt happier after the apology because he believed it made the victim feel good. Simply the fact of apology, irrespective of its sincerity, seems to have had a positive effect on some victims and offenders.

Governing the conferencing process

Shaping self-identities and individual behaviour The process of moulding people's identities and shaping their attitudes and conduct referred to in the previous subsection is not restricted to the pre-conferencing stage. It continues during the conference itself. Some data from this study indicate that various techniques were employed towards that end by those facilitating conferences.

The following example (which has been already mentioned earlier in the context of the discussion of the 'plurality of voices') may demonstrate how subtle techniques used by conference facilitators may shape one's self-identity and behaviour during the restorative justice process. During the conference which was attended as part of this study, there was a participant (let us name him George) – the brother of an offender – whom the conference facilitator wanted to silence during the conferencing process. The facilitator explained that she feared that he might influence the process in an undesirable way. To achieve her objective, the facilitator purposefully did not prepare a chair for George (chairs with names of those who were going to sit on them were arranged in a particular order beforehand).

When at the start of the conference the offender's family, including George, entered the room, the facilitator greeted them and asked if they wanted drinks. George said he wanted a cup of tea. He behaved in a very confident fashion and started chatting to people in the room. Before drinks were served, the participants were invited to take their seats. At this point George discovered that there was no chair for him. He seemed unpleasantly surprised and informed the conference facilitator that he could not see his chair. Instead of adding a chair to the circle where the main participants were going to sit, the conference facilitator expressed surprise and said, 'Oh, George, I did not expect you would come too! Why don't you sit somewhere at the back?'. (In reality, the conference facilitator did expect that he would come to the conference). George obeyed and sat behind the circle of main conference participants, together with people who were merely observers. At this point the conference participants were asked to remind the facilitator which drinks they wanted. When George's turn came, he said he did not want any drinks (as pointed out earlier, when he walked into the room he said he wanted a drink). He looked upset, and his behaviour had notably changed. He no longer acted in the same confident fashion as he did when he entered the room. He sat there silently and did not participate in the conferencing process for a considerable period, until victims started asking him questions. During an interview conducted after the conference, he said that the sitting arrangements discouraged him from active participation in the conferencing process.

This example illustrates how determining seating arrangements may influence participants' behaviour in a way desired by facilitators. It also demonstrates that what may appear as insignificant statements (such as the facilitator expressing surprise and saying that she did not expect a person to come to the conference) and behaviour (the facilitator making a conference participant sit behind the main circle) may subtly force someone to adopt a self-identity which the facilitator wanted them to adopt. Initially, a person entered the room feeling he was an important guest there and intending to participate actively in the restorative justice process. Minutes later, he was made to feel that his presence was unimportant and his participation was not very welcome.

Among other subtle techniques employed by conference facilitators to influence the behaviour of participants was a skilful employment of praise and encouragement to elicit certain aspirations and conduct from conference participants. At the start of the conference which was observed, the offenders were generously praised for changing their attitudes following the offence. Such a beginning of the conference probably at least to some degree shaped self-identities of conference participants and interactions that followed. The offenders were encouraged to act so as to live up to the identities of reformed characters, willing to admit their past mistakes and make amends. From the start of the conference victims were discouraged from being too harsh on offenders: the victims were invited to believe – or at least consider a possibility – that offenders were capable of becoming law-abiding citizens.

Other uses of praise by conference facilitators in order to promote desirable behaviour were observed. For example, after the second part of the conference, as the offender's family were leaving, they expressed pessimism and doubts about their ability to successfully implement the rehabilitation plan. A facilitator responded by praising them for their performance during the conference and developing the rehabilitation plan, assured them that what they had just done was 'a breakthrough' and 'a way forward' and encouraged them to stick to the plan.

A notable technique used by facilitators to channel a conference in a desirable direction is a skilful use of questioning. What happens, for example, if an offender does not apologize in a conference spontaneously? The following extract from an interview with a facilitator illustrates how asking an offender the right questions can promote an apology:

> So, what I would say, allowing time for composure, so there would be a silence, and I might say something like: 'I am getting the sense that you don't know how to say what you want to say... Do you want to say something?'
>
> 'Yes'. (A long pause).
>
> 'So is this thing you want to say, is it difficult for you to say it?'
>
> 'Yes'. (Another long silence).
>
> 'Would it help if you and I went outside and talked about how we did this [in the pre-conference meeting]?'.
>
> Say you've had the silence... Because I am a facilitator and I know what a young person wants to say because we discussed that in our [pre-conference meeting], I might prompt them and say:
>
> 'Do you remember when I came to see you and we talked about such-and-such a thing? Can you remember what you said to me?'
>
> 'Yes.'

> 'Is this something you want to share now?'
>
> 'Yes.'
>
> 'So, do you want to say something, or would it help if I reminded you?'
>
> Or, if [the offender] really can't speak: 'Would you like me to share that?'
>
> That has happened in a couple of times where you've got a person who really has been stuffed up. But again, you wouldn't go rushing in there and say, 'Well, when I came to see you, you told me this, this, this and this'. It's about trying to get them to… You are asking them, 'Would it help? I know it is difficult. I think everybody here is finding that this isn't an easy meeting and we all appreciate what effort it is taking for people to speak. Would it be helpful…' It might be that the mum goes outside and comes in with him again or whatever. It is not so much… You are not putting words into their mouth. You are trying to get them to say the words they have already spoken to you.

Facilitators do not literally put words into anybody's mouth. However, they do seem to have a great deal of power over what people say and how they behave.

Yet another technique used by facilitators in the process of governing the conferencing process involved creating a particular atmosphere in the conferencing room. As noted above, at the very beginning of the conference which was observed as part of this study, Youth Offending Team workers read out short reports in which they generously praised the offenders for making a lot of progress in recent months and being of reformed character. That way of starting a conference set a positive mood for the interactions that followed.

Carefully selecting the venue of the conference could be another way of creating a desirable conference environment. The conference observed as part of this study took place in a church. This setting probably encouraged certain emotions and behaviours and inhibited others, since the atmosphere was conducive to confession, repentance and forgiveness (as the father of one of the offenders pointed out). A friend who came to that conference to support a victim acknowledged in the interview: 'I think the fact that the conference was in a church helped a lot because people respect the church, so emotions were constrained'.

Managing restorative justice's emotions

Several other victims pointed out that negative emotions during conferences were carefully restrained by facilitators. They noticed that facilitators endeavoured to create a calm, quiet and subdued emotional atmosphere in the room. For example, in one interview a victim pointed out:

> I think it was handled well, professional. It was very laid back, everybody has got a chance to say what they wanted to say, no one was shouting at anybody. And I think the way it was controlled was the right way, because the people who controlled it were ladies with very soft voices. There were no harsh voices, it was just laid back, and I think it went extremely well.

In another interview a victim also felt that the emotional atmosphere during the conference was 'very quiet ... very subdued'.

Conference facilitators themselves consider emotional expression during conferences very important. One facilitator emphasized that he encouraged and assisted emotional expressions: 'I do make it clear to people that they are not to be worried about being emotional ... Some people may get afraid of expressing their emotions, but I try to make them comfortable with their emotions'.

How exactly do conference facilitators handle emotional tension and outbursts during conferences? It appears from the interviews and observations that facilitators are equipped with an array of techniques enabling them to manage the conference and channel emotions in a desirable direction (such as indirect mediation between victims and offenders before the conference; excluding from participation certain people; deciding in advance where particular conference participants are going to sit; imposing ground rules and re-iterating them; calling a 'time out' and refocusing discussions when conference facilitators feel necessary; skilful questioning, re-phrasing statements, re-focusing discussions, re-directing issues; using body language and eye contact to express disapproval; stopping the conference and re-starting it and so on). These techniques may be extremely subtle, but appear effective in managing the conferencing process, dispersing negative emotions and channelling the process towards a desired transformation.

A conference facilitator said in the interview that managing a conferencing process requires a lot of skill and knowledge of when it is right to act in a particular fashion, for example, to call 'time out' in order to 're-group' emotions (as she explained in the interview). She gave an example of a conference when the offender's mother was crying throughout the restorative meeting. The conference facilitators decided not to stop the conference and try to comfort the mother. They thought it was important for victims to see that the offender's mother was upset and ashamed because of what her son had done and disapproved his actions. It was also believed to be constructive for the offender to see his mother crying because it could have an impact on his attitudes and future behaviour.

The facilitator also emphasised in the interview that experiencing strong emotions may have an educational effect on offenders: '...you have to have the emotion for it to be a learning experience. ... for the learning to sink in ... you actually have to ... reflect on it and feel it'.

A successful conference is considered one where negative emotions are transformed into positive ones. During a number of conferences, it appears that positive emotional transformation took place. Those who initially felt nervous, scared and even terrified found themselves more relaxed as the conference progressed. One offender described this process: 'I was frozen at first. ... I couldn't talk. When I talked, I was shaking. But after I got used to it'.

Several offenders said that the 'turning point' for them was the apology. After they had apologized, they felt much better. Several victims pointed out that they started feeling more comfortable when they actually saw the offenders and started talking with them.

However, it seems that in some cases such emotional transformation did not occur. Some victims said they remained nervous throughout the conference. Even after offenders apologized and promised not to re-offend, it appears it had little effect on some victims' fears.

Indeed, in some cases the atmosphere became even more tense as the conference progressed, as the following quote from an interview with an offender's mother suggests:

> It was quite tense. It was relaxed to start with, and then [the offender] started to get fed up, lost interest. Then it started to get quite tense, because he wouldn't answer [the conference facilitaror's] questions, he wouldn't apologize to the policeman. He thought it was all a waste of time, and he was tired, and hungry, and fed up.

Several offenders and their supporters said they felt increasingly angry during conferences. One such offender felt that way because he thought he was punished for something that was the right thing to do, given the circumstances. What exacerbated his anger was that his father took the side of the victim. This conference culminated in a conflict between the offender and his father. The father threatened to hit the offender and eventually walked out of the room. The offender walked out too. This offender described the conference's dynamics in the following way:

> My sisters were just sitting there, they didn't know what to say … my mom was trying to stick up for me. And my dad, whatever I was saying, my dad was trying to say something smart, by taking the micky out of what I said. …At the end I walked out … because everybody was getting at me…

Another offender felt angry as the conference progressed because he thought that a police officer who was present at the conference was making unfair accusations against him. The offender said in the interview that he found it difficult to restrain his emotions and curb the desire to hit the police officer. As soon as he returned home after the conference, he started hitting pillows to release his anger.

In a different case the mother of two offenders admitted in the interview that she (as well as her own mother) got very angry during the conference when the victim (head teacher of the school which the offenders had set on fire) started criticizing the offenders. She confessed that she wanted to punch the teacher. She believed that the school authorities (who took no action against bullying of her son and instead blamed her son for provoking the bullying) triggered the behaviour of her sons and felt that the boys

> …got the blame for everything that went on in that school. … And [the school authorities] said it was [my sons'] fault. Even in this conference meeting they said it was all [my sons'] fault. That's what they said. My mum was sitting there, and she told me she wanted to get up and punch [the head teacher]. I mean, I would've done as well, but there was the police there and everybody.
>
> (From interview with the offenders' mother)

What seems to unite these cases where conferences failed to achieve desirable emotional transformation is that there was a perception on unfairness on the part of some conference participants[31].

In the conference observed as part of this study, after the offenders had apologized and one victim had expressed her forgiveness, the facilitators announced a coffee break during which participants talked to each other in a more relaxed environment. Following the break, everybody in the room seemed more cheerful, and those who cried throughout the first part of the conference smiled for the first time. However, there was one exception: the mother of one offender did not join other participants during the coffee break, refused an offer of a drink and sat on her own, looking very upset and distressed. During the interview she confided that the conference made her feel very bad:

> I think [I felt that way] because the old lady – she kept addressing me personally. I found that extremely stressful. I found that very upsetting and very disturbing. I know it was her way of coping with it and dealing with it, but I found that incredibly hard. I really didn't like that at all. If it hadn't been for the boys, I would've gone.

The interviewee in question said that she 'walked out of that meeting feeling like scum'. She also pointed out that conference organizers promised that the result of the conference would engender positive feelings. However, her experience demonstrated that it had the opposite effect, as a quote from an interview with her demonstrates:

> [The conference organizers] have said to me, 'You'll walk out of there, saying 'yeah, that was a good thing''. And I told them afterwards, 'No. You told me that I would walk out of here saying that was a good thing, and I'm not saying it'. … If I had known and I'd had a choice, I would never have gone. There was one stage in the meeting where if it hadn't been for the boys, I would have walked out. I felt bad.

One explanation why this conference failed to produce positive emotional transformation in this offender supporter may be that she was not prepared for the intensity of emotions which a conference may generate. Later in the interview she emphasized that she had not been made aware prior to the conference how difficult it would be to face victims. In response to the question about her expectations prior to the conference, she explained:

> [The conference] was not quite what we had expected. I expected it to be as it was ran, like the victims were asking questions... But we weren't prepared for the intensity of the victims looking straight at you. That was a bit disturbing.

However, as mentioned earlier, this offender supporter was different from other participants in the conference which was observed. Other participants appeared to have experienced a positive mood change. So, facilitators seem to have been

31 Shapland et al (2006) report that in their study one of the reasons why conferences or mediation were unsuccessful was the rejection by one of the parties of their pre-cast role, for example, an offender attempted to deny responsibility or tried to blame others.

successful in creating desirable emotional transformations in the vast majority of crime stakeholders.

Managing the second part of the conference

During the second part of the conference, professionals control and lead the process, as well as mould outcomes, very much in the same subtle fashion as during the first part. In the conference which was observed, the second part differed from the first not only because of the absence of victims, but also because professionals played a much more prominent role than they did during the first part. It was observed that professionals encouraged the family to confess their problems, diagnosed and classified those problems and articulated behaviours which conference participants needed to adopt in order to resolve their predicaments. An extract from the notes taken during an observation of this stage in the conferencing may illustrate these processes of confession, diagnosis and prescribing a 'cure':

> Offender's father: I find it frustrating. I try to improve things but people aren't listening…
>
> YOT worker: Lack of respect for your opinion.
>
> Father: Yes.
>
> [The mother and brother of the offender (whom we shall call Chris) start arguing about who does most housework].
>
> Brother: I can't do everything!
>
> Mother: You don't do a thing!
>
> Father: It's about helping everyone!
>
> Facilitator: Who doesn't do the cooking, does the dishes. [Continues instructing the family how to share household responsibilities].
>
> Brother: I saw my parents [who hardly ever talk to each other] recently sitting next to each other, and I was shocked – they are talking to each other!
>
> YOT worker: It's a lack of respect!
>
> Brother: When I'm off in the army, it'll be back.
>
> Conference facilitator [addressing the offender]: [Chris], when they are being petty, tell them that they are being petty.
>
> Mother: He mediates between us.
>
> Facilitator: It's too much pressure on him to mediate. [Chris], just say to them they are petty.

Father: I work hard, bring money into the home. But what I see is a mess in the house.

Facilitator: I'm worried that Chris is caught in your problems.

Father: I want a normal home, everyone working together.

Facilitator: You need a few hours on Saturday. You need time when you are all together.

Mother [interrupts]: I hate to hear that he [her husband] is bringing money. I was brought up not to do anything. He was brought up to work in the house.

YOT worker: Perhaps your husband shouldn't remind continuously that he's bringing all the money.

To sum up, during observations, it did not appear that a de-professionalized form of justice was witnessed. Professionals staged and orchestrated the process and subtly shaped its outcomes. What happened during restorative justice encounters usually was a consequence of a careful preparation and skilful management of the process by conference facilitators. Importantly, this was accomplished in a very careful and virtually invisible way, so that conference participants may not even have realized how significant the input of facilitators was. This may explain the finding mentioned earlier that several victims who were interviewed said that they felt uncomfortable about the 'passive' role the restorative justice professionals appeared to play and wished that the professionals had provided a greater input.

What was observed in the course of this research was not de-professionalization, but rather a *transformation* of the role of the professionals in the criminal justice process. They no longer pushed people directly involved in – and affected by – a conflict out of the arena, effectively turning them into passive onlookers. Indeed, an active participation of crime stakeholders was crucial if a conference were to achieve desirable outcomes[32]. That participation required that they confess their thoughts and feelings to facilitators who diagnosed how their attitudes had to be changed and helped them construct and adopt particular mentalities and behaviours.

A new ethical orientation?

As has been discussed in Chapter Two, proponents propose to conceptualize restorative justice as a new 'paradigm' of justice. They argue that restorative justice offers a new moral framework, characterized by different values and presenting a distinct alternative to the conventional ways of thinking about crime and justice. How true would it be to say that restorative justice, as practised in the project of this study, embodied a different ethical orientation?

Important in the context of this discussion is the fact that the project received referrals from the criminal justice system after they had been processed by the system. This meant that by the time a case entered the restorative justice project,

32 So, the findings mentioned above that the vast majority of participants in conferences felt they were actively involved in the process should not be surprising.

a lot of definitional work had already been done (Zernova 2006). What constitutes 'crime', who is the 'victim' and who is the 'offender' in a given case, or the very fact that there is a 'victim' and an 'offender' in a particular situation has already been determined within the framework of criminal law (cf. Shearing 2001). This enabled the criminal justice system to effectively direct and shape the restorative process and outcomes see Dignan (2005, 173-5) and Shapland et al (2006b, 508-9) for discussion of this problem). In some cases, this may be deeply problematic, as some examples from this research demonstrate.

One of the case studies involved an assault by one girl on another girl from the same school. The girl classified by the criminal justice system as an 'offender' could not be interviewed. However, it appeared from conversations with the restorative justice project workers that in reality she was a victim, and the girl labelled by the system 'victim' was in reality an offender who had bullied the other girl for a long time and started a fight on the occasion leading to the criminal prosecution. Following the fight, the girl who had started it called the police and made a complaint. The system defined the incident as an 'assault', the girl making the complaint as a 'victim' and the other girl – an 'offender'.

What the system had classified as an 'assault' was effectively taken out of the context and responded to as an isolated incident without a prior history (that is, bullying of the girl defined by the criminal justice system as an 'offender' by the 'victim' for many years). By the time the case came to the restorative justice project, the over-simplifying and misleading labels 'victim' and 'offender' had already been assigned, and a particular ethical framework had been pre-established. That framework was based on the questionable assumption that the 'victim' was absolutely blameless and the 'offender' totally culpable, which failed to reflect the reality of the situation.

Another case study involved damage by fire of school buses and the administrative part of a school. According to the mother of the 'offenders' and a conference organizer, one of the 'offenders' had been severely bullied by students from his school. He complained to teachers about bullying, but teachers did not help him. Instead, they blamed him for provoking the bullying. The 'offender' and his brother decided to damage the school buses on which the bullies travelled to the school. The boys hoped that it would prevent the bullies from getting there. Damaging the administrative section of the school was a way of retaliating against teachers who ignored the complaints of the 'offender', and, instead of helping him to stop the bullying, blamed him. The 'offender' and his brother were prosecuted, punished and ordered to attend a family group conference, where they had to apologize to the 'victims' – school authorities – for the damage they had caused.

The imposition of the criminal justice system's classification of 'victim'/ 'offender' clearly failed to capture the complexities of this case and distorted more than it revealed[33]. The system took no notice of those who had severely bullied one of

33 Another problem created by the adoption of the criminal justice system's classification victim/offender was alluded to in a complaint by a victim that during preparation for the conference facilitators attempted to place the offender and the victim on the same level and behaved as if the offender had not done anything wrong. Acting as neutral parties and not

the 'offenders'. The criminal damage was defined as the only event worth attention. This one event was pulled out of a deeper terrain, and the events which had preceded – and to a large degree led to – it were ignored. The case came to the restorative justice project with definitions already attached and the moral framework already pre-established, and the conference proceeded within that framework.

As the above examples demonstrate, when a restorative programme gets referrals from the criminal justice system, it is guided by the moral compass of the system. Restorative justice is being dictated to by the system regarding the distinction between 'victim' and 'offender', the definition of 'crime' in a given case, and how cases should be dealt with. The submission by restorative justice to such dictates may force it to operate on the basis of false assumptions and distorted views of reality and provide ethically questionable responses to situations (Zernova 2006).

Another consequence of restorative justice adopting the framework of criminal law is that whatever falls within the legal definitions of 'crime' is being placed within the scope of restorative justice, while other instances of injustices, violence and hurtful behaviour are considered to be outside restorative justice (as long as no obvious breach of criminal law is involved). This creates artificial distinctions between legitimate and illegitimate instances of violence, harms, and injustices and arbitrarily limits the scope of restorative justice (Sullivan and Tifft 2001, 1998, 2000a, 2000b; Pavlich 2005). Some of the case studies can serve as illustrations of this problem.

In one case, an incident of an assault by one girl on another girl was defined as crime. Therefore, it fell within the scope of restorative justice. However, the events which preceded and directly related to the assault – continual bullying of the victim by a group of girls, friends of the offender, over many years – escaped the legal definition of 'crime'. Consequently, those events fell outside the ambit of the restorative paradigm. No doubt, the incident of assault which led to the restorative justice conference was hurtful for the victim. However, it appears from interviews with the victim and her mother that even more hurtful was the continuous bullying over the years. To avoid the bullying, the victim had to change several schools. She was too afraid to go outside her house, unless accompanied by her mother. The girl stopped going to school and often did not leave home for weeks. Eventually, she

---

taking sides is, of course, an important ingredient of the role of a mediator or a facilitator. It needs to be pointed out that this neutral position might fit very well in civil mediation or Zwelethemba-type projects where disputes arrive to restorative meetings without prior intervention by the criminal justice system and without the offender either being found guilty or having admitted guilt (see Chapter One for more detail). In those circumstances there is no 'victim' and 'offender': there are equal parties to a conflict or a dispute. However, the situation within the project of this research was different. Cases came to restorative justice conferences with problems being pre-defined as 'crimes' which had the 'offender' (whose guilt was either established by the court or admitted by him- or herself), and the 'victim' (whose innocence was beyond question). In such circumstances, it was not unnatural for victims to assume that people organizing conferences should treat the respective parties consistently with the pre-established roles – 'victim' and 'offender'. As mentioned above, a number of victims felt uncomfortable and were rather confused when facilitators refrained from expressing disapproval of the offending behaviour in conferences.

had to move to another town and stay with her father, which meant she had to live separately from her mother and siblings.

Another case study (which will be discussed in more detail in the next chapter) also demonstrates the artificial distinction between legitimate and illegitimate violations of people and injustices resulting from the adoption of legal definitions of crime. This case also shows how the scope of restorative justice may be limited as a consequence of criminal law determining what should fall within the restorative paradigm, and what should stay outside. We learn from that case that a situation where a 16 year old boy has nowhere to live and goes without food for days is legitimate and thus outside the scope of restorative justice. Bullying of the local youth by a police officer is not defined by the criminal justice system as 'crime' and therefore is outside the ambit of restorative justice. Beating up a person fails to be classified as 'crime', and thus falls outside restorative justice, if the individual who does the beating up wears the police uniform. Yet, pushing a police officer in order to stop him beating up a person is considered a crime and thus within the restorative paradigm.

A broad implication of restorative justice subjecting itself to the authority of criminal law and accepting that some violations of people and injustices are legitimate and others are not – depending on whether or not they have been proscribed by criminal law – is that the scope of restorative justice is limited in such a way as to uphold the values and the agenda of the criminal justice system. Restorative justice effectively imitates the ethical and ideological orientation of the system and fails to provide an alternative moral 'lens'.

Yet this study has found some evidence hinting at a possibility that during family group conferences information could be revealed which could challenge the definitions imposed by the criminal justice system and bring to the attention the events preceding a particular criminal incident. In one case involving assault the conference never took place, but a person who did the preparatory work for the conference and with whom the case was discussed believed that had the conference taken place, perhaps it could have brought to light the fact that the 'victim' started the fight on the occasion leading to the criminal prosecution and the conference, as well as the fact that the 'victim' continually bullied the 'offender' over the years. It was also suggested by the conference organizers that the 'victim' feared that information unfavourable to her would be disclosed during the conference and would become known to her parents. That fear prompted her to take steps in order to prevent the conference taking place. So the 'victim' approached the 'offender' a few days before the conference in the school, apologized to her and proposed that they should become friends. The surprised 'offender' accepted the proposal. At the request of the 'victim' and with the consent of the 'offender' the family group conference was cancelled.

Had the conference gone ahead, it could well be that information disclosed there would have led to the conference participants re-considering who was the 'victim' and who was the 'offender' and looking at the incident of an assault leading to the conference in a somewhat different light. The conference could have enabled the truth to emerge and the reputation of the 'offender' to be cleared in the eyes of the conference participants and perhaps some others. Is there a problem, then? If there is a potential that during conferences the misapplied labels could be challenged, is there still a ground for concern? There probably is, for at least two reasons. The first reason relates to the fact that restorative justice in this project operated post-sentence. When a case comes to the restorative justice project after it had been processed by the criminal justice system and during the conference it transpires that, say, a person defined as 'offender' was not as culpable as the criminal justice system made it appear, this would not lead to the removal of a criminal record of the 'offender'. Thus, had the conference in the case study in question taken place, the reputation of the 'offender' could have been cleared in the eyes of those who attended the conference and maybe some others (which, no doubt, is very important), however, she would still have a criminal record. Secondly, it is far from obvious that the evidence challenging the definitions imposed by the criminal justice system would necessarily come to light and would be taken seriously during conferences. Three case studies provide examples. In those cases the offenders did not see themselves as offenders. However, they did not even attempt to present their side of the story in conferences, because they thought no one would listen to them.

Conclusion

This chapter looked at a number of aspirations of restorative justice advocates in the light of empirical findings. These findings suggest that within this restorative justice project most of these aspirations have been hardly realized.

The validity of the claim that restorative justice presents an alternative to offender rehabilitation becomes questionable when one considers the presence of various elements of the offender welfare model within the project. Importantly, the vast majority of conference participants perceived restorative justice as a form of offender rehabilitation. A number of victims felt that they were invited to conferences to help offenders, and that the main – or even the only – beneficiaries of the process were offenders. Another important finding is that victims felt that conference facilitators adopted an over-sympathetic approach towards offenders, typical of the traditional offender welfare model of criminal justice.

Some findings make one doubt the validity of the claim that restorative justice is a victim-centred justice. However, other findings suggest that at least occasionally the interests of victims were given a priority. Also, a number of interviewees felt that victims, as well as offenders, got benefits out of conferences.

The empirical evidence puts into question the claim that the restorative justice process is characterized by voluntariness. For a number of offenders, conference attendance was court-ordered. But even where the attendance was not court-ordered, it was not necessarily voluntary in the purest sense. Coercion within restorative justice is not limited to official legal sanctions. There may be other sources of coercion which are more covert and complex in nature. Also, it is misleading to think of coercion in 'either/or' terms: either coercive or voluntary. This way of thinking is too naïve and fails to reflect the intricacies of what really happens.

The findings from this study indicate that the degree to which crime stakeholders were empowered within this project was limited. While an appearance could be created that conference participants were key decision-makers, the criminal justice system retained the overall control over how cases were responded to. At the same time, some data may suggest that the 'empowered' crime stakeholders could be used to promote the achievement of the goals of the criminal justice system.

The empirical findings also suggest that restorative justice in this project can hardly be seen as a community-based justice. Restorative justice professionals had control over who represented community and allocated to the community a very limited role. While certain findings suggest that some community members seemed to be wiling to take part in the process of offender reintegration, other findings indicate that some community representatives felt uncomfortable about their enlarged role in the criminal justice process and wished for a greater professional input.

It has been suggested that present restorative practices are not characterized by de-professionalization. Rather, they present a transformation of the role of professionals. Professionals no longer turn crime stakeholders into passive onlookers. Far from it, they require stakeholders to take an active part. In doing so, restorative justice professionals subject conference participants to hardly noticeable moral and psychological pressures and enticements in order to make them adopt particular self-identities created under the guidance of the professionals. Professionals effectively mould the restorative process and its outcomes, while masking that fact from conference participants who may be under an illusion that conference facilitators played a 'passive' role and the crime stakeholders were the main decision-makers.

This chapter has further argued that restorative justice as practised in this project has failed to provide a moral framework distinctive from that of the criminal justice system. This was the result of the project adopting concepts 'crime', 'victim' and 'offender' as dictated by criminal law. It has been illustrated how the adoption of the criminal justice system's foundational concepts forced restorative justice process to imitate the system's ethics.

The only restorative ideal which seems to have been achieved in this family group conferencing project (at least in the eyes of most conference participants) is to create an alternative to punishment. The vast majority of interviewees, including offenders, did not perceive conferences as a form of punishment.

Chapter Five will return to these findings and attempt to explain why most aspirations of restorative advocates have not been realized in this family group conferencing project.

Chapter Four

Problematic Ideals and a Problematic Relationship

Introduction

The previous chapter has looked at restorative ideals and recorded experiences of participants in family group conferences. This chapter will continue analysing some restorative aspirations, providing empirical evidence. The ideals of reparation and achieving peace and harmony in the aftermath of crime will be discussed. The chapter will also look at the relationship between restorative justice and the criminal justice system and examine some implications of the dependence of restorative justice on the system. It will re-visit concerns of certain critics sceptical of practising restorative justice in close alliance with the criminal justice system which have been outlined in Chapter Two and support them with empirical evidence. The chapter will conclude by questioning some current trends within restorative justice practice, in particular, large-scale and state-sponsored implementation of restorative justice.

The ideal of reparation

As has been discussed in Chapter Two, a common theme within the restorative justice discourse is that crime causes harm and that doing justice involves repairing that harm. Consistently with the restorative aspiration to repair crime's harm, the statement of principles of this restorative justice project postulated that '[t]he primary focus of conferences will be the offence that has been committed and reparation to the victim', and one of the project's official goals was '[t]o resolve the offence and facilitate reparation of any loss or damage to the satisfaction of victims'. That is, crime was viewed as causing harm or damage, which needed to be repaired in order to achieve justice.

When crime and justice are conceptualized thus, a number of questionable assumptions seem to be made. Firstly, it is assumed that crime necessarily causes harm. Secondly, it is assumed that reparation of that 'harm' is desirable. It is assumed that the status quo was just and fair, characterized by 'right relationships' between individuals and groups, and thus is worth restoring. Such assumptions may be problematic.

One of the case studies from this empirical research can demonstrate problems inherent in understanding crime as causing harm and justice as reparation of that harm. The case involved a police officer and a boy who pushed the officer, trying to defend a friend from a violent attack by the police officer in question. The criminal justice system defined pushing the officer as 'assault' and referred the case to the restorative justice project. In accordance with the restorative justice theory, it was assumed that in the aftermath of crime (the assault on the police officer), the offender needed to take steps to undo the harm caused by the crime. It was decided that such reparation could be achieved if the offender apologized to the police officer during a family group conference.

What seems to have been overlooked in this case is that no obvious harm was caused to the victim when the offender pushed him. Indeed, the victim did not consider himself a victim. He told this to conference organizers when he was invited to attend the conference. During the interview he mentioned the same. What seems to have been additionally overlooked was that when the police officer was being 'harmed' (that is, when he was pushed by the offender), the police officer himself was in the process of causing harm by hitting the offender's friend.

The offender felt he was made to apologize for something that he believed was the right thing to do, given the circumstances and refused to offer a sincere apology[1]. This caused in him feelings of anger, resentment and unfairness (to use his own words, 'the whole thing was unfair'). In addition to generating a sense of injustice in the offender, the conference led to a serious conflict between him and his father. The father was upset by the fact that his son did not want to apologize to the officer and threatened to hit the boy. The boy thought it was unfair that his father did not believe his version of the events and took the policeman's side. The conflict culminated in the father throwing his son out of the house soon after the conference, with the result that the boy had nowhere to live and nothing to eat for days.

The aforementioned conference aimed at repairing the harm (which was presumably caused by the crime, in accordance with the prescription of the restorative justice theory). Yet, upon closer examination, it appears that the result for some was a much greater harm and suffering than the 'harm' which the conference was supposed to repair.

The same case study demonstrates problems inherent in adopting the 'status quo's' definition of crime as authoritative and determinative of how crime should be responded to. It was presumed that the status quo – or the pre-crime state of affairs – was right and just. Crime violated that status quo. Following this reasoning, to achieve justice in the aftermath of crime, we should aim at restoring the status quo. To accomplish this, the offender was required to take some kind of reparative action towards the victim, such as making an apology.

What seems to have been disregarded is that the pre-crime state of affairs was not necessarily right and fair, and therefore its restoration would not necessarily achieve justice. It is quite likely that forcing the offender in this case study to apologize

1 One of the conference facilitators who was interviewed, when expressing her views on the matter, said that if she were the offender in that case, she would not apologize to the police officer either, given the past behaviour of the officer (bullying local young people) and the fact that the officer was acting violently against a boy on the occasion leading to the 'assault' and subsequently the conference. According to the conference facilitator in question, she was not the only person who held that view. Some people in the Youth Offending Team dealing with the case also said that they would not have apologized, had they been that offender.

to the police officer (who beat up his friend and who, according to several people involved in the case, continually bullied local young people) has had the effect of legitimizing violent and abusive behaviour on the part of the police officer and served to perpetuate pre-existing oppressions and injustices.

This case study demonstrates some of the problems inherent in making reparation of harm a universal restorative justice principle. Restorative justice in this project operated in the name of reparation of harms presumably caused by crimes, while avoiding ethical discussions of whether, for example, harm may exist outside crime, or whether some definitions of crime may be questionable, or whether reparation of crime's harm is necessarily desirable and morally right in a particular circumstance. Allowing reparation of harm to determine the focus of restorative justice effectively reduces the ethical work that needs to be carried out in responding to a complex situation to a narrow set of questions (Who has harmed whom? What harm has been caused? What needs to be done to repair the harm?), and various other considerations may be simply left outside the ethical enquiry (Pavlich 2002b, 1). This leads to pre-determined outcomes which may be ethically questionable.

The ideal of peace and harmony

It is fundamental to the restorative justice philosophy that crime ruptures human relationships. Healing broken social bonds, a reduction of hostility and fear and a creation of a positive and peaceful relationship becomes one of the main concerns of justice (Zehr 1990; Claassen 1996; Mika and Zehr 2003).

While most restorative justice proponents aspire towards restoring peace and harmony damaged by crime, some critics whose ideals were outlined in Chapter Two question that aspirations at least in some circumstances. They argue that the problem with the assumption that reconciliation of conflicting parties is a universally desirable outcome is that it seems to overlook the fact that a conflict in a particular case may not be necessarily a self-contained problem or dispute between people directly involved. It is quite possible that the conflict may be much bigger and deeper and may have social-structural roots (for example, poverty, inequalities of power, marginalization of certain individuals and groups). In such cases, peaceful resolution of an individual conflict may not necessarily reduce the social inequalities and injustices which might have generated the conflict in the first place. Instead, it may neutralize and expunge from the society a potentially disruptive conflict, thus serving to preserve the status quo, no matter how unjust it may be (Mika 1992; Pavlich 1996a, 2005; Dyck 2000). Some of the empirical findings from this study might suggest that it is far from obvious whether it is always desirable to 'heal' the relationships ruptured by the crime, so as to reduce hostility, create peace between individuals involved and restore the social equilibrium which existed prior to the offence.

In some case studies there appeared to be hints that what in reality could be social problems were effectively reduced to interpersonal and individual problems and responded to accordingly. Thus in one case an assault by a black girl on a white girl (whom she never met before) was responded to as a self-contained conflict between two people, with the offender's drunkenness and aggressiveness being defined as the source of the problem. Yet, it may well be that this incident stemmed from a social (as opposed to individual) problem – racial hatred. While a successful reconciliation between the victim and the offender in this case might have assisted the victim by reducing her fear of the offender, it did not challenge the broader social and cultural conditions from which that individual instance of assault might have originated, allowing those conditions to persist and produce more victims.

Another case study might be an example of a situation where the problem could have been wider than the way in which the criminal justice system defined it. There is some evidence (mainly conversations with conference organizers, notes kept in the restorative justice project and an interview with the girl defined by the criminal justice system as a 'victim') pointing to a conflict much deeper than a fight on a particular occasion between two girls, which was the focus of the conference. It appears that the 'victim' was from a middle-class wealthy family, and the other girl (correspondingly defined by the system as an 'offender') – from a disadvantaged low class background. The 'victim' looked down upon the 'offender' and made fun of her dressing style, music she listened to, as well as her attitudes and values. What in reality could have been a conflict with social-structural roots – classism, economic inequalities and social prejudices – was reduced to an interpersonal conflict between the two girls. The achievement of reconciliation between the girls – the ultimate goal of restorative justice – has hardly reduced prejudices and inequalities at the social-structural level. The existing injustices were preserved and protected through quickly and effectively neutralizing and expunging from the society a potentially disruptive conflict. The discussion of politically controversial issues was evaded by presenting the problem as an interpersonal dispute. A peace accord was concluded between two people whose interests might be in much lesser harmony than mediators facilitating their reconciliation made them believe.

A different case study might also provide an example of a restorative justice intervention diffusing and trivializing conflicts that could be a result of wider social structures and inequalities. In the family group conference (which was observed), when asked by victims why they committed burglaries, the offenders explained that they did not want to be looked down upon — or excluded from – a group of friends simply because they could not afford to buy certain things. They committed burglaries to obtain money necessary to buy designer clothes, cigarettes and some other items they felt they needed in order to maintain a certain status in the eyes of their friends.

The case was responded to on the assumption that it involved an interpersonal conflict between the victims and the offenders and resulted from individual faults located within the offenders (such as lack of empathy and lack of discipline). However, there is a possibility that what in reality gave rise to the crime – or at least created strong pressures to commit it – were much deeper social problems (such as economic inequalities and materialistic values in the society).

As has been argued by certain critics (see Chapter Two), there is a potential danger that through reframing wider social problems as intra- or interpersonal ones and achieving peaceful resolutions in individual cases, conflicts stemming from social-structural inequalities and other social ills may be efficiently neutralized and potential challenges to inequalities of wealth and power and other injustices in the society may be prevented. The above examples from the case studies might be seen as offering some empirical support for the critique which questions the aspiration of mainstream restorative justice advocates to restore peace and harmony in the aftermath of an offence.

It may be argued that the above examples do not demonstrate a problem inherent in restorative justice. All they demonstrate is that the process dealt only with one aspect of the problem and overlooked others. Yet it will be suggested here that neutralizing and individualizing conflicts may or may not be inherent in restorative justice, depending on how restorative justice is conceptualized and practised. Trivialization and diffusion of conflicts with social-structural roots is likely if restorative justice accepts the authority of criminal law, upholds the agenda of the criminal justice system and is narrowly conceived and reduced to practices such as victim-offender mediation programmes or family group conferences which occur under the aegis of the criminal justice system and are facilitated by system-oriented practitioners.

Some additional evidence supporting the claim that wider and deeper social problems and conflicts could be individualized and neutralized within the context of this study is that only those were allowed to participate in restorative justice processes who were likely to endorse and support values of the criminal justice system. People who could potentially challenge those values and whose participation could influence the process of the conference in a direction deemed undesirable by the conference organizers subscribing to the values of the criminal justice system tended to be excluded from conference participation. It is quite possible, for example, that the discussion focus during the restorative justice conference in the case study involving burglaries by offenders who wanted to impress their friends with designer outfits mentioned above could have been different had the offenders' friends been invited to participate. Yet, their participation was prevented and thereby a discussion of politically contentious issues was avoided. Voices of people whose property rights were violated were heard, the wrong done against them was acknowledged, and the values of respect for property were upheld. Voices of those who could tell what it is like to be a young person from a poor low class family in a society ridden with inequalities of wealth and obsessed with materialistic values were effectively silenced.

Somewhat similarly, in the case study involving the assault on the police officer (discussed earlier), there were people whose participation could potentially bring perspectives and views very different from those that were presented in the conference which was controlled by professionals and dominated by adults. Had the young people from the local community who were allegedly bullied by the police officer been invited to attend, a new angle could have emerged from the conference. Instead of focusing on values of authority and respect for those in power and further silencing voices of those who are already disempowered and marginalized, the restorative justice conference could have uncovered abuses of power, oppressions and injustices and offered a forum for a political debate. Instead of individualizing and privatizing the conflict and conceptualizing it as a problem located within the individual offender, perhaps a much deeper and wider conflict between the powerful and the powerless in the society could have been unveiled and brought to the forefront of the political arena.

Restorative justice in the shadow of the criminal justice system

As noted in Chapter Two, many restorative justice advocates wish to transform the criminal justice system by refocusing it towards restorative goals. To achieve this, some want to divert cases from the system until restorative processes start permeating the system (McCold 2000), and some wish to install restorative justice into the very heart of the system (Bazemore and Walgrave 1999b). Other writers, however, have expressed concerns about operating restorative justice in a close relationship with the system (Harris 1989; Morris 1995). This study can add to the debate about the relationship between restorative justice and the traditional criminal justice system empirical findings illustrating some implications of the alliance between restorative justice and the system.

The project studied here worked alongside the criminal justice system. As a leaflet which was given to potential conference participants prior to conferences explained, restorative justice 'works alongside the formal justice system but the law means it cannot replace it'. Restorative justice in this project depended on the system in several important ways, and, as will be argued below, such dependence had numerous negative consequences.

Dependence for funding

The criminal justice system was the main funder of this project. This put certain pressures on the project workers. In particular, if they wanted to ensure continuing funding, they needed to demonstrate that progress was made towards the goals desired by the system. The project dealt with juvenile offenders, and the most important goal of its major funding body was defined in section 37 of the Crime and Disorder Act 1998: 'It shall be the principal aim of the youth justice system to prevent offending by children and young persons'.

Probably unsurprisingly, this empirical study found that a lot of importance within the project was attached to prevention of re-offending, with the consequence that some needs of victims were overlooked (see Chapter Three). One of the conference facilitators during an interview criticized this situation and concluded: 'Let's face it, the money is there because of crime agendas rather than victim agendas'. Being funded by the criminal justice system meant that restorative justice was made to a large degree to serve the agenda of the system, with the effect that the restorative ideals were diverted from the original vision of creating an alternative way of doing criminal justice (Zernova 2006).

Dependence for referrals

Cases were referred to the project of this study after the sentencing stage. That is, cases entered the project either after the court had ordered offenders to attend a conference, or after the court had ordered an assessment for a conference, and the assessment recommended a conference.

The fact that cases came to the project after they had been processed by the criminal justice system had at least two implications. One implication – that a particular ethical framework had been pre-established by the criminal justice system which directed and shaped the restorative justice process and outcomes – has been discussed in the previous chapter. The second implication was that a prior intervention by the criminal justice system could frustrate the achievement of restorative objectives. This can be illustrated by a case study which involved an incident of assault and robbery carried out by a group of boys against another boy. On the advice of their lawyers, the offenders pleaded not guilty. This triggered a criminal trial, with the victim being forced to testify in court. According to a conference organizer in that case, the victim interpreted the 'not guilty' plea as a way for the offenders to say: 'we did not do it, he [the victim] is lying'. What the victim understood as an accusation of dishonesty was even more painful for him than being assaulted and robbed. Also, the interrogation by lawyers during the court process was very distressful for him. It appears that the criminal justice process added to the suffering caused to the victim by the crime. The offenders were found guilty and were ordered to attend a family group conference and apologize to the victim. However, he refused to come to the conference, which probably was not surprising in the light of the painful experiences he had to go through during the criminal trial.

There is no way of knowing what would have happened in this case had it not been processed by the criminal justice system first and had it come to the restorative project directly. But cases like this are probably unavoidable as long as restorative justice depends on the criminal justice system for referrals and is preceded by the criminal justice system's intervention. Achieving objectives of the criminal justice system (such as establishing guilt in this case) may frustrate the restorative justice goal of healing victims. Indeed, it may add to the injuries caused by the crime.

In another case where a prior intervention by the criminal justice system had compromised the achievement of restorative justice objectives, a conference took place after the offender had served his prison sentence. The offender in this case stole a bus, drove it away and severely damaged it. During the conference, it was suggested that the offender should do some work for the victims – the bus company – to repair, at least partly, the harm he had caused. The offender refused to work for the victims because he felt that he had already been punished enough for his crime in prison. Had it not been for the earlier intervention of the criminal justice system, perhaps the offender would have been more inclined to try to repair some of the damage and thus bring the resolution of the case closer to the restorative justice ideal.

Somewhat similarly, an offender's parents in a different case study objected to their son writing a letter of apology to his victims because they felt it was an additional punishment on the top of imprisonment. Again, had the criminal justice system not intervened prior to the conference, perhaps writing a letter of apology to victims would not have been perceived as an excessive punishment.

Dependence on system-oriented practitioners

Another way in which restorative justice within this project was affiliated with the criminal justice system was through conference facilitators subscribing to the system's values and promoting the goals of the system. This affiliation was not obvious. The project operated outside the criminal justice system (it was based within the social services department), and the project practitioners proclaimed themselves neutral parties, working within a moral framework very different from that of the system.

Yet, on a closer examination, it appears that the role they played was not as neutral as the practitioners claimed it was. By facilitating cases within the framework pre-established by the criminal justice system and directing the restorative process towards outcomes sanctioned by the system, facilitators have implicitly surrendered their neutrality and practised allegiance to the system and its values. Facilitators encouraged conference participants to accept that framework, embrace self-identities of victims and offenders as defined by criminal law and perform the expected roles, enabling a case to be processed consistently with the ideology of the criminal justice system. This prevented a possibility of ethical discussions about, for example, what exactly – if anything – constitutes crime in circumstances, and who – if anybody – is the victim and who is the offender[2].

As has been argued in the previous chapter, through multiple private meetings, skilful questioning, use of encouragement and praise, re-phrasing statements, re-focusing discussions, invoking feelings of guilt and empathy and using other psychological tools, conference organizers and facilitators subtly pressurized offenders to embrace identities of repentant selves, willing to admit their past mistakes, make amends and become law-abiding citizens. In doing so, facilitators effectively assist the achievement of the objectives of the criminal justice system, however they employ a model of power very different from that employed by the system itself (Pavlich 1996a, 1996b). This power aims not at suppressing its subjects but at producing a particular type of individual selves with certain aspirations and attitudes. This power is exercised in a masked fashion, hiding its presence from its subjects. It may operate outside the state, but for the purposes of promoting the state agenda (Pavlich 1996a, 1996b). The resulting alliance of the two political forces – the power of the criminal justice system and the power of conference facilitators – enables the state to effectively control troublesome individuals at a distance.

In the restorative justice process victims were encouraged by facilitators to adopt particular mentalities, part of which involved a belief that crime is a 'community problem', for which the 'responsibility lies with the community'[3]. If victims internalize this belief, they may assume a greater responsibility for preventing crime in their communities and rely less on the criminal justice system. Likewise, the self-identities which facilitators invited offenders' families to adopt were those of empowered selves capable of handling their problems. Under the guidance of conference facilitators, families developed prevention of re-offending plans which they had to implement after conferences, effectively governing their children on behalf of the state.

---

2 It appeared from informal conversations with facilitators that in some cases they did not agree with the framework prescribed by the criminal justice system. Yet, they felt obliged to limit their personal opinions to informal discussions and structured restorative responses within the framework dictated by the system.

3 As stated in a leaflet handed to victims by conference organizers.

Thus with the help of restorative justice professionals the objectives of the criminal justice system could be secured through victims and offenders' families acting as agents of the state. In the eyes of offenders, disapproval of their offending behaviour comes from victims, and the enforcement of a certain conduct comes from their families. If this provokes resistance and rebellion on the part of offenders, the rebellion would be directed at their families and other community members, rather than the state.

An additional finding hinting at loyalty of restorative justice professionals in this project to the criminal justice system emerged when they were asked how they wanted to see the future of restorative justice. Restorative justice professionals had a rather ambitious vision for the development of restorative justice and imagined a particular type of a relationship between restorative justice and the state justice. They wanted to put restorative justice 'on some serious government agendas', have restorative justice departments as part of local government, guaranteed state funding, standardized training and 'a central thing employed by the government to go out and teach people what the fundamentals [of restorative justice] are' (using words of one facilitator). These proposals for the evolution of restorative justice clearly indicate a strong attachment of the practitioners to the idea of a state-sponsored and state-managed restorative justice.

Marginalization issue

Before concluding this chapter, two other comments will be made concerning the relationship between restorative justice and the criminal justice system and certain current trends in the development of restorative justice.

As has been noted in Chapter Two, proponents of the diversion and integration models of restorative justice debate which of the models is more likely to succeed in transforming the criminal justice system. It is argued by advocates of the integration model that the diversion model is likely to lead to marginalization of restorative justice and unlikely to influence events in the criminal justice arena. However, its proponents refuse to accept this criticism. Both models – diversion and integration – envisage, and aspire towards, a large-scale state-managed implementation of restorative justice and a transformation of the criminal justice system, even though they suggest adopting different routes toward that destination.

It is suggested here that perhaps the debate between advocates of the diversion and the integration models needs to be refocused. Instead of evaluating the chances of either model to implement restorative justice on a large scale with the aim of transforming the state justice system, maybe we should ask: would the state-sponsored implementation of restorative justice on a large scale be necessarily a desirable phenomenon? There are numerous historical examples of centrally-managed large-scale social reforms leading to disasters and inadvertently bringing about suffering for millions. Besides, there is something inherently authoritarian and imperialistic about grand centrally-managed schemes. Maybe it would be wise to reject large-scale 'top-down' social transformations in favour of 'bottom-up' piecemeal changes and local strategies? Maybe keeping restorative justice low-profile and refraining from developing – and attempting to implement – large-scale centrally-managed schemes could benefit restorative justice in the long term? It is unfortunate that a possibility of restorative justice developing in this direction seems to have been rejected by most leading restorative justice advocates without being discussed seriously.

Choosing allies

Another issue which has received little attention within the discourse on restorative justice is a possibility and desirability of restorative justice movement forming coalitions with grassroots social movements whose aims are consistent with those of restorative justice (as suggested by Pavlich (1996a) and Morris (2000)). Grassroots social movements opposing oppressions and injustices could be more appropriate allies for restorative justice than the state justice system in the quest for justice. Forming alliances with such movements could benefit restorative justice by significantly widening its agenda and escaping the present situation where the application of restorative justice is limited to wrongs, harms and injustices which fall within the legal definitions of crime. Also, such coalitions could be stronger in their struggles against injustices, social inequalities and dominations, than groups and movements working in isolation. In time, the development of alliances between restorative justice and grassroots social movements could lead to the creation of a way of doing justice which potentially could present an authentic alternative to the state-sponsored, professionalized and legalized justice.

Conclusion

This chapter focused on two restorative ideals – the ideal of reparation and the ideal of restoring peace and harmony violated by a criminal offence. The problems resulting from making reparation of harm a universal restorative principle were discussed. The danger of restorative justice operating to individualize and diffuse conflicts which may have social-structural roots (as argued by critics of the 'ideology of harmony' dominant in the present restorative theory and practice whose views were presented in Chapter Two) was highlighted. Finally, the chapter looked at the relationship between restorative justice and the criminal justice system in the project studied here and argued that the reliance of restorative justice on the criminal justice system may be problematic because it forces restorative justice to serve the agenda of the system and uphold its ideology. Additionally, it has negative implications for individual cases. Finally, the desirability of large-scale state-led implementation of restorative justice was questioned and it was suggested that perhaps the restorative justice movement needs to re-consider who its allies should be.

Chapter Five

Restorative Ideals Re-examined

Introduction

This book began by outlining and discussing some ideals and aspirations of restorative justice proponents. It also identified some debates and concerns within the restorative justice movement and concerns of critics. It proceeded to report some findings from a study conducted in a family group conferencing project and explore aspirations of restorative advocates in the light of the empirical data. What are the implications of the findings from this empirical study for restorative justice theory and practice? What are the conclusions of this book?

Before the restorative ideals and the empirical findings are revisited, the reader should be reminded that the size of this study precludes the author from making any statistically significant claims about restorative justice. But making such claims is not really an intention. Rather, the intention is to add to the restorative justice debate some experiences and perceptions of the interviewees. The intention is also to bring into the debate about restorative justice some arguments based on the insights which the interviewees have confided in the course of this study, as well as the author's observations. Additionally, the intention is to see what problems and tensions may arise when restorative ideals are pursued in practice.

Restorative justice in the eyes of proponents and conference participants

One issue that seems to emerge from the empirical data is the discrepancy between the meanings which restorative justice theorists attach to certain actions and the interpretations of those actions by lay participants in restorative justice interventions.

Whose concept of punishment?

An example of such divergence of understandings is the question of whether restorative justice is an alternative to punishment or an alternative form of punishment. Heated conceptual debates of this issue are taking place within the discourse on restorative justice (see Chapter Two). Many theorists consider painful measures imposed in consequence of an offence a punishment. Yet, it appears that the meaning which participants in restorative justice conferences attach to the concept 'punishment' differs. Painful and unpleasant sanctions, which are ordered by the court in response to a criminal offence and which can be judicially enforced, may not necessarily be seen as punishment by people who have been subjected to those sanctions.

It has been suggested in Chapter Three that the model of power employed by conference facilitators could have masked the punitive aspects of restorative sanctions. Conference organizers employed a model of power in relation to offenders which aimed not at constraining and repressing legal subjects but at producing a particular type of individual selves with certain aspirations and attitudes. Some of the beliefs those selves possessed were: wanting to say 'sorry' to victims, perceiving conferences as being for offenders' own benefit and seeing those who subjected offenders to restorative sanctions as their friends and helpers. Even if conferences were painful experiences, the above beliefs probably discouraged offenders from interpreting restorative justice as punishment.

Whose understanding of coercion?

Another discrepancy between the interpretations of restorative experiences by certain theorists and some participants in family group conferences relates to the idea of coercion. It is claimed by some restorative justice advocates that restorative justice is characterized by voluntariness (Marshall 1996; Council of Europe 1999; McCold 2000; UN 2000), and this fundamentally distinguishes restorative process from its repressive and coercive legal counterpart. However, as noted in Chapter Three, some of the offenders and their supporters who were interviewed did not feel that their participation in the restorative process was completely voluntary, even when conferences were not court-ordered. They felt that people organizing the conferences and Youth Offending Team workers were 'quite pushy' (as one offender expressed it) in trying to persuade them to attend conferences. A degree of informal pressure was exerted over them, which made them agree to participate in conferences, even though they did not particularly want to do so.

It appears that when certain restorative justice proponents claim that the restorative justice process is voluntary, they seem to equate coercion to formal judicial coercion, backed up with legal sanctions. What seems to be overlooked is that coercion does not need to come from state authorities and does not need to have the force of the law attached to it. It may take a very different form, yet secure the same results – obedience and compliance – without resorting to forceful legal methods. The insights of the interviewees who felt that their consent to participate in conferences was obtained through subtle informal pressures suggest that the claims that restorative justice process is voluntary are misleading.

Desirability of de-professionalization

Yet another disparity between the views of proponents of restorative justice and those of lay conference participants revolves around the idea of stakeholder empowerment and de-professionalization of the restorative justice process. As argued in Chapter Two, it is one of the key aspirations of the restorative justice movement to return the conflict 'stolen' from lay people by professionals to its rightful 'owners'. If experts specializing in conflict-handling should have a role, their function should be limited to merely helping to stage conflicts. Their role should be restricted to that of 'resource-persons … not domineering, not in the centre' (Christie 1977, 12).

Yet the findings of this study suggest that the 'passive' (as perceived by a number of participants) role of 'neutral'[1] facilitators adopted by restorative justice professionals during the first part of the conference made several victims feel uncomfortable. Facilitators delegated disapproval of offending behaviour to victims and refrained from expressing their personal views. However, some victims wished that instead facilitators would have actively engaged in the disapproval and stated their professional opinion.

Perhaps this insight needs to be considered by restorative justice proponents who advocate assigning to facilitators a 'neutral' role of persons who merely help to stage restorative encounters. Clearly, this type of role is not necessarily what all victims want. Some might feel uneasy, being the only people in the conference to express dissatisfaction with offending behaviour and might want to have people in a position of authority to join them in reprimanding offenders.

But, of course, if facilitators discard their 'neutral' role and join victims in active disapproval of the offending behaviour, in the eyes of offenders they may no longer be 'carers' and 'helpers' to whom offenders would be willing to reveal their thoughts and feelings. The offenders would be less willing to submit to the guidance of facilitators in the process of structuring offenders' self-identities in relation to the situation leading to the conference. This would seriously reduce the chances of success by facilitators in procuring certain attitudes and behaviour on the part of offenders. Yet, embracing such mentalities and conduct by offenders is necessary for the achievement of the outcomes desired by facilitators.

Restorative realities

The author's observations made in the course of this study and interview findings may add to the restorative justice discourse some insights and arguments about what may happen when restorative ideals are put into practice. Three topics will be discussed below. The first concerns the debate about the place of offender rehabilitation in restorative justice. Findings shedding light on the relationship between offender rehabilitation and restorative justice in this project will be revisited and problems that may emerge when attempts are made to pursue restoration and rehabilitation simultaneously will be described. The second topic relates to the role of professionals in restorative justice. Findings concerning the function of restorative justice professionals will be summarized. The claim of certain proponents that restorative justice is characterized by de-professionalization and individual empowerment of crime stakeholders will be questioned. The allegiance of restorative justice

1 Although facilitators may present themselves as 'neutral' parties and may succeed in making participants believe that they are not taking sides, it is far from obvious that the role they play is indeed neutral. Facilitators (tacitly) adopt the framework pre-established by the criminal justice system, and this framework presupposes that the victim and the offender are not equal parties: one of them is innocent and the other culpable (cf. mediation in civil matters, although some question the neutrality of mediators even in civil matters – see Pavlich 1996a). By agreeing to facilitate a case within that framework, facilitators have implicitly surrendered their neutrality.

professionals to the criminal justice system will be criticized. The third topic is the potential of restorative justice to produce relational and personal transformations in its participants. Some factors identified by this study which may hinder the personal transformation process will be suggested.

Offender rehabilitation

Some advocates present restorative justice as an alternative to the offender rehabilitation paradigm. Others observe a conceptual compatibility of the restorative and rehabilitative approaches and wish to combine them (see Chapter Two).

As discussed in Chapter Three, this study has found that in this restorative justice project the vast majority of conference participants thought that the purpose of conferences was to make offenders understand the consequences of their actions. The participants hoped that this understanding would prevent the offenders from doing similar things in the future. Making offenders realize the wrongfulness of their behaviour was also the most frequently mentioned reason why victims agreed to attend conferences[2]. Among the main achievements of the conferencing process the one stated most frequently was making offenders appreciate the human costs of their actions and the belief that this might stop re-offending. A number of interviewees thought that the only, or at least the main, beneficiaries of the conference were offenders. Half of the victims felt that they were invited to conferences to help keep offenders out of trouble, rather than get any benefits for themselves. That is, some victims felt that they were used (even though with their own consent) to rehabilitate offenders. The second part of the conference was dedicated solely to offender welfare and prevention of re-offending, and a substantial part of the content of pre-conferencing reports focused on identifying needs and problems of offenders and suggesting ways to meet those needs and solve problems. If one combines these

2 This finding is important in the light of the findings by other researchers which demonstrate low attendance rates by victims in other restorative justice experiments (for example, Maxwell and Morris 1993; Holdaway et al 2001; Karp and Walther 2001; Crawford and Newburn 2003). This study might suggest that when conference organizers invite victims to attend conferences, placing more emphasis on helping juvenile offenders stay out of future trouble might be an effective method of encouraging victims' attendance. This suggestion is supported by another finding: when meeting offenders, adult victims often think that it could have been their own child or grandchild, and this thought promotes victims' desire to help offenders. It appears that at least some victims have a general sense of social responsibility towards young people and are happy to attend conferences for the benefit of offenders. The suggestion that conference facilitators, when inviting victims to attend a conference, might want to place more emphasis on helping offenders may be criticized on the ground that it encourages the use of victims for the benefit of offenders. Yet, even if this criticism is valid, it is weakened by the fact that victims must *consent* to be used that way. If such consent is given, the ethical problem ceases to exist, or at least is minimized. However, some findings from this study which have been discussed in Chapter Three cast doubt on the freedom of such consent. There is a serious danger of conference organizers subjecting victims to moral and psychological pressures in obtaining their agreement to participate.

findings, the alliance of family group conferencing and the offender rehabilitation paradigm becomes obvious.

It needs to be pointed out that this (over?)-emphasis on offender rehabilitation and welfare fits rather well with the role of guides and carers adopted by professionals within the restorative justice process and the model of power employed by them – the power aimed at governing individual behaviour through subtle techniques of discipline and structuring individual mentalities (Pavlich 1996a).

This study has also found some empirical evidence which suggests that drawing a sharp distinction between restorative justice and offender rehabilitation (as done by certain restorative proponents) may not be the best way of 'selling' restorative justice to members of the public. It emerged from interviews that what many victims want is an intervention which reduces chances of re-offending by young people.

However, the fusion of restorative justice and rehabilitation is not always easy (Zernova forthcoming). Some findings demonstrate tensions resulting from attempts to combine the two approaches. These tensions can be traced back to the conflicting assumptions lying beneath the restorative and rehabilitative paradigms. One such tension is between the restorative desire to hold offenders accountable and the traditional welfare/rehabilitative attitude towards sanctioning as irrelevant and inappropriate. There is some evidence suggesting that professionals in this project were rather reluctant to sanction offenders. As a result, several victims in this study complained that they felt uncomfortable during conferences because of what they saw as the conference facilitators' adoption of a non-blaming approach towards offenders, as has been discussed in Chapter Three. These findings demonstrate that combining the restorative approach (which requires sanctioning offending behaviour) with the traditional offender welfare or rehabilitation approach (which views offenders as deserving sympathy, rather than condemnation) is not always easy. There is a tension between the philosophies underlying the two approaches, and getting the balance wrong has a potential to disadvantage victims who may feel that their needs were ignored and that they were used for the benefit of offenders.

Another tension is between promoting the interests of victims and those of offenders, which in some situations may conflict. When this project supplemented its existing child care and protection practice with criminal cases, it faced a challenge of incorporating new matters into the core of its services. In the past the project's clients were children or young people and their families. Now a new recipient of the services was added – victims of crime. Their simple presence – let alone their unique needs and the centrality allocated to them by the restorative paradigm – was something that practitioners had to come to grips with. So, in one case study, referred to in Chapter Three, a facilitator started the conference by asking a young offender if it was okay to start and did not ask a victim of assault (also a child) a similar question. In a different case a young victim of assault felt vulnerable and intimidated during the conference because the offender had more supporters than the victim did. As explained in Chapter Three, this was to a large degree a fault of the conference organizers who required that as many members of the offender family attended the conference as possible, so as to mobilize them in the process of offender rehabilitation. In the endeavours to promote offender rehabilitation, the need of the victim to feel secure was overlooked.

It can be argued that the instances where the interests of victims were neglected, while those of offenders were advanced (possibly at the expense of victims) can be attributed to implementation mistakes on the part of the project and its practitioners. In a well-implemented restorative programme, needs and interests of victims and offenders should not be in conflict. Victims and offenders have a common interest in putting things right (Johnstone 2002, 19), and meeting certain needs of one stakeholder in crime often simultaneously meets some of the needs of the other. Promoting interests of one party should not result in losses for the other – this is not a 'zero sum game' (Williams 2005, 92).

However, this study has found some evidence which may indicate an apparent lack of harmony in some cases between the interests of the victim and the offender even in the absence of obvious implementation errors. One case study referred to in Chapters Three and Four involved a young victim who was seriously traumatized by the offence (robbery and assault) and an offender of a similar age who demonstrated no remorse and made abusive and threatening remarks directed at the victim during preparation for the conference. The conference organizers felt that facing the victim and hearing his story could benefit the offender by hopefully penetrating his indifference and psychological techniques used by him to shield himself from realizing the human costs of his behaviour. At the same time, there was a real danger that exposing the victim to the unremorseful offender could traumatize him even further. The conflict between the competing concerns in this case was resolved by prioritizing the interests of the victim and excluding the unremorseful offender from participation in the conference.

Most restorative justice proponents will probably agree that in cases of conflicts between interests of victims and offenders, such as in this one, interests of victims should come first. Otherwise, victims would be effectively exploited for the benefit of offenders and victimized for the second time. However, adopting the formula that the interests of the victims should always be given priority is problematic.

One problem is that it may not always be easy to establish what exactly is in the interests of victims[3]. In the case involving the unremorseful offender, it seemed to be assumed that it was in the interests of the victim to be protected from an exposure to the offender. Yet, at least arguably, there was a possibility that when confronted with the victim, the unremorseful offender could change his attitudes, and seeing that change could be healing for the victim. Also, it can be argued that simply confronting the offender in a safe environment and telling him what he thought about him could be a therapeutic and empowering experience for the victim, and thus in his interests. A quote from an interview with another young victim who was very afraid of the offender before the conference supports this argument:

> ...[meeting the offender] helped me on the mental side, because I know that I sat in front of him and told him what I think of him, that he is a coward ... everything under the sun

---

3 An obvious way of determining what is in the interests of victims is, of course, to ask them. However, they may not always know what is in their interests. At the same time, a suggestion that people other than victims themselves – such as conference organizers – may know better what is in the victims' interests will be a dangerous one, having a strong paternalistic flavour.

> I felt at that point. But in a sense, it's also helped me … I mean, a few weeks after that I met him, and he looked at me, and I looked straight back at him, because he knew exactly what I was going to say. Yeah, it has helped me on the mental side.

Another problem with adopting the principle that in cases of conflicts between interests of victims and offenders, the interests of the former should prevail is that it is not always obvious who is the victim – if there is one – in a particular case. Although cases came to this restorative justice project with clear definitions of who was the 'victim' and who was the 'offender' (cf. Shearing 2001), some findings from this study suggest that sometimes these definitions could be misleading and could conceal more than reveal (see Chapter Three; also Zernova 2006). Prioritizing interests of 'victims' as defined by the criminal justice system in some cases may lead to ethically questionable outcomes.

The role of restorative justice professionals

The power of facilitators Findings from this study suggest that de-professionalisation would not be a correct description of the restorative justice process. It appears that when proponents claim that the restorative justice process is de-professionalized, they attach a particular meaning to the concept 'de-professionalization'. It seems that this concept is understood as an absence of legal professionals who push stakeholders in crime off the stage, 'rob' them of their conflicts and problems and deprive stakeholders of an opportunity to participate in finding solutions to their disputes. Professionals, however, need not resort to such drastic methods in order to control the process and mould the outcomes of a restorative justice encounter. More subtle techniques and less visible forms of power may be employed in the management of the conferencing process, as has been discussed in Chapter Three.

De-professionalization is therefore not a feature of the restorative justice process. Rather, the process is characterized by a *transformation* of the role of professionals and an adoption by professionals of a different model of power. This power is not designed to constrain and repress its subjects. Rather, it aims at moulding individual behaviour through subtle techniques of discipline and shaping individual attitudes and subjective aspirations through encouraging and pressuring people to embrace particular self-identities (Pavlich 1996a, 1996b). During private meetings preceding conferences and during actual conferences, the role of restorative justice professionals was to diagnose and classify the problem, articulate the visions of individual selves which stakeholders in crime needed to adopt, assist the stakeholders in accepting particular mentalities and guide their actions during the conferencing process towards desired outcomes.

Importantly, the exercise of this mode of power would not be possible if individuals subjected to it were pushed out of the problem-resolution arena. Rather, it requires active participation of such people. During private meetings before conferences and during the actual conferences, under the guidance of facilitators, individuals need to reveal their feelings and thoughts relating to a problematic situation which led to the conference. Then, with the assistance of facilitators, conference participants need to perform an ethical introspection in order to identify the aspects of their selves which should be changed if the problematic situation were to be resolved. Then, conference participants need to transform their present selves and embrace particular self-identities in relation to a particular situation (Pavlich 1996a, 1996b).

It needs to be pointed out that there is some scope for the participants to resist the power of facilitators and refuse to adopt the identities which facilitators encourage and subtly pressurize them to embrace. This happened in one case study where the offender refused to make a genuine apology and walked out of the conference. However, prior to conferences, facilitators carefully evaluate the attitudes of potential participants, and, if it appears that a particular participant is unwilling to adopt a certain self-identity and play an expected role, it is unlikely that the person would be allowed to participate in a restorative justice encounter. Those who have been allowed to participate, yet 'misbehave' during the process get subjected to subtle pressures and micro-punishments by conference facilitators (such as eye contact, body language, interrupting a 'misbehaving' participant and inviting another participant to talk, reminding them of the ground rules with a tone of disapproval in the voice and so on), making them to comply with the roles expected of them and behave in a particular fashion. If this still does not work, a person may be asked to leave the conference, or the conferencing process may be stopped.

If the argument that facilitators have a great deal of power in shaping the restorative process and moulding outcomes is valid, the question arises: is this a problem? It probably is, at least within the context of this study. What makes the exercise of power used by facilitators problematic is not necessarily the fact in itself that facilitators can exercise that power. Rather, the problem is that the power of facilitators within the project studied here was used to reinforce the authority of criminal law and to promote the agenda and values of the criminal justice system. Upholding criminal law and facilitating the achievement of the objectives of the system through restorative interventions was a direct consequence of this restorative justice project functioning as an extension of – or a complement to – the criminal justice system and depending on the system for funding, referrals, legal framework and facilitators loyal to the system.

So the problem may be not so much the power of facilitators in itself, but its relation to the power of the criminal justice system and the ends towards which this power is used. Had restorative justice liberated itself from the dictates of the criminal justice system, had it refused to accept the authority of criminal law, and had restorative justice practitioners refused to practise allegiance to the system, the power of facilitators could be used to seek to achieve objectives very different from those which it seeks to achieve at present. For instance, instead of using their power to promote reparation of 'harms' resulting from breaches of criminal law so as to restore the status quo, facilitators could use their power to seek to uncover and bring to the forefront of the political arena social harms and injustices which tend to escape legal definitions of 'crime' and thus help activate collective challenges to such injustices.

'Democratic professionalism' or colonization by the 'systems people'? Some critics have noted the emergence of the class of 'restorative justice professionals' and the gap between restorative justice theory (which leaves virtually no role for

professionals) and practice (of which professionals are an integral part). Olson and Dzur (2003, 2004) see the emergence of this new class of professionals as a desirable development and introduce the concept of 'democratic professionalism' which involves professional expertise directed toward facilitating public participation. According to Olson and Dzur,

> The emerging role of restorative justice professionals ... responds to the continued need for conventional criminal justice procedural fairness while also meeting the new demands of community participation during a time of declining civic engagement. De-professionalization is not an option, we believe, but reconstructing professional roles to share authority and responsibility with lay people strikes us as a realistic and desirable development.
>
> (2003, 89)

Others, however, are less optimistic about the emerging group of professionals in the restorative justice field. Sullivan and Tifft, for example, are suspicious of the new class of restorative experts whom they refer to as 'correctionalists':

> Unfortunately, within the restorative justice movement, we now see an increasing number of experts funded by the government or private agencies who travel around the country directing seminars or giving talks on restorative justice, but who ironically seem to have little interest in the full range of restorative justice issues or who seem to have any sense of what restorative forms of justice require structurally.
>
> (Sullivan and Tifft 2001, 21)

Sullivan and Tifft's main concern about this current trend within the movement is that these new experts subscribe to the existing political economy and adopt a very narrow vision of restorative justice. For Sullivan and Tifft (2001), restorative justice is not something that is done in response to harms (especially harms defined by criminal law), but a way a relating to others whenever we enter into human interactions. Yet the restorative experts tend to promote restorative justice as a correctional programme underpinned by values of the existing justice system and fail to understand it as justice requiring radical transformations in social relationships and arrangements from the most personal to the most global levels.

Another advocate for whom restorative justice is 'a way of life', Wonshé (2004), uses an analogy of different clans from a tribe building a metaphorical bridge between the criminal justice system and community to describe the current trends within the restorative justice movement. One clan is the 'systems people' – the group who are 'the most visible and audible', who are 'in the centre of construction, hurredly moving around as though they were in charge, busily – sometimes frantically – carving out pathways, passing out blueprints and soliciting volunteers' (Wonshé 2004, 254). The second group near the bridge, much quieter and more slow-moving, do not have a name unifying them, but are 'connected by heart and spirit' (Wonshé 2004, 254). Wonshé describes the process occurring within the restorative justice movement as 'colonization' of the field by the 'systems people' (2004, 255-7).

The concerns of critics who are worried about the 'systems people' colonizing restorative justice and promoting a particular vision of it – the vision which serves the objectives of the criminal justice system – may be relevant in the context of this study. Chapter Four argued that conference facilitators in this project were criminal justice system-oriented in the sense that they subscribed to the values of the system and processed cases within the ideological framework imposed by the system, facilitating the achievement of the system's goals. It has been also highlighted that restorative justice practitioners in this project were strongly attached to the idea that restorative justice should evolve in close alliance with the state justice system and envisaged large-scale state-sponsored restorative reforms.

Individual empowerment Advocates praise restorative justice for empowering stakeholders in crime to resolve their problems the way they wish (Marshall 1996; McCold 2000; Braithwaite 2003a). Yet, if this claim is looked at in the light of the roles played by professionals within restorative justice and the model of power employed by them in shaping individual identities of conference participants and in controlling the restorative process and outcomes, the empowerment of stakeholders becomes questionable. It appears that they are 'empowered' to participate in the restorative process and develop outcomes as long as their actions and decisions fit with, and promote, the agenda set out by professionals.

As has been argued in Chapter Three, within the project of this study victims were 'empowered' to ask questions and express their feelings. They did not have any real say over the disposal of offenders. They could not attend the second part of the conference as observers, let alone as active participants. That is, victims were empowered only to the extent which did not endanger the monopoly of the criminal justice system over how individual cases should be responded to. Incidentally, educating offenders about consequences of their actions served to promote the objectives of the criminal justice system, because it might provoke empathy in offenders and prevent them from doing similar things in the future. Also, the unpleasant experience of having to face victims and answer their questions might deter offenders from further wrongdoings.

Victims were informed that family group conferencing offered them more power than the traditional criminal justice process. Thus a leaflet given to them before conferences described restorative justice as 'a new approach to resolving crime' which enabled victims 'to have a greater say'. It also claimed that within restorative justice '[v]ictims ... have much more influence than they would have in the Courts and the outcomes are more acceptable to them'. Thereby victims were assured that they were luckier than other victims who did not have an opportunity to participate in a restorative encounter. Such assurance masked the fact that the role which victims were allowed to play was in reality insignificant.

Offenders were 'empowered' to meet victims and explain their side of the story. Yet it is important to look at these opportunities offered to them in the light of the finding that several offenders felt that their offending behaviour was justified in the circumstances, but did not even attempt to present their version of the events. With one exception, they submissively complied with the requirements of the restorative process, admitted a wrongdoing and offered an apology.

Under the guidance of a conference facilitator and a YOT worker families of offenders were 'empowered' to create a plan for the prevention of re-offending (which had actually been developed to a significant degree by professionals long before the conference and recorded in a pre-conference report), to implement that plan and to ensure compliance with it through utilizing informal pressures. That is, families were 'empowered' to assist the state in governing their children, helping to ensure that they become law-abiding subjects.

These data suggest that not only the degree of individual empowerment of crime stakeholders in this restorative project was minimal, but also conference participants could be used to achieve the state justice system's goals. At the same time, they could be made to believe that they were the key decision-makers in their case.

Transformative potential

Transformation of relationships Proponents of restorative justice aspire to facilitate healing of social bonds broken by crime. This study has found some evidence of positive relational transformations taking place in this family group conferencing project. So a number of victims reported that prior to conferences they had various negative pre-conceptions about their offenders and were surprised to see that their assumptions were incorrect[4]. In the words of one such victim, the offenders 'were quite meek and mild, and just ordinary boys really, from ordinary families, nothing like I expected'. A conference facilitator similarly pointed out that in her experience victims tend to imagine their offenders in very negative ways before they meet them. However, seeing them breaks down pre-conceptions and invites victims to change attitudes towards offenders[5].

When asked whether their attitudes towards offenders changed after the conference, some victims answered positively: they felt reassured by offenders. Some victims reported feeling less angry towards offenders. Several victims said that they and offenders 'parted like friends really, everybody shook hands at the end' (using the words of one such victim).

A good example of conferences producing positive relational transformations would be a victim who described his feelings towards the offender after the offence in the following way:

> I would've liked to strangle the little bugger myself, because the damage that's been incurred was just excessive. I mean he's actually hit the ambulance, he damaged a number of the vehicle panels, he's done component damage underneath… I would have liked to just strangle the little bugger. I was very angry.

---

4 A finding consistent with those of Hoyle et al (2002, 36).

5 As this facilitator explained,

> Everybody that you go to [prior to a conference] have a preconceived idea about what this young person might look like. The classic quote is: 'I expected to find a monster, and what I saw was a little boy.' What she already knew was that this 'monster' had committed this offence. What she opened up her mind to was a possibility that that could be different. Having opened up her mind to that, she saw it was different, and it helped because it gave her a different angle on it.

After he had met his offender in the conference, this victim ended up offering him an apprenticeship in his company and comforting the offender's mother and assuring her that her son will be all right.

However, it needs to be noted that several victims said they did not have negative attitudes towards their offenders in the first place, so no drastic relational transformations took place as a result of a restorative encounter. Some victims found it difficult to say whether their attitudes towards offenders had changed and had mixed feelings about offenders following the conference. Yet others said that even after the apology offered by offenders, they still felt fear and distrust towards offenders[6].

Transformation of people Writing in the context of mediation, Bush and Folger (2005) argue that mediation process has a capacity to transform people taking part in it. One ingredient in that change is what Bush and Folger describe as 'recognition'. In their own words, '[r]ecognition means the evocation in individuals of acknowledgment, understanding or empathy for the situation and the views of the other' (2005, 22, emphasis omitted). This process involves becoming responsive to other parties' problems and experiencing concern for fellow human beings, despite conflict with them. 'Recognition' implies transformation of people from self-centred beings into caring and compassionate ones.

Some findings from this study suggest that some conference participants might have experienced transformations of the kind described by Bush and Folger. Once they had met their offenders, a number of victims demonstrated sympathy, kindness and generosity towards them. One such victim, when facing the offender, appeared to be willing to share the blame with him. That victim admitted that he had left the car running, thereby facilitating the theft. Another victim gave the offender a lift after the conference and, as has been metioned earlier, was willing to give him driving lessons during weekends.

Some victims and their supporters said that they felt respect towards offenders when they apologized, as this quote from an interview illustrates:

> Victim supporter: To apologize is to become an adult. … Saying it takes a lot of guts, and you know that you are becoming responsible… After you apologize to another person in front of other people – that sort of thing takes a lot of nerve. Everybody said it, and I said it. I said, 'thanks for apologizing. I know it takes a lot of guts to apologize, to admit your mistakes.'

---

6 One such victim of burglary said she had fears about meeting the offenders in the street, even after their apology at a conference. Another victim of burglary said he was scared that the offender might burgle him again, despite the apology and a promise not to repeat his wrongdoing given in the conference. In his own words,

> After it happened, and for a long time afterwards, every single time I would pass by the bathroom I would expect the window to be broken. I expected it to happen. And even now, every morning when I come out, I always look and see that my window is not broken. I always leave the lights on now. I always leave the alarms on, et cetera, et cetera.

A number of victims and victim supporters also said they felt sorry for offenders' mothers, who were present at conferences and some of whom cried. One victim said that after the conference he attempted to comfort the mother of the offender. In his own words,

> ...[the offender's mother] couldn't speak. She was so distraught, she couldn't speak. She was just so devastated, just tears from the moment we started until the moment we stopped. She couldn't speak. And all the way through she just kept crying. Just floods of tears. … The most moving moment was when I kissed his mother and said 'it'd be all right'. You know, it was quite moving, because she was just so devastated.

Or, to quote a victim supporter who sympathized with both the offender and her mother in another conference:

> I felt for [the offender's] mother, because I know how ashamed I would have been if one of my children did that. I'd be so embarrassed and ashamed, so I felt sorry for the mum. And as soon as she walked in the door, she wasn't bolshie. She was embarrassed, and she was upset, you know. … It was quite tearful as well. I was crying, and [the offender's] mum was upset. Everybody was upset. I think it's because we've realized that it was a big mistake. It should have never happened. It was the influence of other people and the drink.

Several offenders and their supporters also sympathized with victims. The following extract from an interview may illustrate this:

> Offender supporter 1: One lady there – when they actually got up and said their 'sorrys' and all that – she started crying, didn't she? I mean, the poor woman had been robbed, right? And she was crying at the letters that they had written to her, you know. I mean, it's unbelievable.
>
> Interviewer: How did you feel about it?
>
> Offender supporter 1: I felt sorry for her.
>
> Offender supporter 2: I felt sorry for her as well.
>
> Offender supporter 1: I mean, she was a really nice woman...

It needs to be noted that while in a number of cases victims and offenders seem to have experienced a better understanding of – and compassion for – the other party, in some cases this did not occur. Some examples have been provided in Chapter Three (section 'De-professionalized justice?') where offenders and their supporters felt increased anger towards victims and even had to curb desire to physically attack them. As has been noted earlier, these were the situations where offenders and their supporters felt that the offenders were falsely accused of a wrongdoing or perceived some other kind of unfairness.

This study has also found that in several cases it seems that the identity of victims affected the attitudes of offenders towards them and determined whether offenders felt empathy towards their victims. If the victim was an individual who had suffered some personal loss or damage as a result of the offence, offenders and their supporters were more likely to report feelings of guilt, remorse and empathic understanding towards the victim. If, however, the victim was a representative of some organization or institution (such as a bus company in one case study, school in another case, the police in yet another case), offenders were less likely to feel repentance and concern for victims and more likely to be angry and defensive. It appears that restorative encounters involving institutional victims were the least meaningful for offenders[7] and less likely to generate their transformation from self-centredness to compassion. One such offender stole a bus and during a police chase hit an ambulance, injuring the ambulance driver. The ambulance driver could not work for many months after the accident. He, the director of the bus company and a policeman who chased the bus came to the conference and expressed their disapproval. In the interview the offender said he felt sorry for the ambulance driver, but not the director of the bus company or the policeman, because, in his words, 'that's their job'.

To sum up, this study has found that in a number of cases conference participants were willing to acknowledge, and be responsive to, other party's situation. However, in some cases this did not happen. These cases tended to involve perceptions on the part of offenders that they were treated unfairly and/or were cases where victims were institutions or organizations, as opposed to private individuals.

The gap

Restorative justice proponents aspire to develop a new model for responding to crime, which would present an alternative to punishment and rehabilitation paradigms. They aim to create a way of doing criminal justice which will place victims at its centre, will empower stakeholders in crime and will be characterized by deprofessionalization. Some also argue that this model of criminal justice should be voluntary. The findings of this empirical study seem to demonstrate a significant gap between aspirations of proponents and practical realities of restorative justice. As has been argued earlier, the description of restorative justice as de-professionalized would be misleading. It is professionalized, although the role the professionals play is different from their role in the traditional criminal justice process. Restorative justice within the project studied here can hardly claim the title of a voluntary justice. Attendance at restorative justice conferences and an apology to victims more often than not was ordered by the court. However, even where it was not, offenders were subjected to subtle informal pressures by conference organizers and YOT workers, trying to make them attend conferences and apologize. Whether restorative justice is an empowering form of justice needs to be looked at in the light of the roles played within the restorative justice process by professionals, who in hardly visible ways manage and orchestrate the process and shape and influence outcomes. As to whether or not restorative justice can qualify as a victim-centred justice, these data send mixed messages. Some evidence suggests that interests of victims were indeed given priority at least in one case, but other evidence indicates that some needs

7 A finding similar to that by Blagg (1985).

of victims were overlooked. Does restorative justice present an alternative to the earlier paradigms of justice? As far as the retributive paradigm is concerned, it is hard to see restorative justice as a true alternative to it, given that restorative justice accepts the authority of criminal law and complements the criminal justice system in the pursuit of its objectives. At the same time, restorative justice adopts a different model of power over its 'clients'. In this sense it might be seen as an 'alternative'. With respect to restorative justice being an alternative to the rehabilitation paradigm, these findings demonstrate that restorative justice attaches a lot of importance to offender rehabilitation and enters into a close alliance with the traditional offender welfare model. So, a better description of restorative justice may be a 'partner', rather than an 'alternative', to the rehabilitative paradigm. How can the gap between the aspirations of advocates of conferencing and practical realities be explained?

Implementation mistakes

Some discrepancies between the ideals and realities probably can be attributed to implementation errors on the part of this restorative justice project and its practitioners.

One example of an implementation mistake was provided by a victim supporter quoted in Chapter Three who did not like the way a conference facilitator started the conference. The facilitator in that case asked the offender but not the victim if they could begin the conference. This omission on the part of the conference facilitator probably can be attributed to implementation failure on the part of the project and its workers (probably resulting from inadequate training and inability by the project worker to understand the victim-focused restorative justice philosophy)[8].

Another example of implementation errors may be suggested by data indicating that participants might have not been prepared for conferences sufficiently well. So, some offender supporters said in interviews that they needed to be better prepared emotionally for the conferencing process. They needed to know in advance what kind of feelings the process may induce:

> Offender supporter 1: …we was told that it wouldn't be easy. We was told it would be very difficult. But I don't think they really made us aware of how difficult it would be. I really think that there could have been emphasis on how hard and what emotions it could evoke on probably everyone's account. … I do think that perhaps we could have been made more aware of... I mean, [the conference organizers] did come around and go through the report with us and things like that... [but] I don't think we were prepared enough to know what was actually going to happen.
>
> Interviewer [to offender supporter 2]: Do you agree?
>
> Offender supporter 2: Yeah. That's totally how I feel about it.

8 An alternative explanation may be attributed to 'systemic' failings on the part of restorative justice operating under the aegis of the offender-centred criminal justice system (see below).

The offender supporters quoted above also said that offenders' parents needed to have more information prior to conferences about the wrongdoings of their children. If they did, it would be less shocking for them to hear victims recount the damage caused. As one offender supporter explained,

> I think there was also things mentioned [in the conference] that we didn't know about, which was also disturbing. We were never reminded or aware of how much damage the boys had done. Nobody told us that – the police, nobody. It never came out in court. I think the only thing that came out was we knew about them kicking the bedroom door in. We knew about the computer being trashed, but we wasn't aware of them literally trashing the houses. Nobody had ever told us that. So, to sit there and hear that on that day was really hurtful. Things like that coming out was like: 'god!' ... if I had known of that before, it wouldn't have been so much of a shock. I mean, I was sitting there and I was absolutely aghast, you know, to think that they did things like that. We had no idea.

This offender supporter was mentioned in Chapter Three, section 'De-professionalized justice?'. She was the participant in the conference which was observed who did not experience a positive emotional transformation. Indeed, she felt worse after the conference. A possible explanation which has been suggested is that she was not prepared well enough for the conference and the emotions it may produce.

Several victims, offenders and their supporters said they simply did not know what to expect when they went to the conference. This finding may be attributed to the failure by conference organizers to explain the conference participants what might happen in the course of a restorative encounter. Some previous researchers of restorative schemes have also found that many participants arrived at meeting with no idea what they were walking into (Miers et al 2001, Hoyle et al 2002). This finding was explained by the fact that facilitators had inadequately prepared participants (Hoyle et al 2002, 18-19).

If victims did not know what to expect in a conference, this makes their consent to take part in restorative justice questionable because they may not have known exactly what they have consented to when they agreed to participate. There is a danger that the lack of knowledge of what to expect during conferences may create a potential for conferences compounding injuries of victims caused by the crime. Besides, if participants in conferences do not know what to expect, they may have little opportunity to think before the conference what they might want to get out of it, what they might want to ask or say, who they might want to bring with them and so on (Hoyle et al 2002, 19). It probably should not be surprising if in such circumstances conferences may fail to achieve their objectives.

Yet another instance where implementation errors on the part of conference facilitators might have impeded realizing restorative ideals was the following. In that case the young victim of assault and robbery expressed quite a lot of anger towards the offender during the interview, and it was clear that the conference failed to achieve reconciliation between the parties. While there may be many factors preventing a restorative resolution in that case, some of them may be attributed to mistakes on the part of facilitators. The facilitators in that case seemed to have failed to create a comfortable conference environment for the victim. He said in the interview that he was made to sit opposite the offender, two or three feet away from him. A tray with hot water and coffee was on the table between them. The victim reported feeling unsafe during the restorative encounter. Additionally, the facilitators have failed to ensure that the victim and the offender have a roughly equal number of supporters. This has compounded the victim's feeling of vulnerability.

The final example of implementation errors that will be mentioned here is the case discussed in Chapter Four where the offender had to apologize to a police officer in a conference for an assault. In that case the offender displayed no remorse during the preparation for the conference and demonstrated no desire to apologize. However, facilitators decided to go ahead with the conference anyway. A day before the conference, the offender was arrested and put in a police cell for 19 hours. An hour before the conference, he was released without any charges being brought. He was picked up at the police station by a social worker and taken to the conference. The offender was tired, angry and hungry when he entered the conferencing room where he was confronted by the police officer to whom he had to apologize and his colleague. Unsurprisingly, the conference was not successful. Probably a better approach in that case would have been to re-schedule the conference (assuming it was decided that the conference had to be held at all).

Restorative justice as a new function of the social services department

Other explanations for the gap between restorative ideals and practice may relate to the context within which this project operated. This family group conferencing project was based within the social services department, which was its second major funder. To enable its continued existence and funding, the project needed to satisfy the department that certain goals were promoted, and those goals related to the welfare of young people in problematic situations, rather than restorative justice issues. As noted earlier, originally the project conducted family group conferences in child care and protection cases. When criminal cases were added to its practice, the original approach to a young person as a victim of his or her circumstances whose needs and welfare were of primary importance seems to have been to a large degree retained. The relationship between this project and the social services department may explain the findings that the offender rehabilitation and welfare received disproportionately more attention than restorative justice matters, creating a gap between restorative aspirations and practice.

Restorative justice as an extension of the criminal justice system

The restorative justice project where this research was carried out operated under the aegis of the criminal justice system and attempted to practise restorative justice within the ideological and structural framework of the system. As noted earlier, this project was dependent on the system in a number of important ways. Firstly, the project was funded mainly by the criminal justice system. This put certain pressures on the project workers. Secondly, the project relied on the system for referrals. This meant that by the time a case came to the restorative justice project, a framework within which the case would be responded to had been already established, the problem had been defined within the framework of criminal law, and labels 'victim' and 'offender' had been attached to people involved. The project also depended on the system for the practitioners subscribing to the values of the system and processing cases consistently with the ideology of the system. The combined effect of these factors was that the restorative justice project effectively functioned as an extension of the criminal justice system, complementing the system in achieving its objectives.

The close relationship between this project and the criminal justice system may explain such findings as the over-emphasis placed on offender rehabilitation, the spin-off of which was neglecting some needs of victims. Also, it may shed some light on the findings relating to the nature and extent of the empowerment of conference participants. They appeared to be 'empowered' only to the degree that did not endanger the achievement of the objectives of the criminal justice system. Indeed, in some ways stakeholders were 'empowered' to *facilitate* the attainment of the system's goals. It should not be surprising that attempts to incorporate restorative techniques in the shadow of the criminal justice system through a piece of legislation (Crime and Disorder Act 1998) the overarching aim of which is prevention of re-offending among juveniles has led to the alteration of the original vision of restorative justice. To a large degree, restorative justice was made to serve the agenda of the system, and when that agenda did not appear to fit well with the aspirations of proponents, those aspirations were abandoned or diluted (Zernova 2007).

It has been further argued that the dependence of restorative justice on the criminal justice system had serious implications for individual cases. Examples have been put forth illustrating how the achievement of restorative goals was frustrated in some cases which were referred to the restorative justice project after they had been processed by the system. Other examples demonstrated how the rigid framework of criminal law, within which restorative justice was forced to operate, failed to capture the complexities of each individual case and how the criminal justice system, by performing the definitional work before a case came to the restorative justice project, had shaped the restorative justice process and influenced outcomes.

Another implication of restorative justice being a servant to the state justice system, depending on the system for ideological framework, is that what in reality may be deeper social problems gets reduced to inter- and intra-personal problems and responded to accordingly. The consequence is that a problem is 'resolved' in a way congruent with the agenda of the criminal justice system, a conflict is quickly expunged out of the society, a possibility of a challenge to the existing social arrangements is prevented, and social injustices and inequalities which may have given rise to a particular conflict in the first place are preserved. Some findings outlined in Chapter Four may suggest that restorative justice operating within the legal framework might serve to individualize problems and neutralize conflicts which may have social-structural roots.

As has been discussed in Chapter Two, many restorative advocates develop models of restorative justice which presume a close relationship between restorative justice and the criminal justice. Other writers are critical of engraving restorative justice onto the existing system, however, their arguments tend to be purely theoretical. The findings of this study may offer some empirical support for the position of these critics.

Problematic ideals

Yet another explanation for the existence of the gap between restorative ideals and realities may relate to the nature of certain ideals. Some of them have not been thought through sufficiently well and may be undesirable or impossible of realization.

An aspiration to create a voluntary form of justice is an example of a restorative ambition which certain restorative justice advocates may wish to re-consider. As has been pointed out earlier, it is misleading to claim that restorative justice is characterized by voluntariness when the threat of judicial punishment is looming in the background of the supposedly 'voluntary' restorative interventions. In such circumstances, the consent of many offenders to participate in restorative encounters was promoted largely by the fear of judicial sanctions, rather than by a voluntary desire to meet victims. Besides, it is a mistake on the part of proponents to equate coercion to *judicial* coercion and limit it to official legal sanctions. This empirical study found that there might be other sources of coercion which are informal and more covert in nature. Also, it is misleading to think of coercion in 'either/or' terms: either coercive or voluntary. Such way of thinking is too naïve and fails to reflect the intricacies and complexities of what really happens. Proponents aspiring to develop an 'entirely voluntary'[9] way of doing criminal justice probably need to re-examine their ambition in the light of the above arguments and accept that totally voluntary restorative justice can hardly ever be possible.

Another problematic ideal of restorative advocates is reparation of harm presumably caused by crime. Defining reparation as an overarching goal of restorative justice appears to be based on the assumptions that crime necessarily causes harm and doing justice requires reparation of that harm.

The empirical findings of this study suggest that such assumptions are problematic. In some criminal offences, it is not obvious that harm has resulted or at least it is not apparent in what sense this may have happened. In such cases there may be nothing obvious to repair. But even if harm clearly has been caused, it is debatable whether its reparation is always desirable. In some cases, far from improving the situation, attempts to repair the harm may lead to negative results. Those who believe that restorative justice should operate in the name of reparation of harm also seem to overlook the fact that reparation of harm would involve restoration of the status quo, which may not necessarily be just and equitable. If the status quo was oppressive and unjust, reparation of harm would effectively restore and perpetuate pre-existing dominations and inequities. One of the case studies discussed in Chapter Four may illustrate these problems.

Pre-defining the goal of restorative justice as reparation of harm also narrows the scope of issues which potentially could have been discussed in deciding how crime should be responded to and thereby significantly limits – and even eliminates – the opportunities for ethical and political debates which could have taken place in the aftermath of an offence. When discussions of politically contentious issues are avoided – and some of the findings discussed in Chapter Four indicate that this did

9 Using the words from the promotional leaflet of the project studied here.

happen in this restorative project – the potential of restorative justice to challenge the existing injustices and bring about meaningful social changes is severely restricted.

Another ideal the realization of which is questionable is the aspiration to craft an alternative to punishment and rehabilitation. Johnstone (2002) and Daly (2002), for example, have argued that the presentation of restorative justice as an alternative to punishment and rehabilitation paradigms is misleading. When proponents criticize punishment and rehabilitation and distinguish restorative justice from them, in essence, they criticize – and contrast restorative justice to – caricatures of both paradigms. The punishment paradigm is presented as either having hurting offenders as the primary reason, or as a simple form of deterrence, and rehabilitation is conceptualized as a highly medicalized model of penal treatment (Johnstone 2002, chapter 5). Such presentations of the two paradigms of criminal justice are inaccurate, and contrasting restorative justice to the caricature images of punishment and rehabilitation is not only deceptive, but also may be damaging. Arguably, the objectives of restorative justice could be achieved more successfully if goals and methods of the rehabilitation and restorative models were combined (Johnstone 2002, 111). Presenting restorative justice as a more constructive form of punishment, rather than an alternative to punishment, could also have practical advantages in promoting it (Daly 2000).

Additionally critics have questioned the attempts to develop the ethical framework for restorative justice which relies on – and is shaped by – a sharp contrast between restorative and traditional criminal justice values on the grounds that it is simply unrealistic. The restorative ambition to manufacture a distinctive ethical orientation to be used in responding to crime is problematic because in reality criminal justice blends a wide range of (often incompatible) values and objectives. This is a result of competitions between various forces aiming to shape the practice in accordance with certain values. Thus social institutions are compromises, rather than pure outcomes of one particular set of values (Garland 1990; Johnstone 2002, 163). It is probably inevitable that seeking a new institution involves keeping some attachments to the past (Pavlich 2005, 120).

It has been further suggested that the extent to which restorative justice really rejects criminal justice values is questionable because restorative justice accepts basic criminal justice concepts (such as 'crime', 'victim', 'offender') and assumptions (such as the assumption that doing justice presupposes a commission of crime). As Pavlich argues,

> ...by positioning its value framework as contingent upon crime, as working in the aftermath of crime, restorative justice paradoxically commits itself to the very moral framework it claims to supplant. ... The restorative quest for a different moral framework of justice grounds itself in the very value orientation it seeks to redress.
>
> (Pavlich 2005, 25, 35)

As noted in Chapter Two, the same critic points out the implicit appeal of restorative justice to the medial model. This appeal is conducted through the emphasis on healing the harms generated by crime and restoration of the presumed 'healthy' order (Pavlich 2005). The language of the medical model masks ethical questions by translating moral problems into technically resolvable issues and thus disables ethical discussions. This limits the ability of restorative advocates to pursue justice through a different ethical framework and makes restorative justice parasitically rely on the very value framework which it aspires to go beyond. Consequently, 'the espoused attempts to find ethical values that surpass criminal justice arenas are muted by a paradoxical commitment to those arenas' conceptual foundations' (Pavlich 2005, 42).

Search for a new ethical framework

Even if a certain degree of attachment to the old legacies when searching for a different ethical framework for restorative justice is unavoidable, what might an attempt to move towards a new ethical framework require? One proponent, Kay Harris (1989), disapproves of certain attempts to develop restorative justice principles and criticizes leading advocates of restorative justice for failing 'to escape the fetters of current ways of thinking' (1989, 35). She emphasizes the dangers of tackling restorative experiments on to the existing criminal justice system, while ignoring value questions. She argues that in making proposals for change, restorative advocates need to be primarily guided by value questions and ethical considerations.

Harris puts forward several moral principles which she recommends as the ethical standards by which reform proposals should be judged. One of the principles proposed is '[w]hatever means you use will become part of the ends you achieve' (1989, 36). Harris challenges claims that such methods as imprisonment, coercion, repression and other means which are inhumane or inconsistent with restorative justice aspirations can be morally acceptable in the pursuit of security and justice. The end does not justify the means utilized in achieving it. Another moral principle is '[n]o ethical decision is exactly transferable from one situation to the next' (1989, 36). Harris believes that it is important to consider the actual effects of actions and decisions on people in terms of how they fit with our values and aims and not simply look to law or some other authority for guidance. Harris suggests as another ethical guideline that '[t]he people with the most ethical right and responsibility to make a decision are the people who will be affected by it' (1989, 36). She refers to the works of Nils Christie (1977, 1982) as a source of support, in particular, his aspiration to limit to the minimum the role of the state and the state justice system and its officials in the conflict-handling process. Harris argues that if returning 'stolen' conflicts to their rightful owners – people directly involved in, and affected by, them – is more than a rhetoric within the restorative justice discourse, restorative justice advocates need to be serious about letting those people exercise power. Among other ethical guidelines is 'do unto others as you would have others do unto you' (Harris 1989, 37). Harris acknowledges that this moral principle may be particularly difficult to follow when we are confronted with people who have offended against us. Yet this principle may be most important in situations when it seems that complying with it is most difficult.

Harris's suggestion that in developing the new paradigm, restorative justice advocates need to be primarily guided by ethical considerations is very important.

Many restorative justice campaigners seem to be too pre-occupied with developing pragmatic plans for the implementation of restorative justice within the existing system. In doing so, they apparently fail to notice that their proposals serve to effectively perpetuate, rather than challenge, the state justice system and the values underpinning it. However, the new paradigm of justice is unlikely to emerge, unless the ethical (as well as structural) framework of the criminal justice system is discarded and different moral values and attitudes are adopted.

Another example of an attempt to create an alternative ethical framework for restorative justice may be found in writings of Sullivan and Tifft (1998, 2000a, 2000b, 2001, 2004). These restorative justice campaigners argue that restorative justice principles derive from a political economy that seeks to take into account the needs of all involved in a given social situation. Therefore, it is necessary to firmly position restorative justice within a concept of justice based on the principle 'to each according to their needs'. Restorative justice should concentrate not only on responding to harms and injustices that have already been done (so as to meet the needs of all involved), but also on creating social arrangements and relationships that take into account needs of everybody from the outset structurally. Needs of all in such a political economy 'are met, but met as they are defined by each person' (2001, 113), and the aim of justice is to achieve 'equal well-being' for everybody. One may agree or disagree with the precise ethical framework proposed by Sullivan and Tifft[10], but what is particularly valuable about these proposals is their revolutionary spirit: they signal a radical re-conceptualization of the restorative justice ethics, rather than clinging to the existing criminal justice system's ethical foundations.

Pavlich offers a rather different approach to developing an ethical framework for restorative justice. He argues that the pursuit of a new ethical discourse might imply conceptualizing the idea of justice not as an entity with an ontological reality, but 'as a never closed, never fully calculable, open and infinite idea that promises new ways to be with others' (2005, 115). Such a way of approaching justice recognizes that ethics is possible precisely because there are undetermined choices. It invites constantly to re-calculate justice and emphasizes the importance of preventing any particular image of justice from being installed as universalizable or necessarily better than others.

Pavlich further suggests that an alternative ethical framework may imply imagining justice without crime (2005, 116-19). There may be different ways of

10 Sullivan and Tifft's idea of restorative justice as needs-based justice raises many interesting questions. Apart from practical questions (for example, how would people's needs be defined in the needs-based economy? Is it only their own perception of their needs that counts? If yes, is it possible that people may misunderstand their *real* needs? What should happen to those members of the society who do not wish to build social relationships in accordance with the principle 'to each according to their needs'?), there is a very important ethical question: How appealing is the concept of justice based on the principle 'to each according to their needs', irrespective of their moral entitlements? Would the adoption of this principle as a universal moral maxim not lead to unethical choices in some – or even many – circumstances? Besides, is there not something inherently authoritarian and totalitarian in suggesting that we all should embrace the same morality and conception of social life?

doing so. The one proposed by Pavlich may take diverse experiences of *injustice* (rather than crime) as the starting point in search for justice[11].

Additionally, it is suggested that images of justice that presume individual victim and offender identities should be resisted. The identity of a victim – which is by definition disempowering – may not be always most suitable if the aim is to transcend victimization and empower individuals. The victim identity individualizes what may be collective injustices. It disables subjects from actively engaging in seeking social transformations so as to resist the pre-existing power relations which may have generated the individual victimization in the first place (Pavlich 2005, chapter 3).

The identity of an individual offender may also not always be appropriate (Pavlich 2005, chapter 4). It implicitly adopts definitions of crime provided by the criminal justice system and sees an individual offender, rather than broader power relationships, as the prime cause of harm. This replicates the criminal justice system's logic which requires individual, rather than systemic, responsibility. It deflects questions of justice from social power relations which may be even more harmful than the act of crime that has been committed. It may also overlook the fact that great harms may be produced and perpetuated by criminal laws themselves (Pavlich 2005, 81). When the emphasis is placed on individual offenders as creators of harm, the politics of restorative justice has offender reform, as opposed to social change, as the primary focus.

The alternative calculations of justice probably would also reject the concept of 'community' as 'something essentially fixed, definable and so potentially closed' (Pavlich 2005, 119) in favour of an open-ended idea of spontaneous solidarity. It is argued that when restorative justice campaigners appeal to fixed and absolute images of community, they create divisions between insiders and outsiders and consequently threats of segregation and exclusions (Pavlich 2001). According to Pavlich, 'communities are identified – implicitly or explicitly – by exclusion. Identifying a community absolutely does not encourage members to face responsibilities to the excluded' (2004, 177). Having rejected the concept of 'community' as a definable entity, instead Pavlich proposes an open-ended idea of negotiating future ways of being with each other. He uses an analogy of a welcoming host receiving guests as a guiding framework for developing practices aimed at redressing injustice (Pavlich 2001, 2004, 2005).

The proposed ethical framework for restorative justice, in Pavlich's own words,

11 Proposals of an early inspirer of restorative justice Nils Christie to imagine justice without crime involve re-defining crime as 'conflict' opening opportunities for norm-clarification (1977, 1982). In his recent book Christie reiterates that '[c]rime does not exist' (2004, 3), discusses a possibility of using 'troubles' as a point of departure and then suggests moving even a step further away from the concept 'crime' and using 'acts' as the first step in an enquiry. The next step involves analyzing the acts that are seen as bad. A penal abolitionist Louk Hulsman, whose ideas have also influenced thinking of some restorative justice writers, similarly argues that 'there is no 'ontological reality' of crime' (1986, 66). Crime is only one of many possible ways to construct social reality. He suggests that crime should be abandoned as a tool in the conceptual frame. Hulsman's preferred focus for an enquiry is 'problematic situations' (1986, 72).

> ...does not claim to be universalizable, nor does it assume a naturally defined ethical subject (e.g. victim, offender, etc.). Rather, it acknowledges its aporetic and ambivalent character, reminding us always of our ethical situation: like the welcoming host, restorative justice participants are required to calculate how to be with others in the future, for which they are profoundly responsible. Yet, no one can predict the outcome of any given – ultimately incalculable and never determinate – ethical decisions.
>
> (2007, 622)

Minimizing the gap?

Proponents of restorative justice envisage an empowering, victim-centred, community-oriented, de-professionalized justice, an alternative to the existing paradigms of justice, which, according to some, would be characterized by voluntariness. The project where this research was carried out falls short of that ideal. Rather, it appears to come very close to the offender rehabilitation paradigm, with some elements of restorative justice added to it. These findings may not present a very encouraging picture. There appears to be a significant gap between the aspirations of proponents and the realities of restorative justice, at least within the scope of this study. Can that gap be minimized? Can a lay-oriented, individually empowering, de-professionalized justice that offers a new ethical orientation ever be possible? Or should the idea of creating a radical alternative to the existing paradigms of justice be rejected as unrealistic?

This book will conclude on a positive note and suggest that a true alternative may be possible. However, it is unlikely to emerge, as long as restorative justice obeys the dictates of criminal law, depends on the criminal justice system in a variety of ways and functions as a servant to the system.

This book has attempted to demonstrate how present restorative justice practice may serve to complement the power of the criminal justice system and facilitate the achievement of wider political aims. Restorative justice may operate outside the state, but for the purposes of promoting the state's agenda and strengthening the state's power. The resulting alliance of the two political forces – the power of the criminal justice system and the power of conferencing – may enable the state to effectively control individuals at a distance. This control is exercised in a masked fashion, concealing the effects, indeed the very existence, of that control from its subjects and consequently reducing chances for resistance on their part (Pavlich 1996a, 1996b). Contrary to the restorative ideal to create an alternative to the criminal justice system, restorative justice in its present form may serve to strengthen the state justice system, rather than to challenge it. If this is so, the development of a true alternative to state-sponsored justice would probably require a radical separation between restorative justice and the state-sanctioned justice. Restorative justice cannot be an 'alternative' to the state justice system, and at the same time operate either within the system or as its extension, bounded by criminal law and colonized by practitioners serving the agenda of the system.

So, what could attempts to achieve – or at least work towards achieving – the divorce of restorative justice from the state justice involve at a practical level? How could restorative realities be brought closer to the ideals of proponents? And how could some of the dangers involved in the present restorative ideals and practices be avoided or at least reduced?

Restorative justice proponents probably need to re-consider their goals and the methods they use in the campaign for restorative justice and reject the idea of large-scale state-sponsored implementation of restorative justice. Firstly, the idea of grand state-sponsored reforms has strong authoritarian overtones and therefore should be treated with great caution. Secondly, there are numerous historical examples suggesting that large-scale top-down reforms often backfire. In the light of historical precedents it may be wise to be suspicious of grand state-managed social transformations. Thirdly, using 'top-down' methods in the restorative crusade fundamentally contradicts the aspiration to be 'a bottom-up movement' which is 'committed to combating oppressive state structures' (Braithwaite 2002c, 563). Finally, keeping restorative justice low-profile may benefit it at this stage, because before a large-scale implementation of restorative justice is attempted, certain changes in public attitudes and social values need to take place. Before radical institutional transformations are carried out, a fundamental shift needs to occur in people's consciousnesses. So, arguably, today restorative justice need not be much more than a 'sensitizing theory' (Zehr 1990, 227) – or a critique which could cause us to think more carefully and critically about our ideologies and actions in the criminal justice arena (and more generally) – accompanied by practical experimentation disengaged from the criminal justice system and designed to explore and refine the restorative vision.

Such practical experimentation will probably require that present funding practices for restorative justice are re-arranged so as to liberate restorative justice from financial dependence on the state and consequently the obligation to follow the dictates of the criminal justice system. Non-criminal justice system funders whose interests and values do not fit well with the restorative philosophy should also be avoided, because such funding bodies are likely to force restorative justice serve their own interests and objectives through financial pressures. If those objectives do not coincide with the restorative principles, restorative ideals are likely to be diluted and put into service of other goals.

Sources of referrals need to be arranged in such a way as to escape the situation where by the time a case comes to a restorative justice meeting, a particular framework within which the case would be responded to has been already established. For example, cases could come to restorative meetings as a result of self-referrals, referrals by relatives, friends, neighbours or non-criminal-justice agencies.

Restorative justice needs to refuse to adopt legal definitions of what constitutes crime and who – if anybody – is a victim and offender. This would prevent attaching to people what may be inappropriate labels which over-simplify and even distort the reality of what happens. This would also avoid situations where events labelled 'crimes' fall within the ambit of restorative justice, while multiple instances of injustices, violence, hurtful and harmful behaviour which happen to escape the legal definitions of crime fall outside the restorative justice realm.

Advocates of restorative justice need to look more critically at the emerging class of experts – restorative justice professionals – who employ their power in the service of political aims of the state justice system. It may be desirable to oppose their attempts to 'colonize' restorative justice, define its meaning and aims and market a particular version of restorative justice which serves the objectives of the state justice system. Proponents need to recognize that the potential of restorative justice to provide a forum where a political debate could unfold is seriously compromised, if not completely extinguished, when the restorative process is orchestrated by professionals aspiring to guide it towards outcomes congruent with the objectives of the criminal justice system.

It is necessary to develop ways of assessing the value of restorative justice which, unlike most current empirical research into restorative justice, are not based on cost-effectiveness of programmes and 'outcome' criteria (see Chapter One) and are not primarily aiming to answer questions which are important to governments and other funding providers.

Restorative justice could have a much wider application than present practices tied up to legally defined crimes and typically restricted to correctional programmes seem to imply, and it could be usefully employed in facing conflicts, problematic situations and injustices on a daily basis. Present restorative practices, pinned to the criminal justice system, are based on a very limited vision of restorative justice. This significantly restricts the scope and focus of the campaign for restorative justice and forces it to evolve in a direction which may not be the most fruitful one.

A broader conception of restorative justice as a way of relating to others or as set of values that could guide human interactions, as proposed by some of its advocates, could suggest much more diverse and widely applicable restorative practices. This broader conception does not necessitate commission of legally defined crimes for restorative principles to become relevant. Conceptualizing restorative justice as a set of values to be used in dealing with everyday problems and conflicts would avoid the situation where the success of the campaign for restorative justice becomes very much at mercy of people with power to determine criminal justice policies and provide or withhold endorsement and funding for restorative initiatives. It would also avoid the present state of affairs where crime stakeholders and ordinary citizens are pushed into the role of clients in restorative programmes, in which the degree of their empowerment is very limited and they can be used to promote broader political goals. Instead, restorative justice could become a truly individually empowering, de-professionalized, lay-oriented practice in which anybody could engage whenever a situation calls for it.

In fact, such restorative practices are probably already common and widespread – simply they are not defined as 'restorative justice'. Building on the work of Louk Hulsman (1986), Gerry Johnstone (2002, 59) notes that only a small percentage of events that could potentially be criminalized are actually defined and responded to as crimes by the criminal justice system. The rest of the potentially criminalizable events are interpreted in many other ways (for example, accidents, disputes, symptoms of an illness, or even legitimate responses to situations) and remain completely outside the state justice system. They are dealt with within the social context in which they occur (family, school, workplace, neighbourhood, circle of friends and so on). If the legal system gets invoked, it tends to be the civil law system. Only in exceptional circumstances the criminal justice system is employed. What this means is that many criminalizable events are probably already dealt with in a way broadly congruent with restorative values. Indeed, it may well be that restorative justice is already a social norm and the state justice response – an exception.

If so, this may suggest a different focus for the restorative crusade. Instead of campaigning for transforming the way crimes are dealt with by the criminal justice system, restorative proponents could campaign for preventing as many cases as possible from being defined as crimes and entering the system in the first place. Restorative advocates could seek to sensitize the public to the adverse social effects of the activities of the criminal justice system; raise public awareness of the benefits of addressing problems, conflicts, harms and injustices in accordance with restorative values; challenge punitive social attitudes and unmask the dangers and losses resulting from people delegating handling their problems to the state justice system. The restorative crusade could endeavour primarily to cultivate social values consistent with the restorative philosophy and encourage their practical application in dealing with everyday conflicts, problems and injustices. If the campaign for restorative justice rejected authoritarian, 'top-down' methods in promoting restorative justice and instead focused on public moral education and the creation of genuine 'bottom-up' alternatives to the state justice system, the society could gradually evolve into one where restorative justice replaces today's state justice.

While it may be easy to imagine how restorative justice could offer an alternative to the state justice system in cases involving non-serious wrongdoings, envisioning restorative responses in very serious cases may be a more challenging task. There may be people who cannot live peacefully among others unrestrained, at least for a time. There may be acts which provoke such strong public reaction that those carrying them out may be themselves in danger of violence and harm from angry members of the public. It may be tempting in such cases to fall back on the state justice system and resort to exclusionary and repressive methods. However, restorative values could guide proponents in the search for possible alternative responses. For instance, in cases where restrictions of liberty are seen as absolutely necessary, restorative values may suggest that those restrictions should be conceived 'as having less to do with buildings, structures, and walls and more to do with human contacts and relations' (Harris 1991, 95). Attempts to create caring and constructive arrangements to maintain certain people safely, especially those who have committed sexual offences, have been already made by groups of ordinary citizens and can be found in circles of support (Cayley 1998, chapter 16). Their underlying philosophy is broadly compatible with restorative values in the sense that it emphasises community hospitality, inclusiveness and support, while helping certain individuals get some insight and making them accountable to community members. Also, perhaps, at least a temporary solution could be offered in some cases by the introduction of sanctuaries, as advocated by Bianchi (1994). A person who had committed a serious act that can trigger strong and potentially violent public reaction could find refuge in a sanctuary until a suitable future for him or her could be negotiated.

Additionally, proponents need to be reminded that it is insufficient for the restorative justice movement to be a 'single-issue' campaign aimed simply at promoting responses to problematic situations, conflicts and injustices in a non-punitive, non-violent, reconciliatory, reparative and individually-empowering fashion. It needs to be acknowledged that what may often appear as an inter-personal dispute or an individual problem may in reality stem from much deeper and wider social problems. Consequently, it is necessary to refuse to limit restorative justice to narrowly conceived practices which individualize disputes and quickly and effectively neutralize potentially disruptive conflicts. It is important that proponents are acutely aware of the inter-related nature of social problems and refuse to accept the social system which causes many of the problems they are fighting against.

Proponents probably need to give more thought to some of the fundamental tenets of the restorative justice philosophy. They may want to refuse to restrict the focus and objectives of restorative justice to the achievement of pre-defined goals (such as reparation of harm and resolution of conflicts). Placing such restrictions on the focus and objectives of restorative practices leads to pre-determined outcomes and limits the ethical discussion of how situations should be dealt with to a narrow set of questions. This prevents a possibility of bringing into light politically contentious issues and consequently reduces – or even eliminates – the potential of conflicts with structural roots to spearhead important social changes.

Advocates of restorative justice may want to consider forming coalitions with grassroots social and political movements, the aims of which are consistent with restorative justice. This could lead to formation of alliances which could take restorative justice to a different level and create a new dispute resolution arena where social oppressions and injustices could be resisted.

While the application of restorative justice values could be vastly expanded, it is important to resist the temptation to view restorative justice principles as absolute moral maxims applicable in every unique circumstance. No doubt the application of restorative values may lead to positive results in some – perhaps even many – situations. Yet, endorsing restorative justice as a universal response to all conflicts, problematic situations and injustices will not help identify, let alone prevent, undesirable consequences. In dealing with some problems and situations restorative values and methods may not be the best ones or may even be inappropriate. Besides, the assumption that restorative justice principles are universalizable or necessarily better than any others reduces the ethical work in every situation to a set of simple questions and a mechanical application of pre-defined rules. It limits moral choices and disables a search for responses which are not centred on a specific set of values (Pavlich 2002b). It prevents us from actively seeking entirely new patterns of social association which may not be seen through the restorative 'spectacles'.

The above suggestions on how restorative ideals could be reformulated and practices changed are not intended as a prescription of what must be done. The intention behind providing the above list is not to outline and advocate an absolute vision of how restorative justice should be conceptualized and practised. Rather, the objective is to identify a gap between present restorative ideals and practical realities and problematize the limitations and dangers inherent in the existing restorative practice and theory. The intention is also to indicate possibility of a different direction in which restorative justice could develop, so as to minimize the present gap between restorative ideals and realities and avoid some of the problems present in today's restorative theory and practice. That suggested direction might alleviate some of the current problems, but itself is unlikely to be free from dangers. Those new dangers, as they emerge, will in turn need to be identified as part of an on-going critique. It is hoped that this book has contributed towards such a continuous critique of present limitations, problems and dangers.

References

Abel, R.L. (1982) (ed.) *The Politics of Informal Justice: The American Experience.* (New York: Academic Press).

Achilles, M. and Zehr, H. (2001) 'Restorative Justice for Crime Victims: The Promise and The Challenge' in Bazemore, G. and Schiff, M. (eds) *Restorative Community Justice: Repairing Harm and Transforming Communities*, 87-99 (Cincinatti, OH: Anderson Publishing).

Ashworth, A. (2002) 'Responsibilities, Rights and Restorative Justice', *British Journal of Criminology.* 43, 578-95.

Auerbach, J.S. (1983) *Justice Without Law?* (Oxford: Oxford University Press).

Auld, J., Gormally, B., McEvoy, K. and Richie, M. (1997) *Designing a System of Restorative Justicez in Northern Ireland, The Blue Book.* (Belfast: The Authors).

Barnett, R. (1977) 'Restitution: A New Paradigm of Criminal Justice', *Ethics,* 87, 279-301.

Barnett, R. (1980) 'The Justice of Restitution', *The American Journal of Jurisprudence,* 25, 117-32.

Barton, C. (2000) 'Empowerment and Retribution in Criminal Justice', in Strang, H. and Braithwaite, J. (eds.) *Restorative Justice: Philosophy to Practice*, 55-76 (Ashgate/Darmouth: Aldershot).

Bazemore, G. (1996) 'Three Paradigms for Juvenile Justice' in Galaway, B. and Hudson, J. (ed.) *Restorative Justice: International Perspectives*, 37-67 (Monsey, NY: Criminal Justice Press).

Bazemore, G. (2000) 'Rock and Roll, Restorative Justice, and the Continuum of the Real World: A Response to "Purism" and Operationalizing Restorative Justice', *Contemporary Justice Review,* 3, 459-477.

Bazemore, G. and Bell, D. (2004) 'What is the Appropriate Relationship Between Restorative Justice and Treatment?' in Zehr, H. and Toews, B., (eds), *Critical Issues in Restorative Justice,* 119-132 (Cullompton: Willan Publishing).

Bazemore, G. and Dooley, M. (2001) 'Restorative Justice and the Offender: the Challenge of Reintegration' in Bazemore, G. and Schiff, M., (eds), *Restorative Community Justice,* 101-126 (Cincinnati, OH: Anderson Publishing).

Bazemore, G. and Elis, L. (2007) 'Evaluation of restorative justice' in Johnstone, G. and Van Ness, D. (eds) *Handbook of Restorative Justice,* 397-425 (Cullompton: Willan Publishing).

Bazemore, G. and O'Brien, S. (2002) 'The Quest for a Restorative Model of Rehabilitation: Theory-for-Practice and Practice-for-Theory' in Walgrave, L., (ed.), *Restorative Justice and the Law,* 31-67 (Cullompton: Willan Publishing).

Bazemore, G. and Schiff, M. (2005) *Juvenile Justice Reform and Restorative Justice. Building Theory and Policy from Practice* (Cullompton: Willan Publishing).

Bazemore, G. and Walgrave, L. (1999a) (eds) *Restorative Justice: Repairing the Harm of Youth Crime,* (Monsey, NY: Criminal Justice Press).

Bazemore, G. and Walgrave, L. (1999b) 'Restorative Juvenile Justice: In Search of Fundamentals and Outline for Systematic Reform' in Bazemore, G. and Walgrave, L. (ed.) *Restorative Justice: Repairing the Harm of Youth Crime,* 45-74 (Monsey, NY: Criminal Justice Press).

Bianchi, H. (1994) *Justice as Sanctuary: Toward A New System of Crime Control.* (Bloomington: Indiana University Press).

Bianchi, H. and van Swaaningen, R. (1986) *Abolitionism: Towards a Non-repressive Approach to Crime* (Amsterdam: Free University Press).

Blagg, H. (1985) 'Reparation and Justice for Juveniles' *British Journal of Criminology,* 25, 267-79.

Blagg, H. (1997) 'A Just Measure of Shame? Aboriginal Youth and Conferencing in Australia', *British Journal of Criminology*, 37, 481-501.

Blagg, H. (2001) 'Aboriginal Youth and Restorative Justice: Critical Notes from the Australian Frontier', in Morris, A. and Maxwell, G. (eds) *Restorative Justice for Juveniles: Conferencing, Mediation and Circles*, 227-242 (Oxford – Portland Oregon: Hart Publishing).

Bottoms, A. (2003) 'Some Sociological Reflections on Restorative Justice' in Von Hirsch, A., Roberts, J. V., Bottoms, A., Roach, K. and Shiff, M. (eds.) *Restorative Justice: Competing or Reconcilable Paradigms?*, 79-113 (Oxford and Portland, Oregon: Hart Publishing).

Bowen, H. and Thompson, T. (1999) 'Restorative Justice and the New Zealand Court of Appeal's Decision in the *Clotworthy* Case', *Journal of South Pacific Law*, 3, available at http://www.vanuatu.usp.ac.fj/journal_splaw/articles/Bowen1.htm

Braithwaite, J. (1989) *Crime, Shame and Reintegration* (Cambridge: Cambridge University Press).

Braithwaite, J. (1998) 'Linking Crime Prevention to Restorative Justice', paper presented at the First North American Conference on Conferencing, Minneapolis, Minnesota, August 6-8, 1998. http://www.iirp.org/library/nacc/nacc_bra.html.

Braithwaite, J. (2000) 'Decomposing a Holistic Vision of Restorative Justice', *Contemporary Justice Review,* 3, 433-440.

Braithwaite, J. (2002a) *Restorative Justice and Responsive Regulation* (Oxford: Oxford University Press).

Braithwaite, J. (2002b) 'In Search of Restorative Jurisprudence' in Walgrave, L. (ed.) *Restorative Justice and the Law*, 150-167 (Cullompton: Willan Publishing).

Braithwaite, J. (2002c) 'Setting Standards for Restorative Justice', *British Journal of Criminology,* 42, 563-577.

Braithwaite, J. (2003a) 'Restorative Justice and a Better Future' in Johnstone, G. (ed.) *A Restorative Justice Reader*, 83-97 (Cullompton: Willan Publishing).

Braithwaite, J. (2003b) 'Principles of Restorative Justice' in Von Hirsch, A., Roberts, J. V., Bottoms, A., Roach, K. and Shiff, M. (eds) *Restorative Justice: Competing or Reconcilable Paradigms?*, 1-20 (Oxford and Portland, Oregon: Hart Publishing).

Braithwaite, J. and Mugford, S. (1994) 'Conditions of Successful Reintegration Ceremonies', *British Journal of Criminology,* 34, 139-171.

Braithwaite, J. and Pettit, P. (1990) *Not Just Deserts: A Republican Theory of Criminal Justice* (Oxford: Oxford University Press).

Braithwaite, J. and Strang, H. (2000) 'Connecting Philosophy and Practice' in Strang, H. and Braithwaite, J. (eds), 203-20 (Burlington, Vermont, US: Ashgate).

Brookes, D. (1998) 'Evaluating Restorative Justice Programs', *Humanity and Society,* 22, 23-37.

Bush, R. and Folger, J. (2005) *The Promise of Mediation: The Transformative Approach to Conflict* (revised edition) (San Francisco: Jossey-Bass Publishers).

Cameron, L. and Thorsborne, M. (2001) 'Restorative Justice and School Discipline: Mutually Exclusive?' in Strang, H. and Braithwaite, J. *Restorative Justice and Civil Society*, 180-194 (Cambridge: Cambridge University Press).

Cayley, D. (1998) *The Expanding Prison: The Crisis in Crime and Punishment and the Search for Alternatives* (Cleveland, OH: Pilgrim Press).

Christie, N. (1977) 'Conflicts as a Property', *British Journal of Criminology,* 17, 1-15.

Christie, N. (1982) *Limits to Pain* (Oxford: Martin Robertson).

Christie, N. (2004) *A Suitable Amount of Crime* (London: Routledge).

Chupp, M. (1989) 'Reconciliation Procedures and Rationale' in Wright, M. and Galaway, B. (eds) *Mediation and Criminal Justice. Victims, Offenders and Community*, 56-68 (London/Newbury Park/New Dehli: Sage Publications).

Claassen, R. (1996) *The Fundamental Principles of Restorative Justice.* http://www.fresno.edu/pacs/rjprinc.html Also reprinted in McCold, P. (2000) 'Toward a Holistic Vision of Restorative Juvenile Justice: A Reply to the Maximalist Model', *Contemporary Justice Review,* 3, 357-414.

Claes, M. (1998) 'The Juvenile Mediation Project in Leuven (Belgium)' in Walgrve, L. (ed.) *Restorative Justice for Juveniles. Potentialities, Risks and Problems,* 367-385 (Leuven: Leuven University Press).

Coates, R.B. and Gehm, J. (1989) 'An Empirical Assessment' in Wright, M. and Galaway, B. (eds) *Mediation and Criminal Justice* (London: Sage).

Consedine, J. (1999) *Restorative Justice: Healing the Effects of Crime* (revised edition) (Lyttelton, New Zealand: Ploughshares Publications).

Council of Europe (1999) *Recommendation N R (99) 19 of the Committee of Ministers to Member States Concerning Mediation in Penal Matters.* http://www.restorativejustice.org/rj3/Government%20Reports/mediationEurope.html

Crawford, A. (2002) 'The State, Community and Restorative Justice: Heresy, Nostalgia and Butterfly Collecting' in Walgrave, L. (ed.) *Restorative Justice and the Law*, 101-129 (Cullompton: Willan Publishing).

Crawford, A. (2006) 'Institutionalizing restorative youth justice in a cold, punitive climate' in Aertsen, I., Daems, T. and Robert, L. (eds) *Institutionalizing Restorative Justice,* 120-150 (Cullompton: Willan Publishing).

Crawford, A. and Newburn, T. (2002) 'Recent Developments in Restorative Justice for Young People in England and Wales. Community Participation and Representation', *British Journal of Criminology*, 42, 476-495.

Crawford, A. and Newburn, T. (2003) *Youth Offending and Restorative Justice: Implementing reform in youth justice* (Cullompton: Willan Publishing).

Cullen, F. and Gilbert K. (1982) *Reaffirming Rehabilitation* (Cincinnati: Anderson).

Cunneen, C. (2003) 'Thinking Critically about Restorative Justice' in McLaughlin E., Fergusson, R., Huges, G. and Westmarland, L. *Restorative Justice: Critical Issues,* 182-194 (London/Thousand Oaks/New Delhi: Sage Publications).

Cunneen, C. (2007) 'Reviving Restorative Justice Traditions' in justice' in Johnstone, G. and Van Ness, D. (eds) *Handbook of Restorative Justice,* 113-131 (Cullompton: Willan Publishing).

Daly, K. (2000) 'Revisiting the Relationship between Retributive and Restorative Justice' in Strang H., and Braithwaite, J. (ed.) *Restorative Justice: Philosophy to Practice*, 33-54 (Ashgate/Dartmouth: Aldershot).

Daly, K. (2001) 'Conferencing in Australia and New Zealand: Variations, Research Findings and Prospects' in Morris, A. and Maxwell, G. (eds.) *Restorative Justice for Juveniles: Conferencing, Mediation and Circles*, 59-83 (Oxford-Portland Oregon: Hart Publishing).

Daly, K. (2002) 'Restorative Justice: The Real Story', *Punishment and Society,* 4, 55-79.

Daly, K. (2006) 'The limits of restorative justice' in Sullivan, D. and Tifft, L. (eds) *Handbook of Restorative Justice,* 134-145. (London and New York: Routledge).

Daly, K. and Immarigeon, R. (1998) 'The past, present, and future of restorative justice: some critical reflections, *Contemporary Justice Review,* 1, 21-5.

Daly, K. and Stubbs, J. (2007) 'Feminist theory, feminism and anti-racist politics, and restorative justice' in Johnstone, G. and Van Ness, D. (eds) *Handbook of Restorative Justice,* 149-170 (Cullompton: Willan Publishing).

Davis, G., Boucherat, J. and Watson, D. (1988) 'Reparation in the Service of Diversion: The Subordination of a Good Idea', *Howard Journal of Criminal Justice,* 27, 127-62.

Declaration of Leven (1997) http://www.sonoma.edu/cja/info/leuven.html. Also in Bazemore, G. and Walgrave, L. (eds) (1999) *Restorative Justice: Repairing the Harm of Youth Crime,* 403-407 (Monsey, NY: Criminal Justice Press).

Dignan, J. (1992) 'Reparing the Damage: Cam Reparation be Made to Work in the Service of Diversion?' *British Journal of Criminology,* 32, 453-72.

Dignan, J. (1999) 'The Crime and Disorder Act and the Prospects for Restorative Justice', *Criminal Law Review,* 48-60.

Dignan, J. (2002) 'Restorative Justice and the Law: the Case for an Integrated, Systemic Approach' in Walgrave, L. (ed.) *Restorative Justice and the Law*, 168-190 (Cullompton: Willan Publishing).

Dignan, J. (2003) 'Towards a Systemic Model of Restorative Justice' in Von Hirsch, A., Roberts, J. V., Bottoms, A., Roach, K. and Shiff, M. (eds.) *Restorative Justice: Competing or Reconcilable Paradigms?,* 135-156. (Oxford and Portland, Oregon: Hart Publishing).

Dignan, J. (2005) *Understanding Victims and Restorative Justice.* (Berkshire: Open University Press).

Dignan, J. and Lowey, K. (2000) *Restorative Justice Options for Northern Ireland: a Comparative Review.* Review of Criminal Justice in Northern Ireland Research Paper 10 (The Stationery Office, Belfast).

Dignan, J. and Marsh, P. (2001) 'Restorative Justice and Family Group Conferences in England: Current State and Future Prospects' in Morris, A. and Maxwell, G.

(eds.) *Restorative Justice for Juveniles: Conferencing, Mediation and Circles*, 85-101 (Oxford-Portland Oregon: Hart Publishing).

Duff, R.A. (1992) 'Alternatives to Punishment – or Alternative Punishments?' in Cragg, W. (ed.) *Retributivism and its Critics*, 44-68. (Stuttgart: Franz Steiner).

Duff, R.A. (1999a) 'Punishment, Communication, and Community' in Matravers, M., (ed.) *Punishment and Political Theory,* 27-43 (Oxford: Hart Publishing).

Duff, R.A. (1999b) 'Penal Communities', *Punishment and Society.* 1, 27-43.

Duff, R.A. (2002) 'Restorative Punishment and Punitive Restoration' in Walgrave, L. (ed.) *Restorative Justice and the Law*, 82-100 (Cullompton: Willan Publishing).

Duff, R.A. (2003) 'Restoration and Retribution' in Von Hirsch, A., Roberts, J. V., Bottoms, A., Roach, K. and Schiff, M. (eds) *Restorative Justice: Competing or Reconcilable Paradigms?*, 43-59 (Oxford and Portland, Oregon: Hart Publishing).

Dyck, D. (2000) 'Reaching Toward a Structurally Responsive Training and Practice of Restorative Justice', *Contemporary Justice Review,* 3, 239-265.

Dyck, D. (2006) 'Reaching toward a structurally responsive training and practice of restorative justice' in Sullivan, D. and Tifft, L. (eds) *Handbook of Restorative Justice,* 527-45 (London and New York: Routledge).

Elliott, E. and Gordon, R. (2005) *New Directions in Restorative Justice: Issues, practice, evaluation* (Cullompton: Willan Publishing).

European Forum for Victim-Offender Mediation and Restorative Justice (ed.) (2000) *VOM in Europe. Making Restorative Justice Work* (Leuven: Leuven University Press).

Foucault, M. (1977) *Discipline and Punish: The Birth of the Prison* (New York: Vintage Books).

Foucault, M. (1978) *The History of Sexuality, vol. 1: An Introduction* (New York: Pantheon Books).

Foucault, M. (1980) *Power/Knowledge: Selected Interviews and Other Writings (1972-1977)* (Brighton: Harvester Press).

Foucault, M. (1981) 'Omnes et Singulatim: Towards a Criticism of 'Political Reason'' in S. McMurrin (ed.) *The Tanner Lectures on Human Values*.(New York: Cambridge University Press).

Froestad, J. and Shearing, C. (2007) 'Conflict resolution in South Africa' in Johnstone, G. and Van Ness, D. (eds) *Handbook of Restorative Justice,* 534-55 (Cullompton: Willan Publishing).

Galaway, B. and Hudson, J. (1996) (eds.) *Restorative Justice: International Perspectives* (Monsey, NY: Criminal Justice Press).

Green, S. (2007) "The victims' movement and restorative justice' in Johnstone, G. and Van Ness, D. (eds) *Handbook of Restorative Justice,* 171-91 (Cullompton: Willan Publishing).

Griffiths, C.T. and Hamilton, R. (1996) 'Sanctioning and Healing: Restorative Justice in Canadian Aboriginal Communities' in Galaway, B. and Hudson, J. (ed.) *Restorative Justice: International Perspectives,* 175-191 (Monsey, NY: Criminal Justice Press).

Hadley, M. L. (2001) *Spiritual roots of Restorative Justice* (Albany, NY: State University of New York Press).

Hadley, M.L. (2006) 'Spiritual Foundations of Restorative Justice' in Sullivan, D. and Tifft, L. (eds) *Handbook of Restorative Justice,* 174-187 (London and New York: Routledge).

Harris, M. K. (1989) 'Alternative Visions in the Context of Contemporary Realities' in *Justice: The Restorative Vision.* (New Perspectives on Crime and Justice. Occasional Papers of the MCC Canada Victim Offender Ministries Program and the MCC U.S. Office on Crime and Justice), 7, 29-38.

Harris, M. K. (1991) 'Moving Into the New Millenium: Toward a Feminist Vision of Justice' in Pepinsky, H.E. and Quinney, R. (eds) *Criminology as Peacemaking,* 83-97 (Bloomington: Indiana University Press).

Harris, M.K. (1998), quoted in McCold, P. (1998) 'Restorative Justice: Variations on a Theme', in Walgrave, L. (ed.) *Restorative Justice for Juveniles: Potentialities, Risks and Problems for Research,* 19-53, 20 (Leuven: Leuven University Press), at 43-44.

Hayes, H. (2007) 'Reoffending and restorative justice' in Johnstone, G. and Van Ness, D. (eds) *Handbook of Restorative Justice,* 426-46 (Cullompton: Willan Publishing).

Hampton, J. (1984) 'The Moral Education Theory of Punishment', *Philosophy and Public Affairs*, 13, 208-38.

Holdaway, S., Davidson, N., Dignan, J. et al (2001) *New Strategies to Address Youth Offending: The National Evaluation of the Pilot Youth Offending Teams.* R D S Occasional Paper No 69 (London: Home Office). http://www.homeoffice.gov.uk/rds/index.html.

Hoyle, C., Young, R. and Hill, R. (2002) *Proceed with Caution: And Evaluation of the Thames Valley Police Initiative in Restorative Cautioning* (York: Joseph Rowntree Foundation).

Hulsman, L. (1986) 'Critical Criminology and the Concept of Crime', *Contemporary Crises,* 10, 63-80.

Johnstone, G. (1996a) *Medical Concepts and Penal Policy* (London: Cavendish).

Johnstone, G. (1996b) 'Towards a Revised Image of the Therapeutic Approach to Offenders', *Law and Critique,* 7, 193-216.

Johnstone, G. (2002) *Restorative Justice. Ideas, Values, Debates* (Cullompton: Willan Publishing).

Johnstone, G. (ed.) (2003) *A Restorative Justice Reader* (Cullompton: Willan Publishing).

Johnstone, G. (2004) 'How, and in What Terms, Should Restorative Justice Be Conceived?', in H. Zehr and B. Toews (eds) *Critical Issues in Restorative Justice,* 5-15 (Monsey, New York: Criminal Justice Press and Cullompton, Devon: Willan Publishing).

Johnstone, G. (2007) 'Critical perspectives on restorative justice' in Johnstone, G. and Van Ness, D. (eds) *Handbook of Restorative Justice,* 598-614 (Cullompton: Willan Publishing).

Johnstone, G. and Van Ness, D. (eds) (2007a) *Handbook of Restorative Justice,* (Cullompton: Willan Publishing).

Johnstone, G. and Van Ness, D. (2007b) 'The meaning of restorative justice' in Johnstone, G. and Van Ness, D. (eds) *Handbook of Restorative Justice,* 5-23. (Cullompton: Willan Publishing).

Karp, D. and Walther, L. (2001) 'Community Reparative Boards in Vermont' in Bazemore, G. and Shiff, M. (eds) *Restorative Community Justice: Repairing Harm and Transforming Communities,* 199-217. (Cincinnati, OH: Anderson Publishing Co).

Levrant, S., Cullen, F.T., Fulton, B., Wozniak, J.F. (1999) 'Reconsidering Restorative Justice: the Corruption of Benevolence Revisited', *Crime and Delinquency,* 45, 3-27.

Marshall, T. (1995) 'Restorative Justice on Trial in Britain' *Mediation Quarterly,* 12, 217-231.

Marshall, T. (1996) 'Evolution of Restorative Justice in Britain', *European Journal on Criminal Policy and Research,* 4, 21-43.

Marshall, T. (1998), quoted in McCold, P. (1998) 'Restorative Justice: Variations on a Theme', in Walgrave, L. (ed.) *Restorative Justice for Juveniles: Potentialities, Risks and Problems for Research* 19-53, 20 (Leuven: Leuven University Press).

Marshall, T.F. and Merry, S.E. (1990) *Crime and Accountability – Victim/Offender Mediation in Practice* (London: Home Office, Her Majesty's Stationery Office).

Martinson, R. (1974) 'What Works? Questions and Answers about Prison Reform', *Public Interest,* 35, 22-54.

Mason, A. (2000) 'Restorative Justice: Courts and Civil Society' in Strang, H. and Braithwaite, J. (eds) *Restorative Justice. Philosophy to Practice* (Darmouth: Ashgate).

Mathiesen, T. (1974) *The Politics of Abolition* (London: Martin Robertson).

Matthews, R. (1988) *Informal Justice?* (London: Sage.

Maxwell, G. and Morris, A. (1993) *Families, Victims and Culture: Youth Justice in New Zealand* (Social Policy Agency and Institute of Criminology, Victoria University of Wellington, Wellington).

Maxwell, G. and Morris, A. (1994) 'The New Zealand Model of Family Group Conferences' in Alder, D. and Wundersitz, J. (eds) *Family Group Conferencing and Juvenile Justice: the Way Forward of Misplaced Optimism?,* 15-36 (Canberra: Australian Institute of Criminology).

Maxwell, G. and Morris, A. (1996) 'Research on Family Group Conferences with Young Offenders in New Zealand' in Hudson, J., Morris, A., Maxwell, G. and Galaway B. (eds.) *Family Group Conferences: Perspectives on Policy and Practice,* 88-110. (Monsey, NY: Criminal Justice Press).

Maxwell, G. and Morris, A. (2000) 'Restorative Justice and Reoffending' in Strang, H. and Braithwaite, J. (eds) *Restorative Justice. Philosophy to Practice,* 93-103. (Dartmouth: Ashgate).

McCold, P. (1996) 'Restorative Justice and the Role of Community' in Galaway, B. and Hudson, J. (eds.) *Restorative Justice: International Perspectives,* 84-101. (Monsey, NY: Criminal Justice Press).

McCold, P. (1998) 'Restorative Justice: Variations on a Theme', in Walgrave, L. (ed.) *Restorative Justice for Juveniles: Potentialities, Risks and Problems for Research,* 19-53 (Leuven: Leuven University Press).

McCold, P. (2000) 'Toward a Holistic Vision of Restorative Juvenile Justice: A Reply to the Maximalist Model', *Contemporary Justice Review,* 3, 357-414.

McCold, P. (2004) 'Paradigm Muddle: The Threat to Restorative Justice Posed by Its Merger with Community Justice', *Contemporary Justice Review,* 7, 1-12.

McCold, P. and Stahr, J. (1996) 'Bethlehem Police Family Group Conferencing Project' (paper presented to the American Society of Criminology, Chicago, 20-23 November 1996. http://www.restorativepractices.org/Pages/bethlehem.html.

McCold, P. and Wachtel, B. (1998) *Restorative Policing Experiment: The Bethlehem Pennsylvania Police Family Group Conferencing Project* (Piperville, Pennsylvania: Community Service Foundation).

McCold, P. and Wachtel, B. (2003) 'Community is not a place: a new look at community justice initiatives' in Johnstone, G. (ed.) (2003) *A Restorative Justice Reader,* 294-302 (Cullompton: Willan Publishing).

McEvoy, K. and Mika, H. (2001) 'Policing, Punishment and Praxis: Restorative Justice and Non-Violent Alternatives to Paramilitary Punishments in Northern Ireland', *Policing and Society,* 11, 359-82.

McEvoy, K. and Mika, H. (2002) 'Restorative Justice and the Critique of Informalism in Northern Ireland', *British Journal of Criminology.* 42, 534-562.

Messmer, H. and Otto H.-U. (1992) (eds) *Restorative Justice on Trial. Pitfalls and Potentials of Victim-Offender Mediation – International Research Perspectives* (Dordrecht, The Netherlands: Kluwer Academic Publications).

Miers, D. (2001) *An International Review of Restorative Justice.* Crime Reduction Research Paper 10 (Lonhdon: Home Office, Policing and Reducing Crime Unit Research, Development and Statistics Directorate).

Miers, D. et al (2001) *An Exploratory Evaluation of Restorative justice Schemes.* Crime Reduction Research Paper 9 (London: Home Office, Policing and Reducing Crime Unit Research, Development and Statistics Directorate).

Mika, H. (1992) 'Mediation Interventions and Restorative Justice: Responding to the Astructural Bias' in and Otto (eds) *Restorative justice on Trial. Pitfalls and Potentials of Victim Offender Mediation – International Research Perspectives* (Dordrecht, The Netherlands: Kluwer Academic Publications), 559-567.

Mika, H. and Zehr, H. (2003) 'A Restorative Framework for Community Justice Practice' in McEvoy, K. and Newburn, , T. (eds) *Criminology, Conflict Resolution and Restorative Justice* (NewYork: Palgrave MacMillan).

Moore, D.B. (1993) 'Shame, Forgiveness and Juvenile Justice', *Criminal Justice Ethics,* 12, 3-25.

Moore, D. B. and O'Connell, T. (1994) 'Family Conferencing in Wagga Wagga: A Communitarian Model of Justice', in Alder, C. and Wundersitz, J. (eds) *Family Conferencing and Juvenile Justice: The Way Forward or Misplaced Optimism* (Canberra: Australian Institute of Criminology), 45-86.

Morris, A. (2002) 'Critiquing Critics. A Brief Response to Critics of Restorative Justice', *British Journal of Criminology.* 42, 596-615.

Morris, A. and Maxwell, G. (2000) 'The Practice of Family Group Conferences in New Zealand: Assessing the Place, Potential and Pitfalls of Restorative Justice' in Crawford, A. and Goodey ,J. (eds) *Integrating a Victim Perspective Within Criminal Justice. International Debates,* 207-225 (Aldershot: Ashgate).

Morris, A. and Maxwell, G. (2001) (eds.) *Restorative Justice for Juveniles: Conferencing, Mediation and Circles* (Oxford – Portland Oregon: Hart Publishing)

Morris, A. and Maxwell, G. (2003) 'Restorative Justice in New Zealand' in Von Hirsch, A., Roberts, J.V., Bottoms, A., Roach, K, and Schiff, M. (2003) *Restorative Justice and Criminal Justice. Competing or Reconcilable Paradigms?*, 257-271. (Oxford and Portland, Oregon: Hart Publishing).

Morris, A. and Young, W. (2000) 'Reforming Criminal Justice: The Potential of Restorative Justice' in Strang, H. and Braithwaite, J. (eds) *Restorative Justice. Philosophy to Practice,* 11-31. (Dartmouth: Ashgate).

Morris, H. (1984) 'A Paternalistic Theory of Punishment', *American Philosophical Quarterly*, 18, 263-71.

Morris, R. (1995) 'Not Enough!' *Mediation Quarterly,* 12, 285-291.

Morris, R. (2000) *Stories of Transformative Justice* (Toronto: Canadian Scholars' Press).

Morrison, B. (2001) 'The School System: Developing its Capacity in the Regulation of a Civil Society' in in Strang, H. and Braithwaite, J. *Restorative Justice and Civil Society,* 195-210 (Cambridge: Cambridge University Press).

Morrison, B. (2007) 'Schools and restorative justice' in Johnstone, G. and Van Ness, D. (eds) *Handbook of Restorative Justice,* 225-350 (Cullompton: Willan Publishing).

Nielsen, M. O. (1996) 'A Comparison of Developmental Ideologies: Navajo Peacemaker Courts and Canadian Native Justice Committees' in Galaway, B. and Hudson, J. (eds.) *Restorative Justice: International Perspectives,* 207-223 (Monsey, NY: Criminal Justice Press).

Olson, S.M. and Dzur, A.W. (2003) 'Reconstructing Professional Roles in Restorative justice Programs' in *Utah Law Review,* 1, 57-89.

Olson, S. M. and Dzur, A.W. (2004) 'Revisiting Informal Justice: Restorative Justice and Democratic Professionalism', *Law and Society Review,* 38, 139-176.

O'Connell, T. (1998) 'From Wagga Wagga to Minnesota', paper presented at the First North American Conference on Conferencing, 6-8 August, 1998, Minneapolis, Minnesota. Available at http://www.restorativepractices.org/Pages/nacc_oco.html.

O'Mahony, D. and Doak, J. (2006) 'The Enigma of 'Community' and the Exigency of Engagement: Restorative Youth Conferencing in Northern Ireland', *British Journal of Community Justice,* 4, 9-24.

Pavlich, G. (1996a) *Justice Fragmented: Mediating Community Disputes under Postmodern Conditions* (London: Routledge).

Pavlich, G. (1996b) 'The Power of Community Mediation: Government and Formation of Self', *Law and Society Review,* 30, 101-127.

Pavlich, G. (2001) 'The Force of Community' in Strang, H. and Braithwaite, J. (eds) *Restorative Justice and Civil Society,* 56-68 (Cambridge: Cambridge University Press).

Pavlich, G. (2002a) 'Deconstructing restoration: the promise of restorative justice' in Wetekamp E.G. M. and Kerner H.-J. (eds) 'Restorative Justice. Theoretical Foundations', 90-109 (Cullompton: Willan Publishing).

Pavlich, G. (2002b) 'Towards an ethics of restorative justice' in Walgrave, L. (ed.) *Restorative Justice and the Law,* 1-18 (Cullompton: Willan Publishing).

Pavlich, G. (2004) 'What are the Dangers as well as the Promises of Community Involvement' in Zehr, H. and Toews, B. (eds) *Critical Issues in Restorative Justice, 173-83* (Monsey, New York: Criminal Justice Press and Cullompton: Willan Publishing).

Pavlich, G. (2005) *Governing Paradoxes of Restorative Justice* (London/Sydney/ Portland, Oregon: Glasshouse Press).

Pavlich, G. (2007) 'Ethics, universal principles and restorative justice' in Johnstone, G. and Van Ness, D. (eds) *Handbook of Restorative Justice,* 615-630 (Cullompton: Willan Publishing).

Pelikan, C. and Trenczek, T. (2006) Victim offender mediation and Restorative Justice: the European landscape' in Sullivan, D. and Tifft, L. (eds) *Handbook of Restorative Justice,* 63-90 (London and New York: Routledge).

Pepinsky, H.E. and Quinney, R. (eds) (1991) *Criminology as Peacemaking* (Bloomington: Indiana University Press).

Pettit, P. (1997) *Republicanism.* (Oxford: Clarendon Press).

Pollard, C. (2001) 'If your only tool is a hammer, all your problems will look like nails', in Strang, H. and Braithwaite, J. *Restorative Justice and Civil Society,* 165-179 (Cambridge: Cambridge University Press).

Pratt, J. (1996) 'Colonization, Power and Silence: A History of Indigenous Justice in New Zealand Society' in Galaway, B. and Hudson, J. (eds) *Restorative Justice: International Perspectives,* 137-155 (Monsey, NY: Criminal Justice Press).

Pranis, K. (2007) 'Restorative values' in Johnstone, G. and Van Ness, D. (eds) *Handbook of Restorative Justice,* 59-73 (Cullompton: Willan Publishing).

Reeves, H. and Mulley, K. (2000) 'The New Status of Victims in the UK: Opportunities and Threats' in Crawford, A. and Goodey, J. (eds) *Integrating a Victim Perspective Within Criminal Justice. International Debates,* 125-145 *(*Aldershot: Ashgate/Dartmouth).

Reitan, E. (1996) 'Punishment and Community: the Reintegrative Theory of Punishment', *Canadian Journal and Philosophy,* 26, 57-82.

Restorative Justice Consortium (2002) *The Statement of Restorative Justice Principles.* Available at http://www.restorativejustice.org.uk/resources/principles.htm_Also reprinted in Johnstone, G. (ed.) (2003) *A Restorative Justice Reader,* 482-4 (Cullompton: Willan Publishing).

Retzinger, S.M. and Scheff, T.J. (1996) 'Strategy for Community Conferences: Emotions and Social Bonds, in Galaway, B. and Hudson, J. (eds) *Restorative Justice: International Perspectives,* 315-36 (Monsey, NY: Criminal Justice Press and Amsterdam, The Netherlands: Kugler Publications).

Roberts, J. V. and Roach, K. (2003) 'Restorative Justice in Canada From Sentencing Circles to Sentencing Principles' in Von Hirsch, A., Roberts, J. V., Bottoms, A., Roach, K. and Schiff, M. (eds.) *Restorative Justice: Competing or Reconcilable Paradigms?,* 237-256 (Oxford and Portland, Oregon: Hart Publishing).

Roche, D. (2002) 'Restorative Justice and the Regulatory State in South African Townships', *British Journal of Criminology.* 42, 514-533.

Roche, D. (2003) *Accountability in Restorative Justice* (Oxford: Oxford University Press).

Roche, D. (2007) 'Retribution and restorative justice' in Johnstone, G. and Van Ness, D. (eds) *Handbook of Restorative Justice,* 75-90 (Cullompton: Willan Publishing).

Ross, R. (2003) 'Returning to the Teachings' in Johnstone, G. (ed.) *A Restorative Justice Reader. Texts, sources, context,* 125-143 (Cullompton: Willan Publishing).

Rothman, D. (1980) *Conscience and Convenience: The Asylum and Its Alternatives in Progressive America* (Boston, MA: Little, Brown.

Sandor, D. (1994) 'The Thickening Blue Wedge in Juvenile Justice', in Alder, C. and Wundersitz, J. (eds) *Family Conferencing and Juvenile Justice: The Way Forward or Misplaced Optimism,* 153-166. (Canberra: Australian Institute of Criminology).

Sawin, J.L. and Zehr, H. (2007) 'The ideals of engagement and empowerment' in Johnstone, G. and Van Ness, D. (eds) *Handbook of Restorative Justice,* 41-58. (Cullompton: Willan Publishing).

Shapland, J. (2003) 'Restorative Justice and Criminal Justice: Just Responses to Crime?' in von Hirsch, A., Roberts, J. V., Bottoms, A., Roach, K. and Shiff, M. (eds) *Restorative Justice: Competing or Reconcilable Paradigms?,* 195-217. (Oxford and Portland, Oregon: Hart Publishing).

Shapland, J. et al (2006a) *Restorative Justice in Practice.* (The University of Sheffield: Centre for Criminological Research).

Shapland, J. et al (2006b) Situating restorative justice within criminal justice', *Theoretical Criminology,* 10, 505-32.

Shearing, C. (2001) 'Transforming Security: A South African Experiment' in Strang, H. and Braithwaite, J. (eds.) *Restorative Justice and Civil Society,* 14-34. (Cambridge: Cambridge University Press).

Sherman, L.W. and Strang, H. (2007) *Restorative Justice: the evidence* (London: The Smith Institute).

Strang, H. (2001) 'Justice for Victims of Young Offenders: The Centrality of Emotional Harm and Restoration', in Morris, A. and Maxwell, G. (eds.) *Restorative Justice for Juveniles: Conferencing, Mediation and Circles,* 183-193 (Oxford-Portland Oregon: Hart Publishing).

Strang, H. (2002) *Repair or Revenge* (Oxford: Clarendon Press).

Strang, H., Barnes, G.C., Braithwaite, J. and Sherman, L.W. (1999) *Experiments in Restorative Policing* (Canberra: ANU). http://www.aic.gov.au/rjustice/rise/progress/1999.html.

Stuart, B. (1996) 'Circle Sentencing: Turning Swords into Ploughshares', in Galaway, B. and Hudson, J. (eds.) *Restorative Justice: International Perspectives,* 193-206 (Monsey, NY: Criminal Justice Press).

Sullivan D. and Tifft, L. (1998) 'The Transformative and Economic Dimensions of Restorative Justice' *Humanity and Society,* 22, 38-54.

Sullivan D. and Tifft, L. (2000a) 'The Requirements of Just Community: An Introduction that Takes into Account the Political Economy of Relationship' *Contemporary Justice Review,* 3, 121-152.

Sullivan D. and Tifft, L. (2000b) *Restorative Justice as a Transformative Process: The Application of Restorative Justice Principles to Our Everyday Lives* (Voorheesville, NY: Mutual Aid Press).

Sullivan D. and Tifft, L. (2001) *Restorative Justice: Healing the Foundations of Our Everyday Lives* (Monsey, NY: Willow Tree Press).

Sullivan, D. and Tifft, L. (2004) 'What Are The Implications Of Restorative Justice For Society And Our Lives?' in Zehr, H. and Toews, B. (eds) *Critical Issues in Restorative Justice,* 387-395 (Monsey, New York: Criminal Justice Press and Cullompton: Willan Publishing).

Sullivan, D. and Tifft, L. (2006) 'Introduction: The healing dimension of restorative justice: a one-world body' in Sullivan, D. and Tifft, L. (eds) *Handbook of Restorative Justice,* 1-16 (London and New York: Routledge).

Taraschi S.G. (1998) 'Peacemaking Criminology and Aboriginal Justice Initiatives as a Revitalization of Justice', *Contemporary Justice Review,* 1, 103-121.

Tavuchis, N. (1991) *Mea Culpa: A Sociology of Apology and Reconciliation* (Stanford University Press, Stanford, California).

Toews, B. and Zehr, H. (2003) 'Ways of knowing for a restorative worldview' in Weitekamp, E.G.M. and Hans-Jürgen Kerner (eds) *Restorative Justice in Context,* 257-71. (Cullompton: Willan Publishing).

Toews, B. and Zehr, H. (2004) 'Preface. Opening the Dialogue' in Zehr, H. and Toews, B. (eds) *Critical Issues in Restorative Justice,* vii-xi (Monsey, New York: Criminal Justice Press and Cullompton: Willan Publishing).

Umbreit, M. (1989) 'Violent Offenders and Their Victims' in Wright, M. and Galaway, B. (eds) *Mediation and Criminal Justice. Victims, Offenders and Community,* 99-112 (London/Newbury Park/New Dehli – Sage Publications).

Umbreit, M. (1994) *Victim Meets Offender The Impact of Restorative Justice and Mediation* (Monsey, NY: Criminal Justice Press).

Umbreit, M. (1996) 'Restorative Justice Through Mediation: the Impact of Programs in Four Canadian Provinces' in Galaway, B. and Hudson, J. (eds.) *Restorative Justice: International Perspectives,* 373-385 (Monsey, NY: Criminal Justice Press).

Umbreit, M. (1999) 'Avoiding the Marginalization and 'McDonalization' of Victim-Offender Mediation: A Case Study in Moving Toward the Mainstream' in Bazemore, G. and Walgrave, L. (eds.) *Restorative Justice: Repairing the Harm of Youth Crime,* 213-234 (Monsey, NY: Criminal Justice Press).

Umbreit, M. (2001) *The Handbook of Victim Offender Mediation: An Essential Guide to Practice and Research* (San Francisco: Jossey-Bass).

Umbreit, M.S. and Coates, R.B. (1993) 'Cross-Site Analysis of Victim Offender Mediation in Four States', *Crime and Delinquency,* 39, 565-85.

Umbreit, M.S., Coates, R.B., Vos, B. (2001) 'Victim Impact of Meeting with Young Offenders: Two Decades of Offender Mediation Practice and Research' in Morris, A. and Maxwell, G. (eds.) *Restorative Justice for Juveniles: Conferencing, Mediation and Circles,* 112-143 (Oxford-Portland Oregon: Hart Publishing).

Umbreit, M.S., Coates, R.B., Vos, B. (2006) Victim offender mediation: an evolving evidence-based practice' in Sullivan, D. and Tifft, L. (eds) *Handbook of Restorative Justice,* 52-62 (London and New York: Routledge).

United Nations, the Economic and Social Council (2000) *Basic Principles on the Use of Restorative Justice Programs in Criminal Matters.* Available at http://www.restorativejustice.org/rj3/UNBasicPrinciples/VanNessarticle.htm. Also reprinted in Johnstone, G. (ed.) (2003) *A Restorative Justice Reader,* 485-488. (Cullompton: Willan Publishing).

Van Ness, D. (1989) 'Pursuing a Restorative Vision of Justice' in *Justice: The Restorative Vision.* (New Perspectives on Crime and Justice. Occasional Papers of the MCC Canada Victim Offender Ministries Program and the MCC U.S. Office on Crime and Justice), 7, 11-27.

Van Ness, D. (1993) 'New Wine and Old Wineskins: Four Challenges of Restorative Justice', *Criminal Law Forum,* 4, 251-76.

Van Ness D., and Strong K.H. (2006) *Restoring Justice. An Introduction to Restorative Justice.* (3rd ed.) (Cincinnati, OH: Anderson Publishing Co).

Von Hirsch, A., Ashworth, A., Shearing, C. (2003) 'Specifying Aims and Limits for Restorative Justice: A 'Making Amends' Model?' in von Hirsch, A., Roberts, J. V., Bottoms, A., Roach, K. and Schiff, M. (eds) *Restorative Justice: Competing or Reconcilable Paradigms?,* 21-41 (Oxford and Portland, Oregon: Hart Publishing).

Von Hirsch, A., Roberts, J. V., Bottoms, A., Roach, K. and Schiff, M. (eds) (2003) *Restorative Justice: Competing or Reconcilable Paradigms?* (Oxford and Portland, Oregon: Hart Publishing).

Walgrave, L. (1995) 'Restorative Justice for Juveniles: Just a Technique or a Fully Fledged Alternative?' *The Howard Journal*, 34, 228-249.

Walgrave, L. (1998) (ed.) *Restorative Justice for Juveniles: Potentialities, Risks and Problems for Research.* (Leuven: Leuven University Press).

Walgrave, L. (1999) 'Community Service as a Cornerstone of a Systematic Restorative Response to (Juvenile) Crime' in Bazemore, G. and Walgrave, L. (eds) *Restorative Justice: Repairing the Harm of Youth Crime,* 129-154. (Monsey, NY: Criminal Justice Press).

Walgrave, L. (2000a) 'How Pure Can a Maximalist Approach to Restorative Justice Remain? Or Can a Purist Model of Restorative Justice Become Maximalist? *Contemporary Justice Review,* 3, 415-432.

Walgrave, L. (2000b) 'Extending the Victim Perspective Towards a Systemic Restorative Justice Alternative' in Crawford, A. and Goodey, J. (eds) *Integrating a Victim Perspective Within Criminal Justice. International Debates,* 253-284. (Aldershot: Ashgate/Dartmouth).

Walgrave, L. (2001) 'On Restoration and Punishment: Favourable Similarities and Fortunate Differences', in Morris, A. and Maxwell, G. (eds.) *Restorative Justice for Juveniles: Conferencing, Mediation and Circles,* 17-37. (Oxford – Portland Oregon: Hart Publishing).

Walgrave, L. (2002) 'Restorative Justice and the Law: Socio-Ethical and judicial Foundations for a Systemic Approach' in Walgrave, L. (ed.) *Restorative Justice and the Law* (Cullompton: Willan Publishing), 191-218.

Walgrave, L. (2003) 'Imposing Restoration Instead of Inflicting Pain' in von Hirsch, A., Roberts, J. V., Bottoms, A., Roach, K. and Schiff, M. (eds.) *Restorative*

Justice: Competing or Reconcilable Paradigms?, 61-78. (Oxford and Portland, Oregon: Hart Publishing).

Walgrave, L. (2007) 'Integrating criminal justice and restorative justice' in Johnstone, G. and Van Ness, D. (eds) *Handbook of Restorative Justice*, 559-79. (Cullompton: Willan Publishing).

Warner, K. (1994) 'Family Group Conferences and the Rights of the Offender', in Alder, C. and Wundersitz, J. (eds) *Family Conferencing and Juvenile Justice: The Way Forward or Misplaced Optimism*, 141-152. (Canberra: Australian Institute of Criminology).

Weitekamp, E.G.M. (2003) 'The History of Restorative Justice' in Johnstone, G. (ed.) *A Restorative Justice Reader. Texts, sources, context*, 111-124. (Cullompton: Willan Publishing).

Wilcox, A., Hoyle, C. and Young, R. (2005) 'Are randomised controlled trials really the 'gold standard' in restorative justice research?' *British Journal of Community Justice*, 3, 39-49.

Williams, B. (2005) *Victims of Crime and Community Justice*. (London and Philadelphia: Jessica Kindsley Publishers).

Wonshé (2004) 'How Does the 'Who, What, Where and How' Affect the Practice of Restorative Justice?' in H. Zehr and B. Toews (eds) *Critical Issues in Restorative Justice*, 253-63. (Monsey, New York: Criminal Justice Press and Cullompton, Devon: Willan Publishing).

Wright, M. (1996) *Justice for Victims and Offenders: A Restorative Response to Crime*. (2nd ed.) (Winchester: Waterside Press).

Wright, M. (1999) *Restoring Respect for Justice*. (Winchester: Waterside Press).

Wright, M. (2003) 'Is it time to question the concept of punishment?' in Walgrave, L. (ed.) *Repositioning Restorative Justice*, 3-23 (Cullompton: Willan Publishing).

Wright, M. (2004) 'The Rights and Needs of Victims in the Criminal Justice Process' in Kaptein, H. and Malsch, M. (eds) *Crime, Victims and Justice: essays on principles and practice* (Aldershot: Ashgate).

Wright, M. (2006) 'Punishment and restorative justice: an ethical comparison', paper presented to Working Group 3, Theoretical Research of COST A21 conference 22-24 November 2006 at Wizsza Szkola Zarzadzania, Warsaw.

Wright, M. and Galaway, B. (1989) (eds) *Mediation and Criminal Justice: Victims, Offenders and Community* (London: Sage Publications).

Wynne, J. (1996) 'Leeds Mediation and Reparation Service: Ten Years' Experience with Victim-Offender Mediation' in Galaway, B. and Hudson, J. (ed.) *Restorative Justice: International Perspectives*, 445-461 (Monsey, NY: Criminal Justice Press).

Yazzie, R. (1998) 'Navajo Peacemaking: Implications for Adjudication-Based Systems of Justice', *Criminal Justice Review*, 1, 123-131.

Yazzie, R. and Zion, J.W. (1996) 'Navajo Restorative Justice: The Law of Equality and Justice' in Galaway, B. and Hudson, J. (ed.) *Restorative Justice: International Perspectives*, 157-173. (Monsey, NY: Criminal Justice Press).

Young, R. (2001) 'Just Cops Doing 'Shameful' Business? Police-led Restorative Justice and the Lessons of Research' in Morris, A. and Maxwell, G. (eds.)

Restorative Justice for Juveniles: Conferencing, Mediation and Circles, 195-226.

Young, R. and Goold, B. (1999) 'Restorative Police Cautioning in Aylesbury – From Degrading to Reintegrative Shaming Ceremonies?', *Criminal Law Review*, 126-38.

Young, R. and Hoyle, C. (2003) 'New, Improved Police-Led Restorative Justice?' in Von Hirsch, A., Roberts, J. V., Bottoms, A., Roach, K. and Schiff, M. (eds.) *Restorative Justice: Competing or Reconcilable Paradigms?* (Oxford and Portland, Oregon: Hart Publishing), 273-291.

Zedner, L. (1994) 'Reparation and Retribution: Are they Reconcilable?', *Modern Law Review,* 57, 228-50.

Zehr, H. (1989) 'Stumbling Toward a Restorative Ideal' in *Justice: The Restorative Vision.* (New Perspectives on Crime and Justice. Occasional Papers of the MCC Canada Victim Offender Ministries Program and the MCC U.S. Office on Crime and Justice), 7, 1-14.

Zehr, H. (1990) *Changing Lenses: A New Focus for Crime and Justice* (Scottdale, PA: Herald Press).

Zehr, H. (1995) 'Justice Paradigm Shift? Values and Visions in the Reform Process' *Mediation Quarterly,* 12, 207-216.

Zehr, H. (2002) *The Little Book of Restorative Justice* (Good Books).

Zehr, H. (2003) 'Retributive Justice, Restorative Justice', in Johnstone, G. (ed.) *A Restorative Justice Reader,* 69-82 (Cullompton: Willan Publishing).

Zehr, H. (2005) 'Evaluation and restorative justice principles' in Elliott, E. and Gordon, R.M. (eds) *New Directions in Restorative Justice. Issues, practice, evaluation,* 296-303 (Cullompton: Willan Publishing).

Zehr, H. and Mika, H. (1998) 'Fundamental Concepts of Restorative Justice', *Contemporary Justice Review,* 1, 47-55.

Zellerer, E. and Cunneen, C. (2001) 'Restorative Justice, Indigenous Justice, and Human Rights' in Bazemore, G. and Schiff, M. *Restorative Community Justice,* 245-263 (Cincinnati, OH: Anderson Publishing).

Zernova, M. (2006) 'Working under the Aegis of the Criminal Justice System: Implications for Restorative Justice Practice', *British Journal of Community Justice*, 4, 67-79.

Zernova, M. (2007) 'Aspirations of Restorative Justice Proponents and Experiences of Participants in Family Group Conferences', *British Journal of Criminology*, 47, 491-509.

Zernova, M. (forthcoming) 'Integrating the Restorative and Rehabilitative Models: Lessons from One Family Group Conferencing Project', *Contemporary Justice Review.*

Zernova, M. and Wright, M. (2007) 'Alternative Visions of Restorative Justice', in Johnstone, G. and Van Ness, D. *Handbook of Restorative Justice,* 91-108 (Cullompton: Willan Publishing).

Zion, J.W. (1998) 'The Use of Custom and Legal Tradition in the Modern Justice Setting', *Contemporary Justice Review,* 1, pp. 133-148.

Zion, J.W. and Yazzie, R. (2006) 'Navajo peacemaking: original dispute resolution and a life way' in Sullivan, D. and Tifft, L. (eds) *Handbook of Restorative Justice,* 91-111 (London and New York: Routledge).

Index

Aboriginal people 7, 13
Australia 13, 52
Canada 16–18
Maori 10–11, 13
Navajo Peacemaking 19–20
Adult offenders 12, 14, 30
Apology 44, 72, 75, 90, 92, 111, 126, 131
Sincere 90, 106, 122
Aspirations of proponents 2, 35, 52, 59, 109, 116, 128, 131–3, 138
Critique of 3, 106–9, 133–5, 142
Disagreements about 35
Australia 12–14, 52

Barnett, R. 36, 43
Bazemore, G. 40–42, 47, 53, 85
Bethlehem experiment 15–16
Braithwaite, J. 13–14, 40–43, 48, 51–2, 72, 84, 139, 133

Canada 8, 16–18
Christie, N. 36, 43, 45–6, 48–50, 55, 84, 87, 116, 135, 137
Circles of support 141
Circles, sentencing 16–19
Criticisms of 18–19
Coercion 15, 28, 46–8, 63, 74–7, 102, 116; *see also* Voluntariness
Community; *see also* Empowerment
Definition of 50, 137
Impact on 18
Moral condemnation 40, 84
Power imbalance 18–19
Role in restorative justice 50
Community–based 48, 50–52, 82–6, 103
Dangers of 52–3
'Competency development' 40
Conference
Plan 62, 79–81
Preparation 61, 87–90, 129–30
Pre–conference report 61, 68, 80, 118, 125
Rationale 67, 73, 118
Conflict
As 'property' 46, 48–9, 116, 135; *see also* Christie, N.
Individualizing 107, 109, 132, 142
Nature of 45–6
Neutralizing 45, 107–9, 132, 142
Social–structural 45, 55, 107–9, 132, 142
Co-option 3, 139
Council of Europe, Recommendation on the Use of Mediation in Penal Matters 29, 60, 74, 116
Crime
Causes of 41, 56, 108
Concept re-defined 55, 105
Legally defined 54–5, 107, 114, 134, 137, 139–41
Prevention of 41, 66–7
Restorative understanding of 1, 37, 42–3
Crime and Disorder Act 1998 26–7, 30, 60, 110, 132
Criminal Justice Act 2003 27
Criminal law 54–5, 57, 99, 100, 103, 109, 112, 122–3, 131–2, 137–8
Criminal justice system; *see also* Diversion model; Integration model
Agenda 109–110, 122, 132, 138
Alliance with 43, 54, 110, 113, 122, 124, 132, 138
Dependence on 29, 53–4, 109–11, 122, 131–2, 139
Goals of 81, 102, 111–12, 122, 124, 125, 132, 134, 139–40
Prior intervention of 77–8, 110–11, 139
Reform of 53, 113
Restorative criticisms of 37, 46–7
Value framework of 54, 98–101, 103, 109–12, 117, 122–4, 132, 134, 136

Daly, K. 3, 39, 42, 62, 134

Declaration of Leuven 44, 47, 74
'Deliberative democracy' 51
De-professionalized 87–98, 117, 121, 123, 128; *see also* Professionals; Facilitators
Discipline
  Techniques of 52, 94, 119, 121–2
Diversion model 53, 113
Domination 86

Emotions 93–7
Empathy 66, 75–6
Empirical research
  Agenda for 31–3, 140
  Problems of 31–3
Empowerment 48–52, 77–82, 102–3, 116–117, 124, 128, 132, 137, 140
  Dangers of 51–3
England
  Recent developments 26–9
Ethics 45, 51–2, 54, 88, 98–102, 106, 112, 121, 135–8, 140–42
Evaluations
  Bethlehem experiment 15–16
  England 27–9
  FGC (Australia) 13–14
  FGC (New Zealand) 11–12
  Pilot YOTs 27
  Referral orders 28
  RISE14
  Thames Valley 15
  Vermont Community Reparative Boards 21
  VOM 10
  Wagga Wagga 13

Facilitator 61, 63–4, 75–6, 83, 116, 122; *see also* Professionals
  Neutrality of 63, 99–100, 112, 117
  Role 112, 117, 121–4
Family Group Conferencing; *see also* Thames Valley Police experiment
  Australia 10–14
  Criticisms of 13
  New Zealand 10–12
  Police-led 12–15
Forgiveness 44
Foucault 52

Government
  At a distance 52–3, 112, 138

Grassroots social movements 114

Harm
  Harmony
  Ideology of 45
  Reparation of 40, 44–5, 65, 105–7, 111, 122, 133
  Restoring 45, 107–8
Harris, K. 54, 56–7, 135, 141
Healing 37, 44, 70, 84, 107, 111, 120, 125
History 7, 10, 19, 30–31
Hollow Water programme 17–18
Hospitality 64–5
Hulsman, L. 137, 140

Ideals of proponents; *see* Aspirations of proponents; Restorative justice, critique of
Implementation
  Large-scale 113, 124, 139
  Mistakes 120, 129–31
  State-managed 113, 124, 139
Indigenous justice; *see* Aboriginal people
Inequalities, social 45, 56, 107–9, 114, 132
Individualizing crime 56
Injustices, social 56, 107–109, 114, 122, 132; *see also* Inequalities, social
Integration model 53, 113

Johnstone, G. 3, 38–40, 42–3, 50, 52, 55, 84, 120, 134, 140
Juvenile offenders *See* Young offenders

Marginalization
  The danger of 53, 113
McCold, P. 39, 41, 47, 50, 53, 74, 77, 116
Medical model 42, 45, 134; *see also* Treatment model

Navajo peacemaking 19–20
Needs-based justice 136
Net-widening 13, 23, 52
New Zealand 10–12
Norm-clarification 46, 55, 137
Northern Ireland 23–5

Offender; *See also* Rehabilitation; Re-offending
  Accountability 37, 70, 119
  Benefit for 9, 63, 84–5, 88, 119
  Concept 56, 134

Empowerment 78–9, 124
Identity 56, 63, 88, 112, 117, 137
Label 56, 99–102, 121, 132, 139
Needs 68, 118
Satisfaction 10, 11, 15
Welfare 61, 68, 118–19
Outcomes 117, 121–2, 140, 142
Pre-determined 107, 142

Paradigm, new 2, 36–8, 55, 57, 119, 129, 134, 136
Participatory justice 46, 48–50, 109, 121, 123; *see also* Empowerment
Pavlich, G. 3, 38, 44–5, 52–6, 100, 107, 114, 117–19, 121, 134, 136–8, 142
Peace
Restoration of 45, 107–8
'Plurality of deliberation' 41, 72, 86
Political debate, staging 46, 133, 140
Power
Model of 112, 116, 119, 121, 124
Process, restorative 2, 51–2, 109
Contrasted with the criminal justice process 46, 49
Fairness of 10, 14–15, 106, 127–8
Professionals 48–50, 61, 63–4, 69, 81, 85–6, 98, 103, 109, 113, 116, 119, 121, 123, 139; *see also* Facilitators
Controlling the process 85, 91–8, 103, 121–2
Punishment 111
As alternative to 38–9, 62–5, 103, 116–17, 134
Restorative justice as a form of 39, 62, 65, 116

Reconciliation 2, 8, 45, 108
Rehabilitation 41–42, 62, 65–70, 72, 79–80, 85, 102, 132, 134, 138; *see also* Treatment
And restorative justice 117–19, 134
Reintegration 40–42, 84–85
Reintegrative shaming 13, 14
Remorse 40, 44, 73, 120, 131
Re-offending 12, 14–15, 18, 29, 61, 71, 110, 118–19, 124, 132
Reparation
Criticism of 45, 106
Material 70, 72
Symbolic 44, 52, 72
See also Harm
Repentance; *see* Remorse
Research findings; *see* Evaluations
Resistance 53, 63, 75, 85, 113, 122, 138
Restorative justice
As ethical orientation 37, 134, 136–8, 140–42; *see also* Ethics
Campaign for
Widening 55, 57, 114, 140–41
Concept of 1–2, 35
Retributive justice 3
Contrasted to restorative justice 1, 37–8
Universality of 30–31
RISE project 13–15

Seating arrangements 91, 130–31
Self-identity 87–88, 91, 112, 122
Self
Techniques of 52, 119, 121
Sex offenders 18, 141
Social change 45–46, 57, 123, 137, 142
State 52, 112–113, 125, 135, 138
Status quo
Restoring 45, 105–107
Sullivan, D. 3, 54–6, 100, 123, 136

Thames Valley Police experiment 14–15
Tifft, L. 3, 54–6, 100, 123, 136
Transformation
Relational 118, 125–6
Personal 118, 126–8
Treatment
An alternative to 39–41, 65–6
Model 39–42
Restorative justice as a form of 66
Merge with restorative justice 41–2, 70

UN Declaration of Basic Principles 29, 46, 74, 116

Values, restorative 2, 52, 54
Vermont Community Reparative Boards 20–21
Victim
Attendance, reasons for 66, 84, 118
Attitudes towards offenders 84, 125
Benefit for 9, 73, 118
Centrality 30, 42–3, 70–73, 102, 119, 128
Concept 56, 134
Empowerment 56, 77–8, 120, 124

Identity 56, 64, 87–8, 112, 127, 137
Institutional 128
Interests of 119–121
Label 56, 99–102, 121, 131, 139
Needs 42, 68, 71–2, 88, 110, 119, 132
Satisfaction 10–12, 14–16
Victim-offender reconciliation/mediation programmes 8–10
Victims' Rights movement 7, 9
Victim Support 60–61, 69–70
Violence, social-structural 54–5
Voluntariness 46–8, 53, 74–7, 102, 116, 133; *see also* Coercion

Wagga Wagga experiment 12–14
Walgrave, L. 39–40, 47, 53, 65
Wright, M. 38, 41

Young offenders 13–14, 25, 29–30, 60–1, 66–7, 69–71, 84, 110, 118–19, 131–2
Youth Justice and Criminal Evidence Act 1999 26–7
Youth Offender Panels 26–8
Youth Offending Team(s) 26–7, 60–61, 116

Zehr, H. 1–2, 8–9, 36–8, 42–4, 139
Zwelethemba experiment 21–3